win
a short break

`D1809978`

Keep in touch and WIN a two-night stay for two in your choice of hotel or B&B

VisitBritain would be delighted to hear what you think of this guide. Please complete the short questionnaire overleaf and send it back to us.

Questionnaires received before 31 October 2006 will be entered into a prize draw to win two nights' stay for two in any hotel or B&B listed in this guide.

Title _____ First name _____

Surname _____

Address _____

Town/City _____ County _____

Postcode _____ Country _____

Mobile _____ Telephone _____

E-mail _____

Which age group are you in?
16-24 ❑   25-34 ❑   35-44 ❑   45-54 ❑   55-64 ❑   65+ ❑

When do you normally buy accommodation guides? (please tick one box)
❑ Easter holidays
❑ Before main summer season, i.e. May
❑ Christmas / end of the year
❑ Anytime – planning a special occasion
❑ Anytime – planning a spontaneous occasion
❑ Anytime – planning a holiday
❑ Spontaneously purchased

How often do you buy accommodation guides? (please tick one box)
❑ Every year
❑ Every 2 years
❑ Every 3 years
❑ Every 4 years
❑ Every 5 years
❑ Single purchase, i.e. I do not replace guide

Do you regularly use any other accessible accommodation guides? If yes, which ones?
_____
_____

What do you find useful about this official tourist board guide?
_____
_____

Is there any other information you would like to see added to this guide?
_____
_____

Have you booked any accommodation through this guide? If yes, which one (establishment and region)?
_____
_____

Would you like to be contacted by VisitBritain in future with news, ideas and special offers?   Yes ❑   No ❑
Would you like to be contacted by VisitBritain's carefully chosen partners with news of more offers?   Yes ❑   No ❑

Please complete, put in an envelope and return Freepost (no stamp required) to:

VisitBritain Commercial Publishing, Freepost RLXU–XLYY–UKLB
Thames Tower, Blacks Road, London W6 9EL

AC06-RRC

official guides to **quality**

Britain's

accessible

places to stay

2006

formerly entitled Accessible Britain

visit **Britain**
publishing

38

72

enjoy Britain's regions

112

150

176

186

Contents

KEY TO SYMBOLS
Inside back-cover flap

VisitBritain

VisitBritain is the organisation created to market Britain to the rest of the world, and England to the British.

Formed by the merger of the British Tourist Authority and the English Tourism Council, its mission is to build the value of tourism by creating world-class destination brands and marketing campaigns.

It will also build partnerships with – and provide insights to – other organisations which have a stake in British and English tourism.

Tourism for All UK

TFA UK is the UK's central source of holiday and travel information for people with access requirements.

It is a registered charity which liaises with government and industry bodies.

Left, clockwise from top
Northern Ballet Theatre, Leeds, West Yorkshire; Hatfield House, Hertfordshire; Brighton Marina, East Sussex; Eisteddfod International Festival, Llangollen; Eilean Donan Castle, Dornie; The Forest of Dean, Gloucestershire

endless possibilities for relaxing short breaks and fun-filled holidays

4

The guide that **gives you** more

This new accessible guide is packed with information from where to stay to how to get there and what to see and do. In fact, everything you need to know to enjoy Britain.

ready, set, go for a quality break

Quality accommodation

Choose from a wide range of quality-assured accommodation. This guide contains an exclusive listing of hotels, guest accommodation, self-catering holiday homes, and hostel and campus accommodation participating in VisitBritain's quality assessment schemes. It also includes camping and caravan parks participating in The British Graded Holiday Parks Scheme. **All accommodation featured in this guide participates in an accessible rating scheme.**

Great days out

Every region has its own special appeal – in each section we give a small selection of attractions not to be missed. For hundreds more ideas go online at visit**Britain**.com, or contact one of the regional tourism organisations for further information.

Travel information

Looking for the best ways to reach your holiday destination? Turn to the back of the guide for useful information and contact details.

Left Start Point, near Kingsbridge, Devon
Right, from top book a cosy winter break;
Holly Farm, Stoke St Gregory, Somerset

How to use this guide

This essential guide for the traveller with accessible needs offers a great choice of accommodation throughout Britain.

Each property in England and Scotland has been awarded an accessible category according to strict criteria. Access Statements are available for properties in Wales. In addition, the quality of the accommodation has been assessed to nationally agreed standards, so that you can book in confidence.

Detailed accommodation entries include descriptions, prices and facilities. Listings include contact details only.

Finding accommodation is easy

Regional entries
The guide is divided into regional sections and accommodation is listed alphabetically by place name within each region.

Colour maps
Use the colour maps starting on page 22 to pinpoint the location of all detailed accommodation. Then refer to the place index at the back to find the page number.

Useful indexes
Indexes at the back of the guide make it easy to find accommodation that matches your requirements and, if you know the name of the establishment, turn straight to the property index for the page number.

Right, clockwise from top time together; no transportation worries; sit back and relax; The St Annes Hotel, Lytham St Annes, Lancashire; Housel Bay, Cornwall

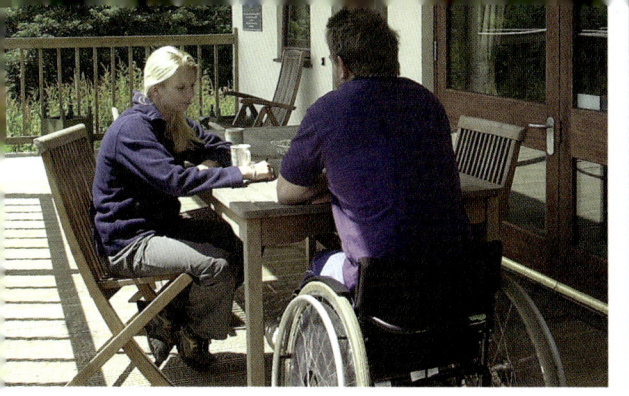

book your accommodation with confidence

Tourism for All UK

Finding suitable accommodation for holidays or to visit relatives is not always easy, especially if you have to seek out ground floor rooms, a step free entrance and all facilities on one level, or large print menus and colour contrast in the bathroom.

Proprietors can sometimes be unaware of accessible needs resulting in disappointment on arrival when you find numerous steps to encounter and you are unable to seat a wheelchair at the dining room table.

For those needing accurate advice, help is at hand.

All-round service

Tourism for All UK (formerly known as Holiday Care) provides information that helps thousands of people arrange a successful holiday or trip every year. This includes equipment hire, respite care centres, accessible attractions, financial help, activity and children's holidays information as well as advice on accommodation.

Tourism for All is the UK's central source of holiday and travel information for people with access requirements.

Finding accommodation

For help in finding suitable accommodation or to make a booking call the Tourism For All reservations line. You may also be able to take advantage of special offers at hotels throughout the UK and overseas. (Note, if you use this service all accommodation in the UK will be assessed by VisitBritain or Tourism for All. Quality ratings for overseas properties are usually based on self-reporting or member's recommendation.)

Making friends

Consider joining the Tourism for All UK 'Friends of TFA' scheme. Members share information and experiences and receive a regular newsletter which highlights new accessible accommodation, attractions and places to go. Membership also gives special discounts on publications and accommodation.

Tourism for All is the UK's central source of holiday and travel information for people with access requirements.

information helpline
0845 124 9971
reservations 0845 124 9973
(lines open 9-5 Mon-Fri)

f (01539) 735567

e info@tourismforall.org.uk

w tourismforall.org.uk

or write to
Tourism for All UK, c/o Vitalise, Shap Road Industrial Estate, Kendal LA9 6NZ

TFA UK is a registered charity, No 279169 and Company Limited by Guarantee No 01466822

Above Carrie-Ann Fleming, Tourism For All UK (front right) with members of the Board outside the call centre in Kendal

Tourism for All UK (TFA) is a charity, formed in 1979. Working with the national tourist boards it has helped to develop the National Accessible Scheme run by VisitBritain, by which accommodation is assessed and rated. The organisation also works with government, speaks at tourism related conferences, promotes good practice and offers consultancy on all kinds of tourism-related access issues.

Improved accessibility throughout the tourism industry is actively encouraged by Tourism for All. Where good practise is established – such as in Chester, and through Cheshire for All, or by Brighton who recently undertook a destination audit, looking at the whole visitor experience from a disabled person's point of view – the charity seeks to celebrate and promote the achievement.

Membership of TFA by local government and industry bodies is an indicator of their commitment to observe their obligations under the Disability Discrimination Act. (Many of these are advertisers in this guide.) Corporate Patrons also support the charity's aims, and include Accor Hotels, InterContinental Hotels, Choice Hotels, Hand Picked Hotels, VisitBritain and the Wales Tourist Board.

Accessible
schemes

England

Serviced accommodation and Self-Catering Holiday Homes

These properties are assessed under VisitBritain's National Accessible Scheme, which includes standards useful for hearing and visually impaired guests in addition to standards useful for guests with mobility impairment.

Accommodation taking part in this scheme will display one or more of the mobility, visual or hearing symbols shown opposite.

Camping and Caravan Parks

These properties are assessed under VisitBritain's National Accessible Scheme for Caravan Holiday Homes and Parks and are categorised for wheelchair users and those with limited mobility.

Accommodation taking part in this scheme will display one of the symbols shown at the foot of the opposite page.

When you see one of the symbols, you can be sure that the accommodation and core facilities have been thoroughly assessed against demanding criteria. If you have additional needs or special requirements we strongly recommend that you make sure these can be met by your chosen establishment before you confirm your booking.

Scotland

All types of accommodation in Scotland are assessed for wheelchair users and those with limited mobility. Entries include one of three mobility symbols shown at the foot of the opposite page.

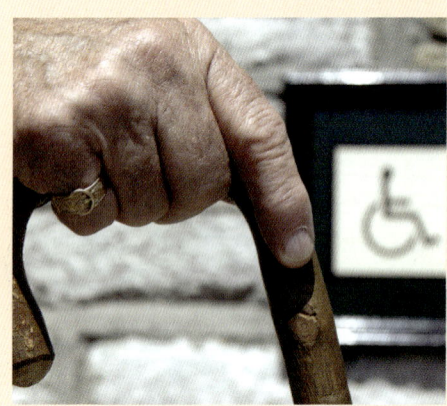

Wales

Owners of all types of accommodation in Wales are required to have a full Access Statement available for guests.

The criteria VisitBritain and national/regional tourism organisations have adapted do not necessarily conform to British Standards or to Building Regulations. They reflect what the organisations understand to be acceptable to meet the practical needs of guests with mobility or sensory impairments and encourage the industry to increase access to all.

What do **access ratings** mean?

England accessible ratings (excluding Camping and Caravan Parks)

Mobility

Typically suitable for a person with sufficient mobility to climb a flight of steps but who would benefit from fixtures and fittings to aid balance.

Typically suitable for a person with restricted walking ability and for those who may need to use a wheelchair some of the time and can negotiate a maximum of three steps.

Typically suitable for a person who depends on the use of a wheelchair and transfers unaided to and from the wheelchair in a seated position. This person may be an independent traveller.

Typically suitable for a person who depends on the use of a wheelchair in a seated position.This person also requires personal/mechanical assistance to aid transfer (eg carer, hoist).

Access Exceptional – is awarded to establishments that meet the requirements of independent wheelchair users or assisted wheelchair users shown above and also fulfil more demanding requirements with reference to the British Standards BS8300:2001.

Visual Impairment

Typically provides key additional services and facilities to meet the needs of visually impaired guests.

Typically provides a higher level of additional services and facilities to meet the needs of guests with a visual impairment.

Hearing Impairment

Typically provides key additional services and facilities to meet the needs of guests with hearing impairment.

Typically provides a higher level of additional services and facilities to meet the needs of guests with a hearing impairment.

Camping and Caravan Parks and all Scottish accommodation

Category 1
Accessible to a wheelchair user travelling independently.

Category 2
Accessible to a wheelchair user travelling with assistance.

Category 3
Accessible to a wheelchair user able to
walk a few paces and up a maximum of three steps.

Quality ratings and awards at a glance

Reliable, rigorous, easy to use – look out for the following ratings and awards to help you choose with confidence:

Quality accommodation ratings

The nationally recognised signs showing stars and diamonds indicate that establishments have been assessed for quality by a trained, impartial assessor and that you can be confident that the accommodation you're booking will meet your expectations.

Hotels and B&B Guest Accommodation

Establishments are awarded a rating of one to five stars (hotels) or diamonds* (guest accommodation) based on a combination of quality of facilities and services provided. Properties in this guide also include townhouses, travel accommodation, farmhouses and inns.

Gold and Silver Awards

These awards are highly prized by proprietors and are only given to hotels and guest accommodation offering the highest levels of quality within their star or

diamond rating, particularly in areas of cleanliness, service and hospitality.

Self-Catering Holiday Homes

Establishments are awarded a rating of one to five stars for increasing levels of quality. High standards of cleanliness are a major requirement, with heating, lighting, comfort and convenience also part of the assessment. Properties in this guide include cottages, barns, houses, bungalows, chalets, flats and studios.

Camping and Caravan Parks

Parks are awarded a rating of one to five stars following an assessment of the quality, cleanliness, maintenance and condition of the various facilities provided. It is not necessary to provide a wide range of facilities in order to achieve a high rating, as the emphasis is on the quality of what is provided.

*Guest Accommodation will be awarded stars from January 2006.

For full details of VisitBritain's quality assurance schemes go online at qualityintourism.com

Hostel and Campus Accommodation

Establishments are awarded a rating of one to five stars for increasing levels of quality and customer care. Hostels provide safe, budget-priced accommodation for young people, families or larger groups and include Youth Hostel Association (YHA) hostels. Campus accommodation comprises educational establishments, such as universities and colleges with sleeping accommodation in halls of residence, or student village complexes. Availability is mainly during the academic vacations.

Enjoy England Awards for Excellence

The prestigious and coveted Enjoy England Awards for Excellence showcase the very best in English tourism and celebrate the people whose contribution to its success is outstanding. Run by VisitBritain in association with England's regions, the awards include categories for Hotel of the Year, Bed & Breakfast of the Year, Self-Catering Holiday of the Year and Caravan Holiday Park of the Year. For more information about the awards and to see the current winners, visit enjoy**England**.com.

Visitor Attraction Quality Assurance

Attractions achieving high standards in all aspects of the visitor experience, from initial telephone enquiry to departure, receive this award and are visited every year by trained assessors.

14

How do we arrive at a **quality rating?**

The process to arrive at a quality rating is very thorough to ensure that when you make a booking you can be confident it will meet your expectations.

a trained assessor has visited before you

Trained assessors visit annually. They award ratings based on the overall quality and ensure that all requirements are met. There are strict guidelines for assessing every type of accommodation.

For hotels and guest accommodation high standards of housekeeping are a major requirement; heating, lighting, comfort and convenience are also part of the assessment. All aspects of the visit are taken into account from the initial telephone enquiry to the standard of services.

For self-catering holiday homes assessors will take into consideration the quality and condition of the fixtures and fittings, the standard of cleanliness and homely, personal touches. The quality of the information provided is also noted.

At camping and caravan parks over 50 separate aspects are taken into account, including landscaping, customer care and cleanliness. Assessors make a sample check of the accommodation provided for hire but the quality of the accommodation itself is not included in the grading assessment.

Accommodation entries **explained**

Accommodation entries contain detailed information to help you decide if it is right for you. This information has been provided by the proprietors themselves.

1 Listing under town or village with map reference

2 Quality rating plus Gold and Silver Awards where applicable

3 Prices
   Hotels – Per room for bed and breakfast (B&B) and per person for half board (HB)
   Guest accommodation – Per room for bed and breakfast (B&B) and per person for evening meal
   Self-catering – Per unit per week for low and high season

4 Accessible rating

5 Establishment name and booking details

6 Indicates when the establishment is open

7 At-a-glance facility symbols

8 Payment accepted

9 Special promotions or facilities

10 Travel directions

2 ★★

B&B per room per night
s **£45.00–£59.00**
3 **d £70.00–£99.00**
HB per person per night
£55.00–£75.00

4

Caley Hall Hotel   **5**

Old Hunstanton Road, Old Hunstanton, Hunstanton PE36 6HH
t (01485) 533486   **f** (01485) 533348   **e** mail@caleyhallhotel.co.uk
w caleyhallhotel.co.uk

General 🐕 P♿ 🍽 ❄

7 Rooms 📶 📺 🍵 📱 🔥 📚 📺

8 Payment Credit/debit cards,
cash/cheques

9 *2 rooms feature specially adapted
bathrooms with level-access
shower. The hotel has no steps.*

Caley Hall Hotel and Restaurant is set around a manor-house dating back to 1648. More recently, the old farm outbuildings have been converted to provide the spacious en suite bedrooms, restaurant and bar. Most of the rooms are on the ground floor, and some feature a four-poster bed or whirlpool bath.

open All year except Christmas **6**
and New Year
bedrooms 15 double, 15 twin,
4 single, 5 family, 1 suite
bathrooms All en suite

In Old Hunstanton, on the left- **10**
*hand side of the A149, just
before the turning to the golf
course.*

Sample detailed entry

**A key to symbols can be found on the back-cover flap.
Keep it open for easy reference.**

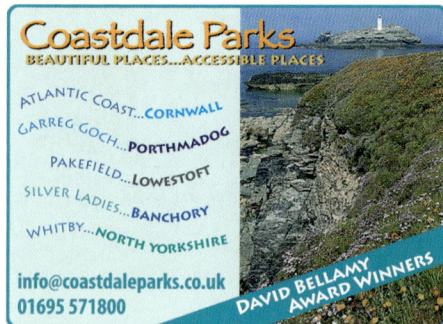
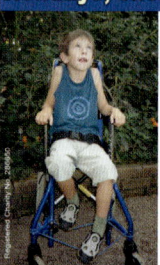
   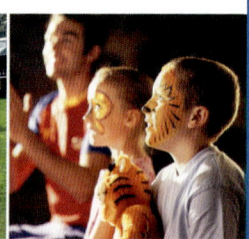

enjoyEngland ✿™
official guides to quality

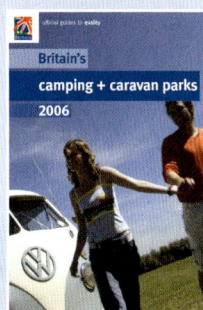

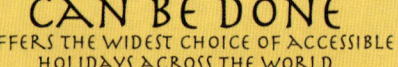

The Caravan Club. Touring for all.

With over 150 Club Sites having wheelchair access to all facilities and 60 having family friendly extras such as baby and toddler washrooms, The Caravan Club leads the way in providing accessibility for all.

The Club offers the largest network of UK Sites in glorious locations with Club Resident Wardens on hand to assist and advise.

Whatever holiday experience you're looking for there's a Club Site to suit you, including 40 Sites open all-year-round.

Whichever Site you choose, you can be assured of excellent facilities, a friendly welcome, and consistently high standards.

THE CARAVAN CLUB

THE CARAVAN CLUB
Our Site Collection
Over 200 quality sites in Britain & Ireland

2006

Map 1

Location
Maps

A   B

1

Every place name with a detailed entry in the regional accommodation sections of this VisitBritain guide has a map reference to help you locate it on the maps which follow. For example, to find Lewes, East Sussex, which has 'Map ref 2D3', turn to Map 2 and refer to grid square D3.

All place names with a detailed entry in the regional sections are shown in blue type on the maps. This enables you to find other places in your chosen area which may have suitable accommodation – the place index (at the back of this guide) gives page numbers.

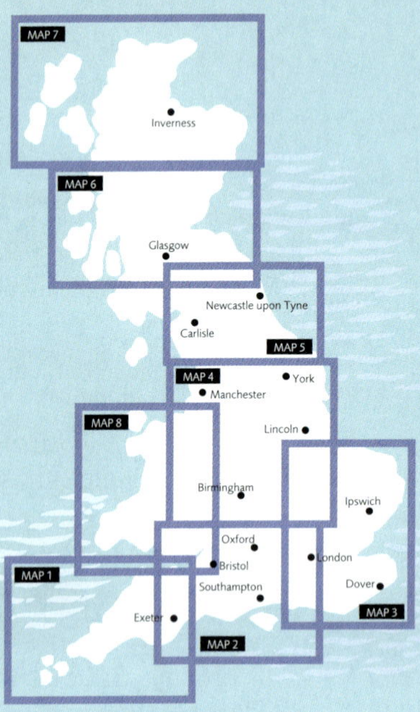

MAP 7

Inverness

MAP 6

Glasgow

Newcastle upon Tyne

Carlisle

MAP 5

MAP 4

York

Manchester

MAP 8

Lincoln

Birmingham

Ipswich

2

Oxford

Bristol

London

MAP 1

Southampton

Dover

Exeter

MAP 3

MAP 2

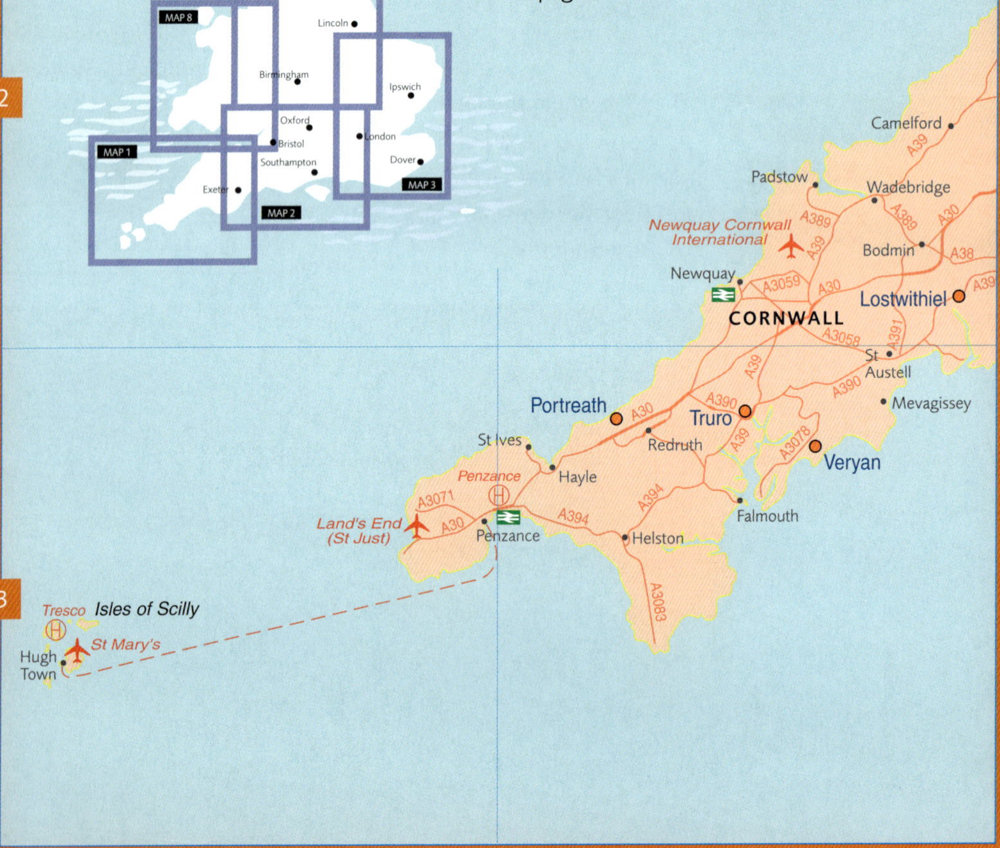

Camelford

Padstow

Wadebridge

Newquay Cornwall International

Bodmin

A38

Newquay

Lostwithiel

CORNWALL

St Austell

Portreath

Mevagissey

St Ives

Truro

Redruth

Veryan

Penzance

Hayle

Land's End (St Just)

Penzance

Falmouth

Helston

3

Tresco Isles of Scilly

St Mary's

Hugh Town

Key to regions: England's West Country

Map 1

Map 2

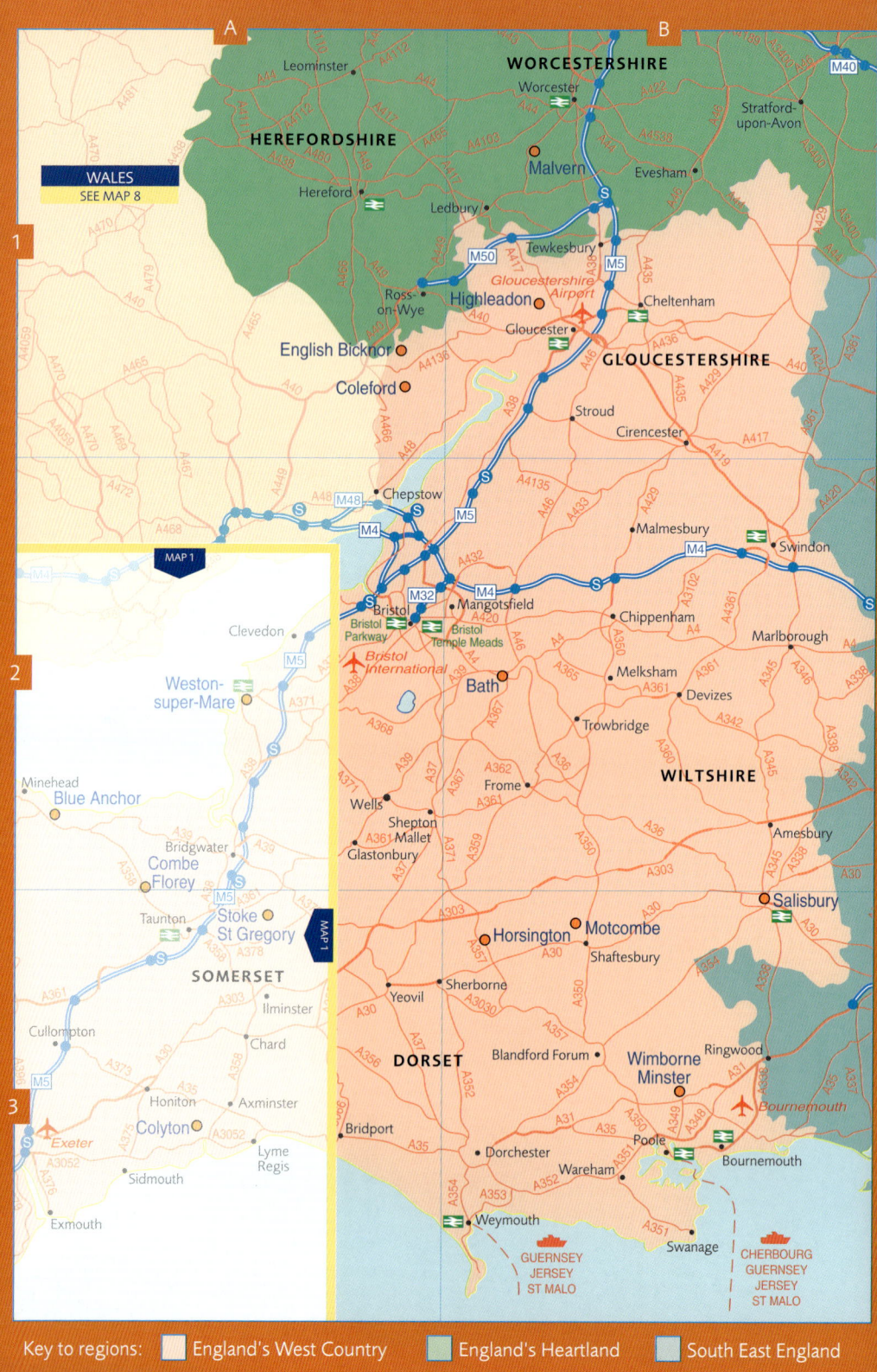

Key to regions: ☐ England's West Country   ☐ England's Heartland   ☐ South East England

Map 2

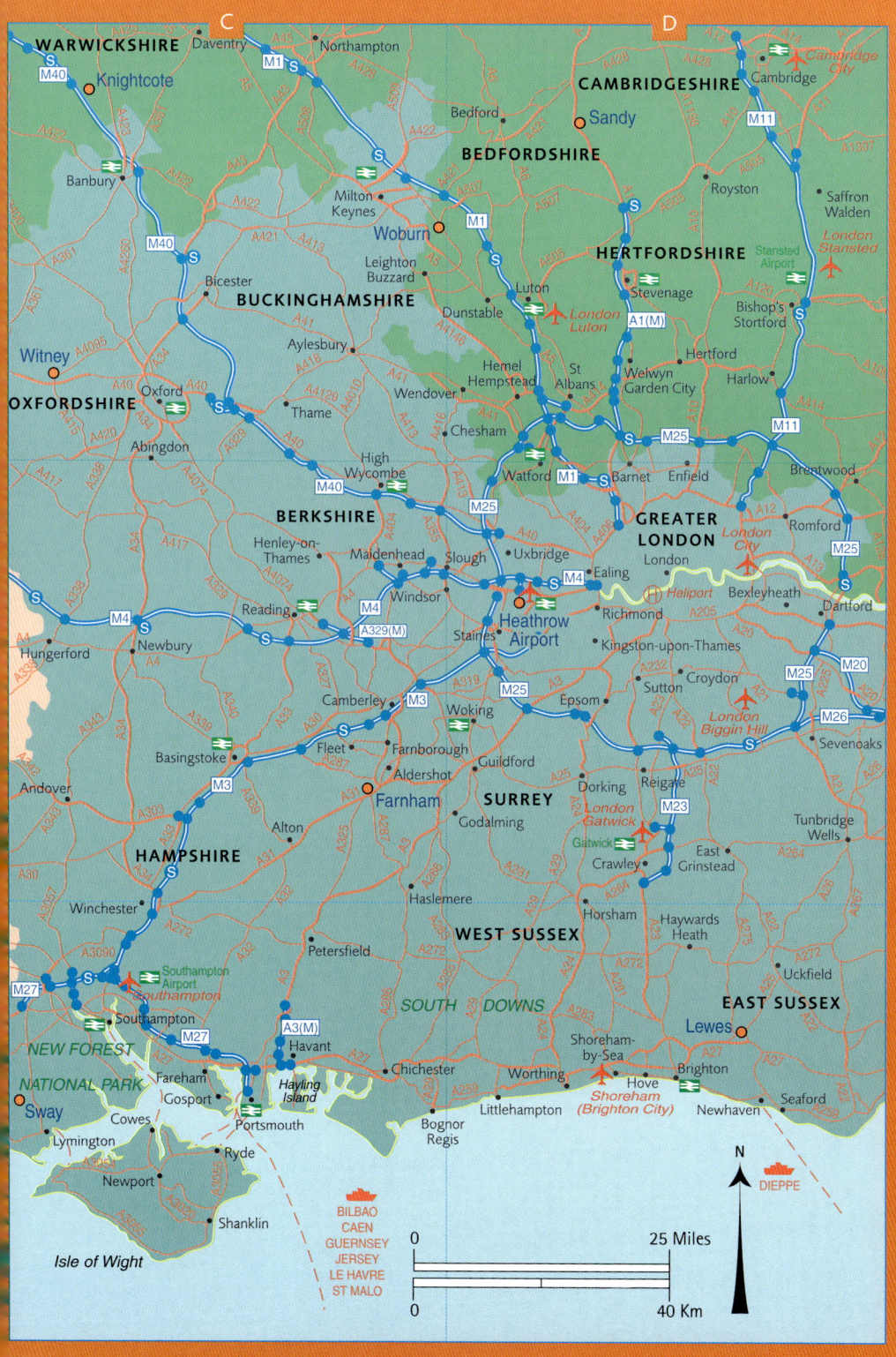

Map 3

Key to regions: England's Heartland South East England

Map 3

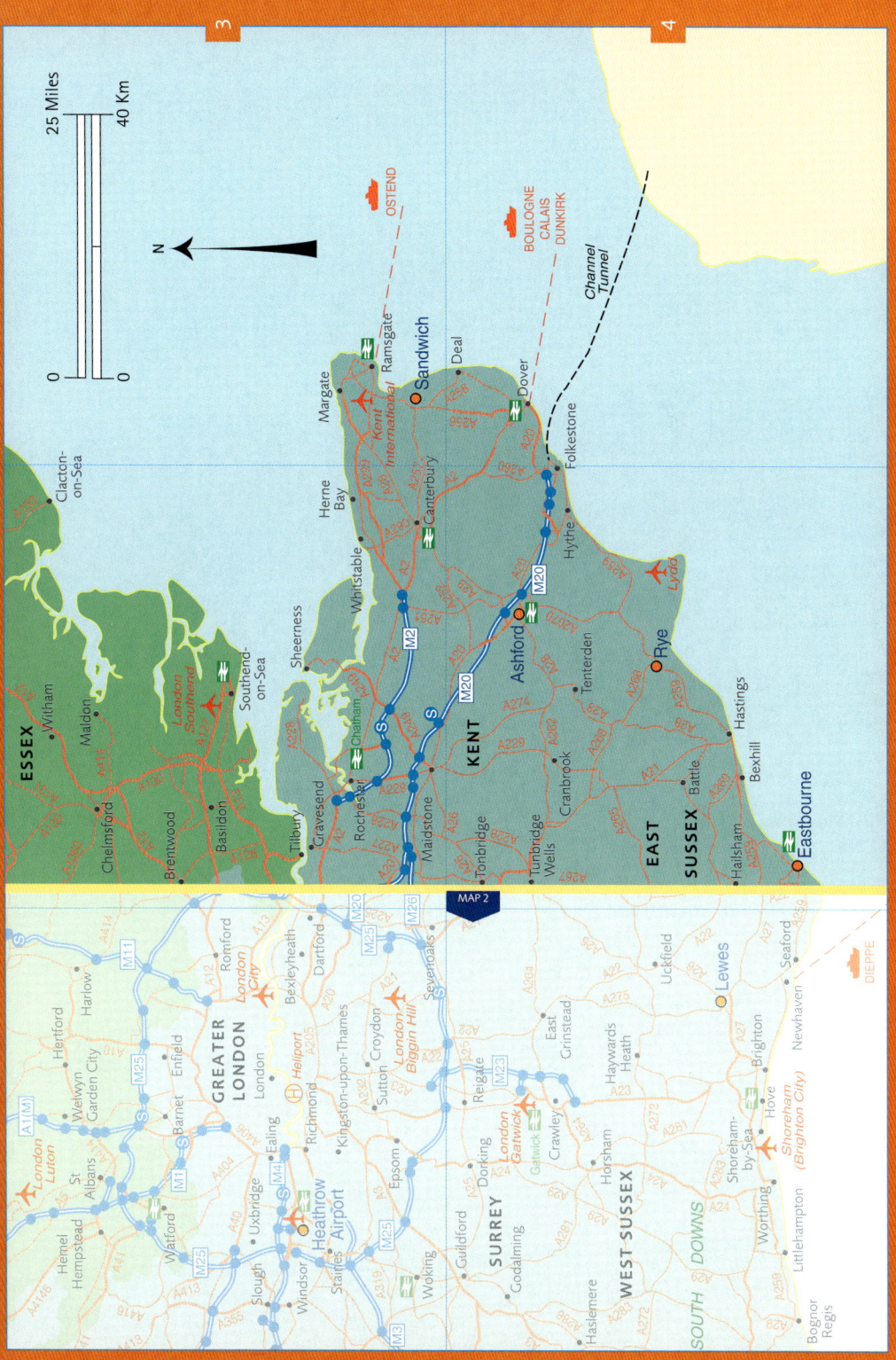

All place names in blue have a detailed accommodation entry in this guide.

Map 4

Key to regions: England's Heartland   England's North Country

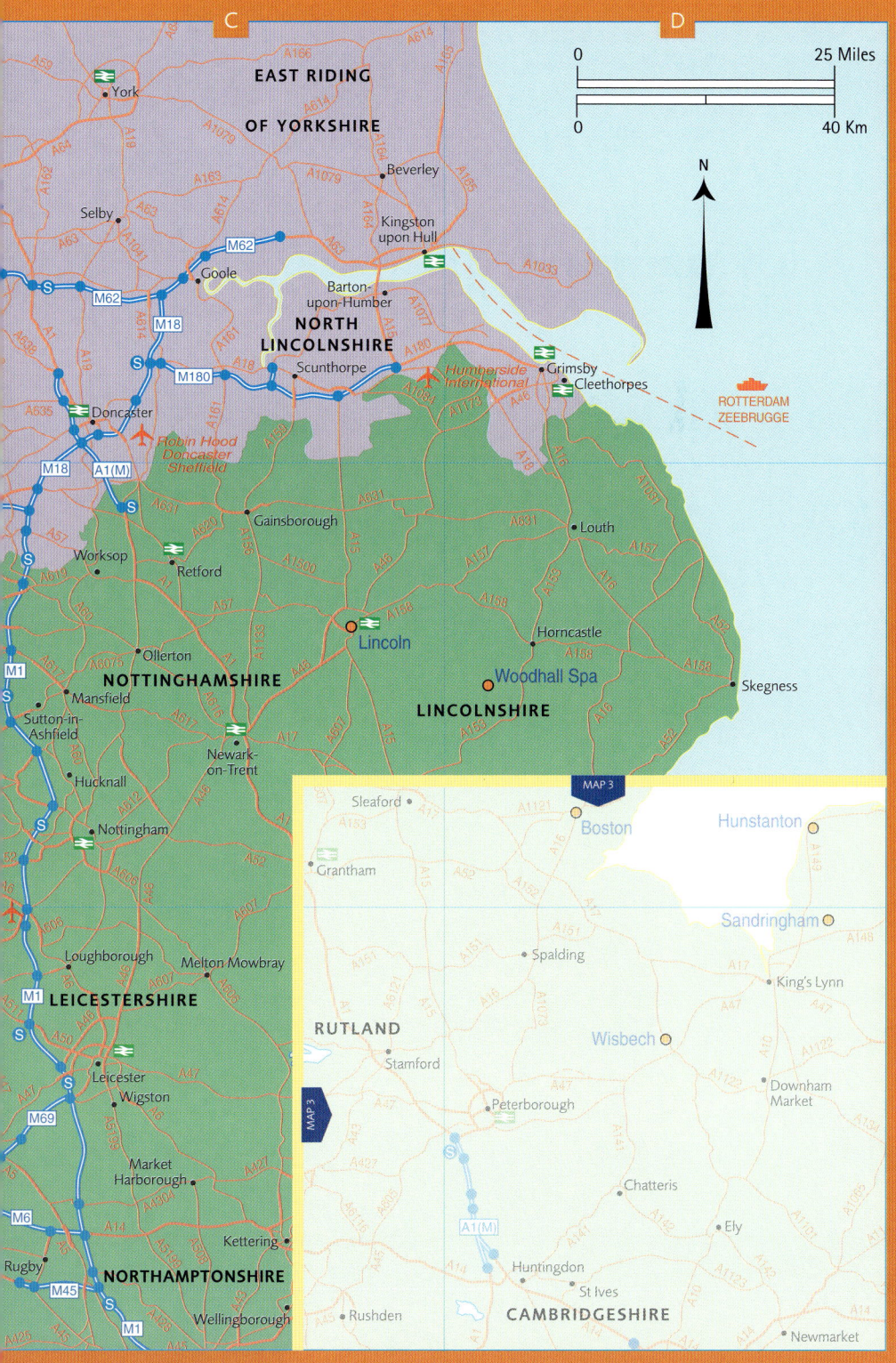

Map 4

All place names in blue have a detailed accommodation entry in this guide.

29

Map 5

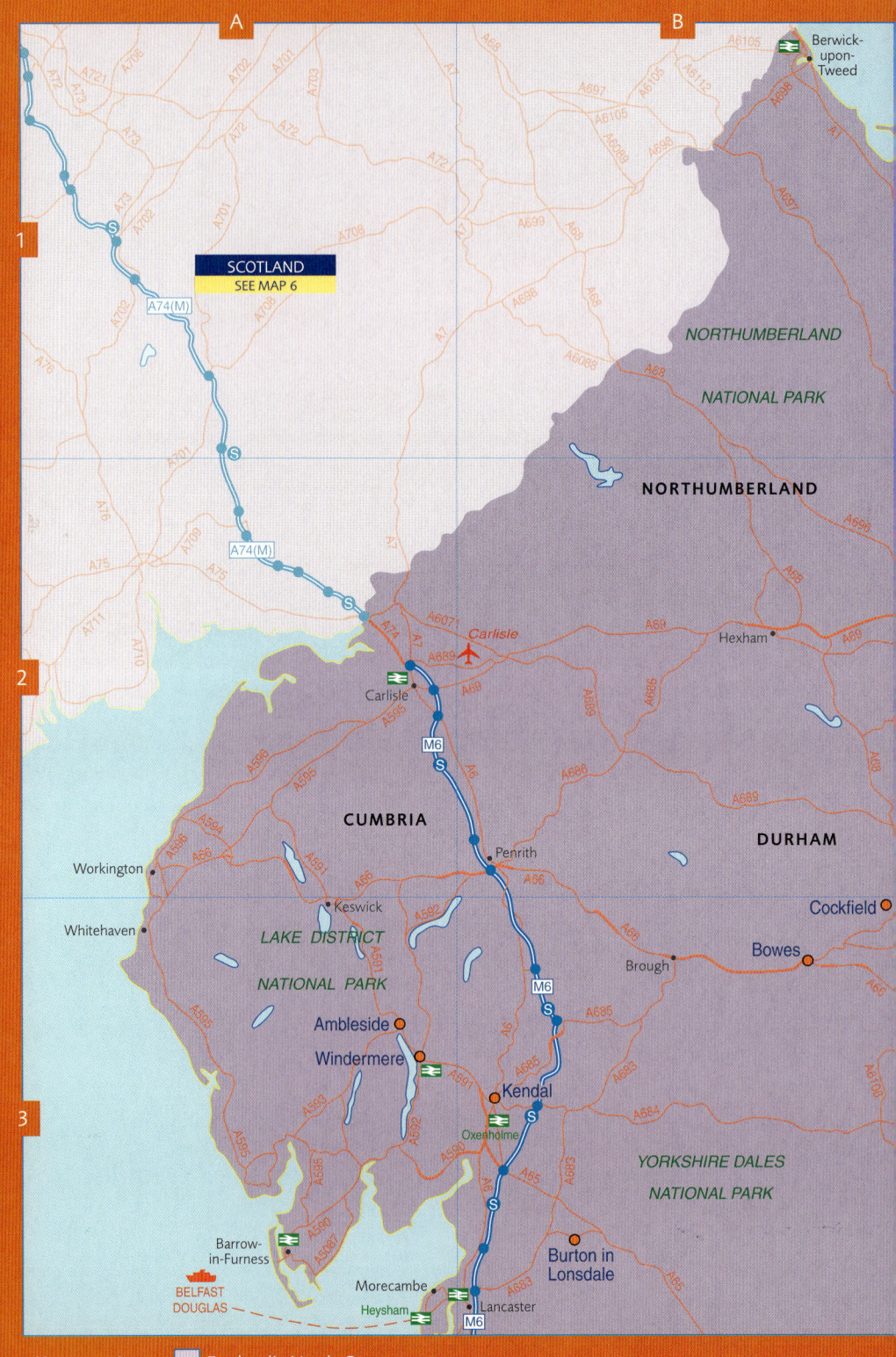

Map 5

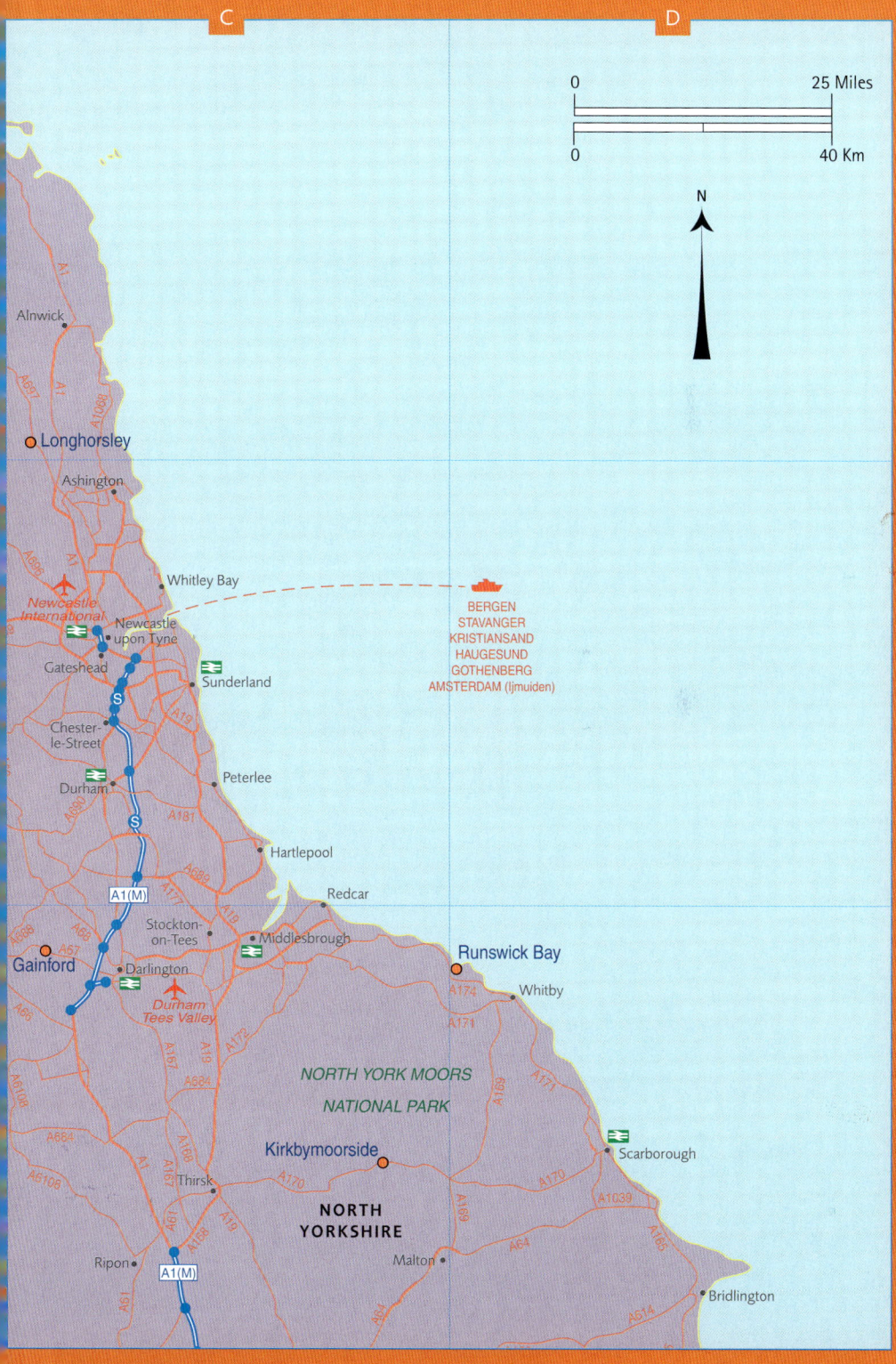

0   25 Miles

0   40 Km

N

C

D

Alnwick

Longhorsley

Ashington

Whitley Bay

Newcastle International

Newcastle upon Tyne

Gateshead

Sunderland

Chester-le-Street

Durham

Peterlee

Hartlepool

A181

A1(M)

Redcar

Stockton-on-Tees

Middlesbrough

Gainford

Darlington

Durham Tees Valley

Runswick Bay

Whitby

BERGEN
STAVANGER
KRISTIANSAND
HAUGESUND
GOTHENBERG
AMSTERDAM (Ijmuiden)

NORTH YORK MOORS

NATIONAL PARK

Kirkbymoorside

Scarborough

Thirsk

NORTH
YORKSHIRE

Ripon

A1(M)

Malton

Bridlington

Map 6

A   B

LOCHBOISDALE
CASTLEBAY

Fort William

Tiree

A830
A861
A82
A861
A884
A868
A849
A849

1

Oban

ARGYLL
AND
BUTE

LOCH LOMOND &

THE TROSSACHS

NATIONAL PARK

STIRLING

Helensburgh

Alexandria
Dumbarton

Greenock
Port
Glasgow

Glasgow
International

M8

Glasgow

Rothesay

Paisley

East
Kilbride

M77

2

Islay

NORTH
AYRSHIRE

Kilmarnock

Campbeltown

Glasgow
Prestwick
International

Ayr

Cumnock

EAST
AYRSHIRE

SOUTH
AYRSHIRE

NORTHERN

IRELAND

3

Stranraer

Gatehouse
of Fleet

Key to regions: ▪ Scotland

Map 6

Map 7

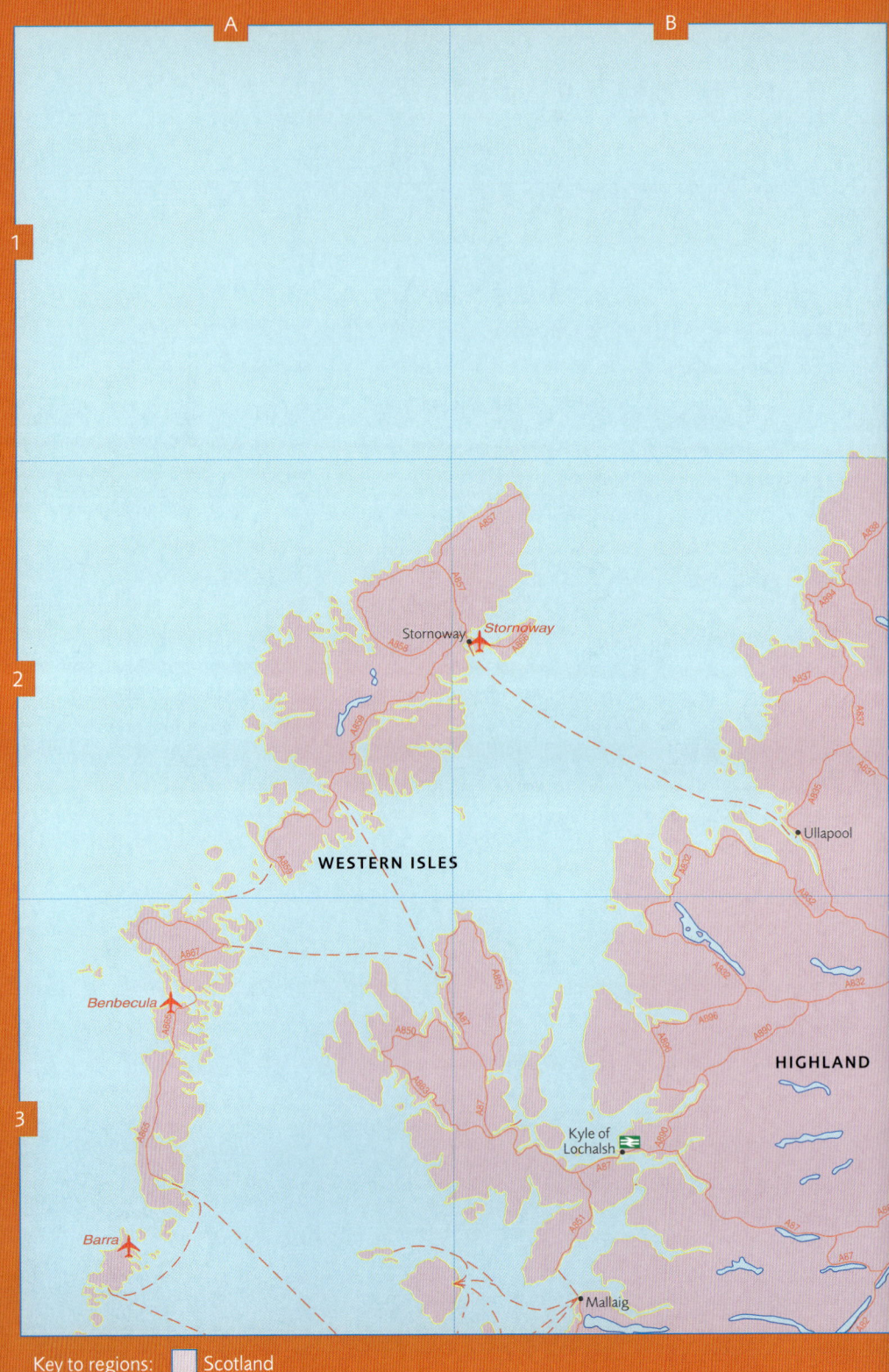

A

B

1

2

Stornoway

Stornoway

Ullapool

WESTERN ISLES

Benbecula

3

HIGHLAND

Kyle of
Lochalsh

Barra

Mallaig

Key to regions: ☐ Scotland

Map 7

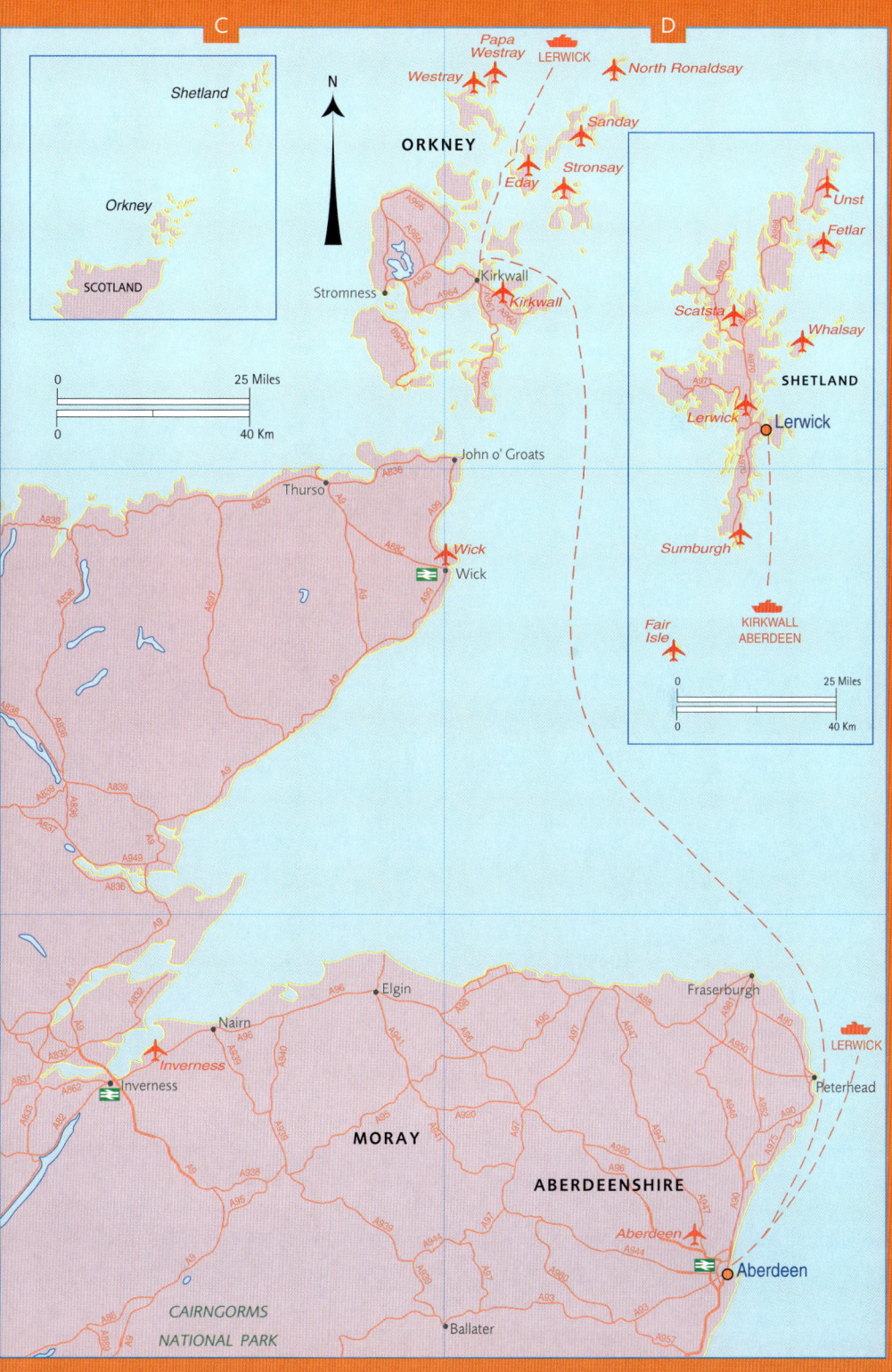

C

D

Shetland

Orkney

SCOTLAND

N

Papa
Westray

Westray

LERWICK

North Ronaldsay

ORKNEY

Sanday

Eday

Stronsay

A966

A986

A965

Stromness

B9041

A964

Kirkwall

Kirkwall

A960

Unst

Fetlar

Scatsta

Whalsay

A971

SHETLAND

Lerwick

Lerwick

0   25 Miles

0   40 Km

John o' Groats

Sumburgh

A836

Thurso

A9

A895

Fair
Isle

KIRKWALL
ABERDEEN

A882

Wick

0   25 Miles

A99

Wick

0   40 Km

A836

A9

A838

A897

A9

A836

A838

A896

A839

A9

A835

A836

A837

A9

Elgin

Fraserburgh

A96

A98

A952

A832

Nairn

A96

A940

A920

A98

A950

LERWICK

Inverness

A82

A96

A95

A97

A947

A90

A862

Inverness

A862

A96

A939

A920

A975

Peterhead

MORAY

A338

A95

A97

A920

A96

A9

A938

A944

A96

ABERDEENSHIRE

A947

A90

A833

A9

A939

A941

A97

A93

A980

Aberdeen

A944

Aberdeen

A93

A857

CAIRNGORMS

A86

A93

NATIONAL PARK

Ballater

A857

Map 8

Key to regions: Wales

All place names in blue have a detailed accommodation entry in this guide.

Never has a rose meant so much

Everyone has a trusted friend, someone who tells it straight. Well, that's what the Enjoy England Quality Rose does: reassures you before you check into your holiday accommodation that it will be just what you want, because it's been checked out by independent assessors. Which means you can book with confidence and get on with the real business of having a fantastic break.

The **Quality Rose** is the mark of England's *official*, nationwide quality assessment scheme and covers just about every place you might want to stay, using a clear star and diamond rating system: from caravan parks to stylish boutique hotels, farmhouse B&Bs to country house retreats, self-catering cottages by the sea to comfy narrowboats perfect for getting away from it all. Think of the Quality Rose as your personal guarantee that your expectations will be met.

enjoyEngland.com

★ ★ ★

SELF CATERING

Our ratings made easy

★	Simple, practical, no frills	◆
★★	Well presented and well run	◆◆
★★★	Good level of quality and comfort	◆◆◆
★★★★	Excellent standard throughout	◆◆◆◆
★★★★★	Exceptional with a degree of luxury	◆◆◆◆◆

Look no further. Just look out for the Quality Rose.
Find out more at enjoy**England**.com/quality

England's North Country

Cheshire   County Durham   Cumbria
East Yorkshire   Greater Manchester   Lancashire
Merseyside   North Yorkshire   northern Lincolnshire
Northumberland   South Yorkshire   Tees Valley
Tyne and Wear   West Yorkshire

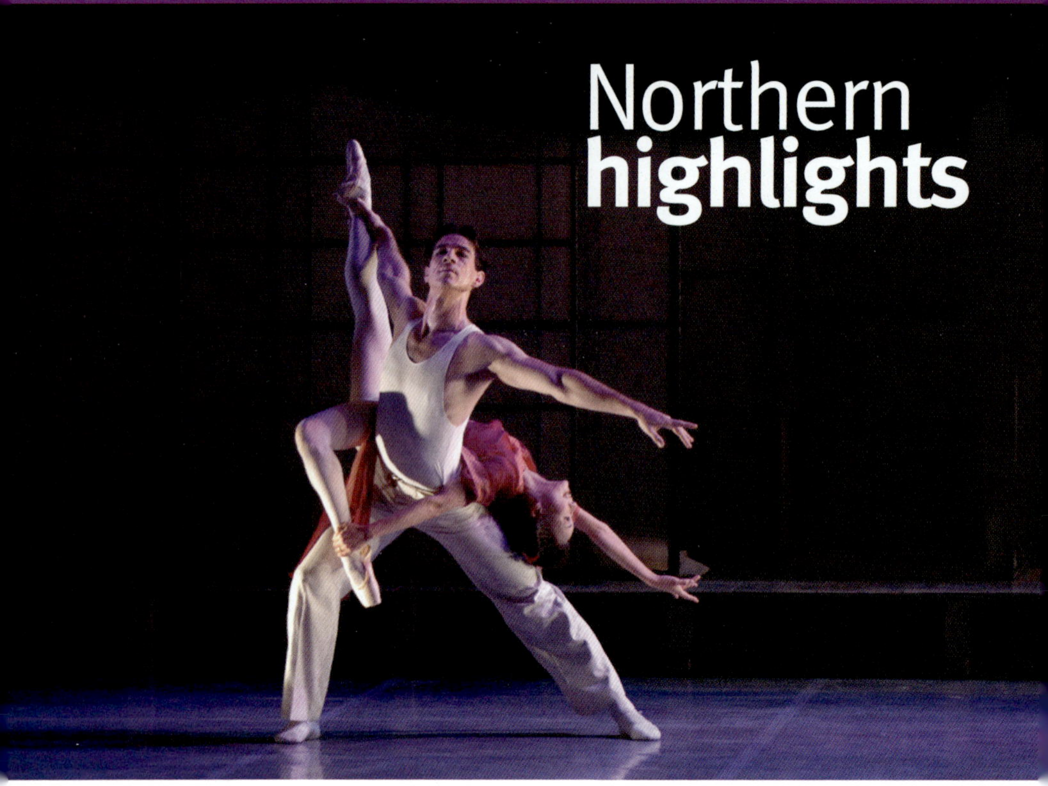

Northern **highlights**

Windswept moors and breathtaking coastlines. Mirrored glass lakes and the magnificent cathedrals of York and Durham. The urban wonders of the Gateshead Millennium Bridge and Urbis in Manchester. There is all-year-round fun and games at Blackpool. It's all just part of an ordinary day in England's proud and historic North Country.

Inspiring landscape

Let the landscape inspire you, just as it did Emily Brontë. For a brilliant metaphor for Catherine and Heathcliff's intense passion, look no further than the raging tempests of the North York Moors. Wander lonely as a cloud in the Lake District – where William Wordsworth and Samuel Taylor Coleridge both lived. Find England's highest mountain, Scafell Pike, and its deepest lake, Wastwater. You're spoilt for choice for National Parks – Yorkshire alone has over 1,000 square miles to explore. The Forest of Bowland, an Area of Outstanding Natural Beauty, is another

Lime-washed cottages in quiet hamlets; grassy fells and dales; sandy beaches with salty tide pools; majestic mountains and gently lapping lakes – simply admire the breathtaking scenery in **Cumbria – The Lake District**. golakes.co.uk

Previous page study famous collections at The Whitworth Art Gallery, Manchester
Above stunning performances at the Northern Ballet Theatre, Leeds, West Yorkshire

unspoilt gem. Blow the cobwebs away along miles and miles of sandy beaches in the North East.

All aboard

Cumbria has 16 lakes as well as beautiful rivers and tarns. Sit back and relax on an island cruise around Windermere or board a steamer on Ullswater, where Donald Campbell broke the water speed record in 1955. On Coniston Water take a trip in style on the restored Victorian steam yacht Gondola. Head north to stunning Kielder Water, Europe's largest man-made lake where a cruiser will drop you off at Tower Knowe Visitor Centre. An exhibition tells the history of the valley from before the ice age to the construction of the dam that created Europe's largest man-made lake. Seabirds? Binoculars at the ready on a Farne Island boat trip. Pick out guillemots, razorbills and thousands of bright-beaked puffins. Spot colonies of grey seals as you turn for home.

Browse the wonderful tapestry of landscapes, flavours and cultural heritage, or stay in a cosmopolitan city

Roman Britain

Imagine Roman soldiers pacing along Hadrian's Wall nearly two millennia ago. The wall was a huge undertaking – 73 miles long and built in six years. Explore the many forts, milecastles and turrets that dot its length. For an insight into life as a Roman soldier, visit

At Roman Eboracum (York) uncover more of our past at **Jorvik**, a reconstruction of a settlement showing how Vikings lived, worked and fought. **jorvik-viking-centre.co.uk**

Housesteads Fort, the most complete base. Find more Roman remains in the walled city of Chester, Britain's best-preserved Roman town – complete with partially excavated amphitheatre. The Dewa fortress – buried beneath the town – now lives on through the Dewa Roman Experience. Imagine the sights, sounds and smells of 2,000 years ago. Turn from history to shopping. Discover The Rows – two-tiered galleries packed with unique and tempting shops.

This sporting life

Get caught up in the passion of the North's great footballing tradition. Drop by the beautiful game's temples of Old Trafford, Anfield and St James' Park. A must for football fans is The National Football Museum at Preston. In March don't miss the Grand National at Aintree, near Liverpool. Feel the excitement as you witness one of the highlights of racing's National Hunt season. Terrifying jumps such as Becher's Brook and The Chair test the skills of runners, riders and punters alike.

Master builders

Be uplifted by the spiritual and physical presence of two of England's most impressive churches. York Minster, the

Step onto a tram for a trip into living history. **Beamish**, England's favourite open-air museum, enthrals with the sights, sounds and scents of yesteryear. **beamish.org.uk**

largest medieval Gothic cathedral in Northern Europe, rose phoenix-like after it was severely damaged by fire in 1984. Arrive at Durham by train and be greeted by the magnificent sight of the 900-year-old cathedral perched high above the city. Not to be outdone, many other buildings match its grandeur. Fountains Abbey, Britain's largest monastic ruin, and adjacent Studley Royal Water Garden, are must-sees. Are your walls at home a bit bare? This wasn't a problem at Castle Howard where Canalettos, Holbeins and Gainsboroughs are just some of the art treasures on display. How about some nice wallpaper? William Morris did a good line – see for yourself in Liverpool's half-timbered Speke Hall. Telly addicts will recognise the exterior of Lyme Park in Cheshire from *The Forsyte Saga*. Movie magic also transformed Alnwick Castle into a location for the Harry Potter films.

A proud industrial heritage

Where did the Industrial Revolution gather pace? In the North Country, of course! Experience its legacy in a multitude of ways. Learn about the days of early industrialisation at Quarry Bank Mill in Cheshire and the Armley Mills Leeds Industrial Museum. Visit Salts Mill at Saltaire World Heritage Site, a 'model' Victorian industrial village. Hear vivid tales at the National Coal Mining Museum in Wakefield, and the award-winning Beamish: The North of England Open Air Museum. Drift along a canal, the essential transport system of the period, past breathtaking countryside and urban heartlands. Imagine once more the romantic age of steam on the Settle-Carlisle or East Lancashire Railway, or wonder at the giant locomotives at the National Railway Museum in York.

City slickers

You can't ignore the vibes of north England's dynamic cities – Leeds, NewcastleGateshead, Manchester, Liverpool, Bradford and Sheffield. Regeneration has helped them give London a run for its money. Vibrant Leeds: by day it's a shopping mecca, by night, it's a buzzing entertainment centre. Stay in chic boutique hotels and splash out in the restored Corn Exchange. Enjoy the renaissance of Newcastle and Gateshead. Be enchanted by the stunning architecture of the Gateshead Millennium Bridge.

Visit the Merseyside Maritime Museum, relax in a waterside bar and relive the heady days of the 1950s at The Beatles Story in Liverpool's award-winning **Albert Dock.** **albertdock.com**

Shop till you drop at the MetroCentre, Europe's largest shopping and leisure centre or be awe-inspired by the amazing Angel of the North. Sheffield's Winter Garden is also a place you won't want to miss. What's more, this is a region that is culturally rich. Check out new artists at the Baltic in Gateshead, the Centre for Contemporary Art, and listen to a favourite score at Opera North. Enjoy a performance at the West Yorkshire Playhouse, Leeds, or spend hours at the National Museum of Photography, Film & Television in Bradford, the most visited national museum outside London.

A musical movement

Explore the cities of Liverpool and Manchester, both with music beating through their veins. Liverpool, named European Capital of Culture 2008, is famed as the birthplace of The Beatles. Trace their history from the world-famous Cavern Club to The Beatles Story, where you can learn all there is to know. If the visual arts interest you,

you'll love Tate Liverpool – an exciting contemporary art space. Manchester also led a musical revolution – this time in the late 1980s and early 1990s. Remember The Stone Roses and The Inspiral Carpets? Head for Salford Quays and the paintings of LS Lowry – his cityscapes are synonymous with Greater Manchester's industrial age. These areas, criss-crossed by canals, are now a thriving arts and entertainment centre. Choose between 50 free museums and art galleries in the Greater Manchester area, or spice up your life on the 'Curry Mile'. Shopping is first rate at The Trafford Centre and Harvey Nics.

further information

England's Northwest
visitenglandsnorthwest.com

One Northeast Tourism Team
(0191) 229 6200
visitnortheastengland.com

Yorkshire Tourist Board
0870 609 0000
yorkshirevisitor.com

Above thunderous waters at High Force, near Middleton-in-Teesdale, County Durham

ALNWICK, Northumberland — SELF-CATERING

★★★★–★★★★★★

Bog Mill Farm Holiday Cottages contact Mrs Ann Mason, Bog Mill Farm, Alnwick NE66 3PA **t** (01665) 604529 **f** (01665) 606972
e stay@bogmill.co.uk **w** bogmill.co.uk

ALSAGER, Cheshire — HOTEL

★★★

Best Western Manor House Hotel Audley Road, Stoke-on-Trent ST7 2QQ
t (01270) 884000 **f** (01270) 882483
e mhres@compasshotels.co.uk **w** compasshotels.co.uk

AMBLESIDE, Cumbria Map ref 5A3 — HOTEL

★★★
SILVER AWARD

B&B per room per night
s £75.00–£120.00
d £130.00–£195.00
HB per person per night
£85.00–£130.00

Rothay Manor

Rothay Bridge, Ambleside LA22 0EH **t** (015394) 33605
f (015394) 33607 **e** hotel@rothaymanor.co.uk **w** rothaymanor.co.uk

Regency country-house hotel in its own landscaped gardens in the heart of the Lake District, renowned for the warm, comfortable, friendly atmosphere and excellent food and wine. Family owned and run for over 35 years, the hotel makes an excellent base for sightseeing. Special interest holidays and mid-week breaks available. Closed 3 to 27 January.

bedrooms 6 double, 4 twin, 1 single, 5 family, 3 suites
bathrooms All en suite

From M6 jct 36 follow A591 to Ambleside. At Ambleside, turn left at traffic lights and left again 0.25 miles further on. Hotel on right.

Access ☺

General 🛋 P♿ ✂ 🍴 ❄

Rooms 🛏 📺 💧 🍵 ⚲ 🖳 🗔

Payment Credit/debit cards, cash/cheques

1 room and 1 suite adapted for wheelchair users; roll-in showers; shower chairs; dedicated wheelchair access; disabled parking.

AMBLESIDE, Cumbria — SELF-CATERING

★★★★

The Larches contact Mrs Susan Jackson, Heart of the Lakes, Fisherbeck Mill, Old Lake Road, Ambleside LA22 0DH **t** (015394) 32321 **f** (015394) 33251
e info@heartofthelakes.co.uk **w** heartofthelakes.co.uk

ARNSIDE, Cumbria — GUEST ACCOMMODATION

♦♦♦♦

Willowfield Hotel 53 The Promenade, Arnside, Carnforth LA5 0AD
t (01524) 761354
e info@willowfield.uk.com **w** willowfield.uk.com

BAMBURGH, Northumberland — SELF-CATERING

★★★★

Dukesfield Farm Holiday Cottages contact Mrs Maria Eliana Robinson, EMR Properties, The Glebe, Radcliffe Road, Bamburgh NE69 7AE
t (01668) 214456 **f** (01668) 214354
e eric_j_robinson@compuserve.com **w** secretkingdom.com/dukes/field.htm

BARDON MILL, Northumberland — GUEST ACCOMMODATION

◆◆◆◆◆
GOLD AWARD

Montcoffer Bardon Mill, Hexham NE47 7HZ **t** (01434) 344138 **f** (01434) 344730
e john-dehlia@talk21.com **w** montcoffer.co.uk

BELFORD, Northumberland — SELF-CATERING

★★★★

Elwick Farm Cottages contact Mrs Roslyn Reay, Elwick Farm, Belford NE70 7EL
t (01668) 213242 **f** (01668) 213783
e w.r.reay@talk21.com **w** elwickcottages.co.uk

BLACKPOOL, Lancashire — HOTEL

★★

Bond Hotel 120 Bond Street, Blackpool FY4 1HG
t (01253) 341218 **f** (01253) 349452
w bondhotel.co.uk

BLACKPOOL, Lancashire Map ref 4A1 — HOTEL

Rating Applied For

B&B per room per night
s £30.00–£45.00
d £60.00–£120.00
HB per person per night
£42.00–£60.00

Century Hotel

406 North Promenade, Blackpool FY1 2LB **t** (01253) 354598
e info@centuryhotel.co.uk **w** centuryhotel.co.uk

In a prime location, the Century Hotel offers excellent facilities for the visually impaired or disabled. Wheelchair access to bedrooms, wet rooms, emergency call system, equipment hire, lifts to all floors. Gold HOAST award.
open All year
bedrooms 4 double, 18 twin, 8 single, 3 family, 2 suites
bathrooms All en suite

Access ☺ 🛏 abc .: ☑ 🐕
General 🛋 P♿ 🍴 🛗
Rooms 📺 ☕ 🛁 🛏 📠
Payment Cash/cheques

BLACKPOOL, Lancashire — HOTEL

★★

New Mayfair Hotel 673-677 New South Promenade, Blackpool FY4 1RN
t (01253) 347543 **f** (01253) 349678

BLACKPOOL, Lancashire — GUEST ACCOMMODATION

◆◆◆◆

Pembroke Private Hotel 11 King Edward Avenue, Blackpool FY2 9TD
t (01253) 351306
e info@neartheprom.com **w** pembrokehotel.com

BLACKPOOL, Lancashire — GUEST ACCOMMODATION

◆◆◆◆
SILVER AWARD

Seabreeze Guest House 1 Gynn Avenue, Blackpool FY1 2LD **t** (01253) 351427
e info@vbreezey.co.uk **w** vbreezy.co.uk

BLACKPOOL, Lancashire — SELF-CATERING

★★★★

Burbage Holiday Lodge Burbage Holiday Lodge, 198 Queens Promenade, Blackpool FY2 9JS **t** (01253) 350159 **f** (01253) 356657
e enquiries@burbageholidaylodge.co.uk

BOLDON COLLIERY, Tyne and Wear — HOTEL

★★★

Quality Hotel Sunderland Junction A19/184, Witney Way, Boldon Business Park, Boldon Colliery NE35 9PE **t** (01915) 191999 **f** (01915) 190655
e enquiries@hotels-sunderland.com **w** hotels-sunderland.com

BOSLEY, Cheshire — SELF-CATERING

★★★

The Old Byre contact Mrs Dorothy Gilman, The Old Byre, Pye Ash Farm, Leek Road, Macclesfield SK11 0PN **t** (01260) 223293 **f** (01260) 223293
e d.gilman@hotmail.co.uk

BOWES, County Durham Map ref 5B3 — SELF-CATERING

★★★★

Units **5**
Sleeps **2–4**
Low season per wk
£180.00–£300.00
High season per wk
£300.00–£500.00

Mellwaters Barn, Barnard Castle

contact Mr Andrew Tavener, Mellwaters Barn,
East Mellwaters Farm, Stainmore Road, Bowes,
Barnard Castle DL12 9RH **t** (01833) 628181 **f** (01833) 628020
e mellwatersbarn@aol.com **w** mellwatersbarn.co.uk

Access	🐕
General	🐕 🏠 🪑 P ✂ ◉ Ⓢ
Unit	🛁 🍴 📷 📶 ♿ 🖥 📱 ♒ 🔥 🪜 📺 📁

Payment Credit/debit cards, cash/cheques, euros

Through platform and stairlifts. Profiling beds, adjustable easy chairs. Adjustable grab rails and wardrobe rails. Other disability equipment available.

Barn Cottages are all fully accessible to disabled people, sleeping up to four per cottage or combined for larger parties. Bedrooms can be twin or double bedded. Level-entry shower or bath with shower over and ceiling hoist. Specially adapted kitchens. Car parking close to entrance. Service dogs welcome.
open All year
nearest shop 1 mile
nearest pub 1 mile

From A1(M) turn onto the A66, signed Brough/Penrith. One mile west of Bowes, take a left-hand turn off the A66, cross Pennine route.

BRAMLEY, South Yorkshire — HOTEL

★★★

Best Western Elton Hotel Main Street, Rotherham S66 2SF
t (01709) 545681 **f** (01709) 549100
e bestwestern.eltonhotel@btinternet.com **w** bw-eltonhotel.co.uk

BUCKDEN, North Yorkshire — SELF-CATERING

★★★★

Dalegarth and The Ghyll Cottages contact Mr & Mrs David & Susan Lusted, 9 Dalegarth, Buckden, Skipton BD23 5JU **t** (01756) 760877 **f** (01756) 760877
e dalegarth@aol.com **w** dalegarth.co.uk

BURTON IN LONSDALE, North Yorkshire Map ref 5B3 — SELF-CATERING

★★★★

Units **2**
Sleeps **1–5**

Low season per wk
Min £230.00
High season per wk
Max £475.00

Brentwood Farm Cottages, Burton-in-Lonsdale

contact Mrs Anita Taylor, Brentwood Farm Cottages, Barnoldswick Lane, Burton in Lonsdale LA6 3LZ **t** (015242) 62155 **f** (015242) 62155 **e** info@brentwoodfarmcottages.co.uk **w** brentwoodfarmcottages.co.uk

General 🐾 🏛 ⌂ P ✂

Unit ♿ 🎛 📺 📻 💿 🔥 🛏

Payment Credit/debit cards, cash/cheques

Electric bed, adjustable side table, commode, elephant's feet to raise the bed/table, intercommunication all available.

Award-winning barn conversion set in tranquil countryside. Centrally located for the Yorkshire Dales, Lake District and Trough of Bowland. A hidden treasure. Central heating, electric bed, bed linen and towels included. Wheelchair accessible. A home from home.

open All year
nearest shop 1 mile
nearest pub 1 mile

M6, jct 34. Go west on A683, take A687 to Burton in Lonsdale. Or leave A65 between Skipton and Kendal at Ingleton. Go west on A687 to Burton in Lonsdale, left onto Barnoldswick Lane.

CARLISLE, Cumbria — HOTEL

★★

County Hotel 9 Botchergate, Carlisle CA1 1QP **t** (01228) 531316 **f** (01228) 401805 **e** info@countycarlisle.com **w** cairnhotelgroup.com

CATON, Lancashire — SELF-CATERING

★★★★

The Croft – Ground Floor Apartment contact Miss Sue Brierly-Hampton, The Croft - Ground Floor Apartment, 4 The Croft, Caton LA2 9QG

CHIPPING, Lancashire — HOTEL

★★★★

The Gibbon Bridge Hotel Chipping, Preston PR3 2TQ **t** (01995) 61456 **f** (01995) 61277

CLAPHAM, North Yorkshire — HOTEL

★★

New Inn Hotel Clapham, Lancaster LA2 8HH **t** (01524) 251203 **f** (01524) 251496 **e** info@newinn-clapham.co.uk **w** newinn-clapham.co.uk

CLEETHORPES, northern Lincolnshire — GUEST ACCOMMODATION

♦♦♦♦

Tudor Terrace Guest House 11 Bradford Avenue, Cleethorpes DN35 0BB **t** (01472) 600800 **f** (01472) 501395 **e** enquiries.tudorterrace@ntlworld.com **w** tudorterrace.co.uk

COCKERHAM, Lancashire — CAMPING & CARAVANNING

★★★★★

Moss Wood Caravan Park Crimbles Lane, Lancaster LA2 0ES **t** (01524) 791041

COCKFIELD, County Durham Map ref 5B3 — SELF-CATERING

★★★★

Units **2**
Sleeps **4–5**

Low season per wk
Min **£150.00**
High season per wk
Max **£340.00**

Stonecroft and Swallows Nest, Bishop Auckland

contact Mrs Alison Tallentire, Low Lands Farm,
Bishop Auckland DL13 5AW **t** (01388) 718251 **f** (01388) 718251
e info@farmholidaysuk.com **w** farmholidaysuk.com

Access	🐾
General	🛁 🏠 🛗 P Ⓢ
Unit	🏠 🏭 📺 🍳 🔥 ⬛ 📺 🔌 🔟 ⚒ 🧺 📗 🗑 🧹 ❄

Payment Cash/cheques

Adapted kitchen, level-entry shower with shower chair, raised toilet seat with handrails, ground-floor bedrooms, turning circles in every room.

Winners County Durham Accessible Award 2002. Comfortable, cosy, accessible cottage. Level-entry shower, ground-floor bedrooms, all linen and towels provided, log fire, original beams, own garden, gas barbeque. Lots to see and do for everyone. Friendly owner-run farm. A truly relaxing holiday. A warm welcome awaits you.

open All year
nearest shop 1 mile
nearest pub 1 mile

Directions on request.

CONISTON, Cumbria — SELF-CATERING

★★★★

Red Dell Cottage contact Mr Philip Johnston, The Coppermines & Lakes Cottages, The Estate Office, The Bridge, Coniston LA21 8HJ
t (015394) 41765 **f** (015394) 41944
e info@coppermines.co.uk **w** coppermines.co.uk

CORNHILL-ON-TWEED, Northumberland — GUEST ACCOMMODATION

♦♦♦♦
SILVER AWARD

The Coach House at Crookham Crookham, Cornhill-on-Tweed TD12 4TD
t (01890) 820293 **f** (01890) 820284
e stay@coachhousecrookham.com **w** coachhousecrookham.com

CRANAGE, Cheshire — GUEST ACCOMMODATION

♦♦♦♦
SILVER AWARD

Padgate Guest House Twemlow Lane, Cranage, Holmes Chapel, Crewe CW4 8EX
t (01477) 534291 **f** (01477) 544726
e lynda@padgate.freeserve.co.uk
w padgateguesthouse.mysite.wanadoo-members.co.uk

CRASTER, Northumberland — SELF-CATERING

★★★★

Craster Pine Lodges contact Mr & Mrs Robson, 9 West End, Craster, Alnwick NE66 3TS **t** (01665) 576286
e pinelodges@barkpots.co.uk **w** crasterpinelodges.co.uk

CROSTHWAITE, Cumbria — SELF-CATERING

★★★★

Greenbank contact Jackie Gaskell, Greenbank, Crosthwaite, Kendal LA8 8JD
t (015395) 68598 **f** (015395) 68598
e greenbank@nascr.net **w** greenbank-cumbria.co.uk

DARLINGTON, Tees Valley — SELF-CATERING

★★★★★

The Mill Granary contact Mr & Mrs Richard & Kate Hodgson, Middleton House,
Ingleton, Darlington DL2 3HG **t** (01325) 730339
e millgranary@aol.com **w** millgranary.co.uk

DREWTON, East Riding of Yorkshire — GUEST ACCOMMODATION

◆◆◆◆

Rudstone Walk Country Accommodation Drewton, Brough HU15 2AH
t (01430) 422230 **f** (01430) 424552

DREWTON, East Riding of Yorkshire — SELF-CATERING

★★★★

Rudstone Walk Country Accommodation contact Mrs Laura Greenwood,
South Lane, Drewton, Brough HU15 2AH **t** (01430) 422230 **f** (01430) 424552
e admin@rudstone-walk.co.uk **w** rudstone-walk.co.uk

EASINGWOLD, North Yorkshire — GUEST ACCOMMODATION

◆◆◆◆

Thornton Lodge Farm Thornton Hill, York YO61 3QA
t (01347) 821306 **f** (01347) 821306
e sue.raper@btopenworld.com **w** thorntonlodgefarm.co.uk

EAST ORD, Northumberland — CAMPING & CARAVANNING

★★★★★

Ord House Country Park East Ord, Berwick-upon-Tweed TD15 2NS
t (01289) 305288 **f** (01289) 330832
e enquiries@ordhouse.co.uk **w** ordhouse.co.uk

EBBERSTON, North Yorkshire — SELF-CATERING

★★★–★★★★★

Cow Pasture Cottage contact Manager, Cow Pasture Cottage, 67 Main Street,
Scarborough YO13 9NR **t** (01723) 859285 **f** (01723) 859285
e ernie@jhodgson.fsnet.co.uk **w** studley-house.co.uk

ELLERBY, North Yorkshire — GUEST ACCOMMODATION

◆◆◆◆
SILVER AWARD

Ellerby Hotel Ryeland Lane, Saltburn-by-the-Sea TS13 5LP
t (01947) 840342 **f** (01947) 841221
e david@ellerbyhotel.co.uk **w** ellerbyhotel.co.uk

GAINFORD, County Durham Map ref 5C3 — SELF-CATERING

★★★★

Units **2**
Sleeps **2–4**

Low season per wk
£220.00–£245.00
High season per wk
£295.00–£395.00

East Greystone Farm Cottages, Darlington

contact Mrs Sue Hodgson, East Greystone Farm Cottages,
East Greystone Farm, Gainford, Darlington DL2 3BL **t** (01325) 730236
f (01325) 730236 **e** sue@holidayfarmcottages.co.uk
w holidayfarmcottages.co.uk

A one-bedroom and two-bedroom cottage stone barn conversion, all on ground level. Situated on working farm in open countryside with lovely views. Easy access to local amenities, attractions and the Dales.

open All year
nearest shop 1 mile
nearest pub 1 mile

Access
General
Unit
Payment Cash/cheques

GOATHLAND, North Yorkshire — GUEST ACCOMMODATION

◆◆◆◆

The Beacon Guest House Goathland, Whitby YO22 5AN
t (01947) 896409 f (01947) 896431
w touristnetuk.com/ne/beacon

GRANGE-OVER-SANDS, Cumbria — HOTEL

★★★
SILVER AWARD

Netherwood Hotel Lindale Road, Grange-over-Sands LA11 6ET
t (01539) 532552 f (01539) 534121
e netherwoodhotel@aol.com w netherwood-hotel.co.uk

HARBOTTLE, Northumberland — GUEST ACCOMMODATION

◆◆◆◆
SILVER AWARD

The Byre Vegetarian B&B Harbottle, Morpeth NE65 7DG t (01669) 650476
e rosemary@the-byre.co.uk w the-byre.co.uk

HARWOOD DALE, North Yorkshire — GUEST ACCOMMODATION

◆◆◆◆

The Grainary Harwood Dale, Scarborough YO13 0DT
t (01723) 870026 f (01723) 870026
w grainary.co.uk

HULME WALFIELD, Cheshire — GUEST ACCOMMODATION

◆◆◆◆

Sandhole Farm Hulme Walfield, Congleton CW12 2JH
t (01260) 224419 f (01260) 224766
e veronica@sandholefarm.co.uk w sandholefarm.co.uk

Bank holiday dates for your diary

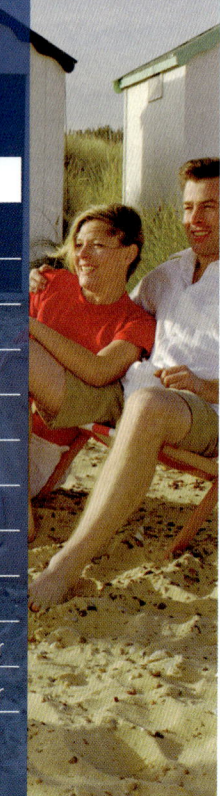

holiday	2006	2007
January Bank Holiday (Scotland)	2 January	2 January
New Year's Day (England & Wales)	2 January	1 January
New Year's Day (Scotland)	3 January	1 January
Good Friday	14 April	6 April
Easter Monday (England & Wales)	17 April	9 April
Early May Bank Holiday	1 May	7 May
Spring Bank Holiday	29 May	28 May
Summer Bank Holiday (Scotland)	7 August	6 August
Summer Bank Holiday (England & Wales)	28 August	27 August
Christmas Day	25 December	25 December
Boxing Day	26 December	26 December

ILKLEY, West Yorkshire Map ref 4B1

★★★★–★★★★★★

Units	**7**
Sleeps	**2–9**

Low season per wk
£325.00–£595.00
High season per wk
£425.00–£1,195.00

Westwood Lodge Ilkley Moor, Ilkley

contact Tim Edwards and Paula Hunt, Westwood Lodge Ilkley Moor, Westwood Drive, Ilkley LS29 9JF **t** (01943) 433430 **f** (01943) 433431 **e** welcome@westwoodlodge.co.uk **w** westwoodlodge.co.uk

Award-winning historic cottages and apartments in our friendly and welcoming country home. The largest cottage has full M2 facilities; the others have ground-floor bathrooms and toilets. Private gardens with parking adjacent to each cottage. Excellent wheelchair-friendly rail/bus links to our door. High-class shops and restaurants nearby.

open All year
nearest shop 0.5 miles
nearest pub 0.5 miles

Thirty minutes from M1/A1/M62/M65. From Ilkley station head up Wells Road (signposted Ilkley Moor). We are on the right just before the 2nd cattle grid.

Access **abc**

General

Unit

Payment Credit/debit cards, cash/cheques, euros

Weekend and mid-week breaks available throughout the year (late availability only during peak periods).

INGLETON, North Yorkshire

◆◆◆◆

Riverside Lodge 24 Main Street, Carnforth LA6 3HJ **t** (01524) 241359 **e** info@riversideingleton.co.uk **w** riversideingleton.co.uk

KENDAL, Cumbria Map ref 5B3

★★★

Units	**1**
Sleeps	**2–4**

Low season per wk
£250.00–£300.00
High season per wk
£300.00–£350.00

Barkinbeck Cottage, Kendal

contact Mrs Hamilton, Barkinbeck Cottage, c/o Barkin House Barn, Gatebeck, Kendal LA8 0HX **t** (015395) 67122 **e** barkinhouse@yahoo.co.uk **w** barkinbeck.co.uk

Converted barn in peaceful, rural location. Ideal for visiting the Lakes and Yorkshire Dales. Level access throughout. Adapted bathroom. One double, one twin bedroom, open fire, panoramic views. Owner maintained.

open All year
nearest shop 5 miles
nearest pub 5 miles

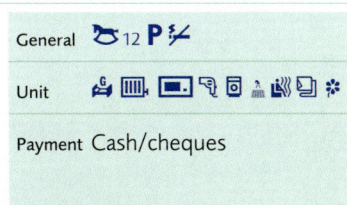

General

Unit

Payment Cash/cheques

KIELDER, Northumberland — SELF-CATERING

★★★★

Calvert Trust Kielder Calvert Trust Kielder, Falstone, Kielder Water, Hexham NE48 1BS **t** (01434) 250232 **f** (01434) 250015
e enquiries@calvert-kielder.com **w** calvert-trust.org.uk

KIRKBYMOORSIDE, North Yorkshire Map ref 5C3 — GUEST ACCOMMODATION

◆◆◆◆
SILVER AWARD
B&B per room per night
s £52.50–£65.00
d £70.00–£100.00
Evening meal per person
Min £30.00

The Cornmill

Kirby Mills, Kirkbymoorside, York YO62 6NP **t** (01751) 432000
e cornmill@kirbymills.demon.co.uk **w** kirbymills.demon.co.uk

General
Rooms
Payment Credit/debit cards, cash/cheques

Sympathetically converted 18thC watermill and Victorian farmhouse providing tranquil, well-appointed accommodation. Large rooms, powerful showers and large, fluffy towels. Guest lounge with self-serve honesty bar and wood-burning stove. Sumptuous breakfasts and pre-booked dinners served in the mill. Sorry no pets and no smoking indoors.

open All year
bedrooms 4 double, 1 twin
bathrooms All en suite

From Thirsk A170 to Scarborough. 1km after Kirkbymoorside roundabout take left turn into Kirby Mills. Entrance to car park is 20m up on right.

KIRKOSWALD, Cumbria — SELF-CATERING

★★★★

Howscales contact Liz Webster, Howscales, Kirkoswald, Penrith CA10 1JG
t (01768) 898666 **f** (01768) 898710
e liz@howscales.co.uk **w** howscales.co.uk

LANGHO, Lancashire — HOTEL

★★★

Mytton Fold Hotel and Golf Complex Whalley Road, Langho, Blackburn BB6 8AB
t (01254) 240662 **f** (01254) 248119
w myttonfold.co.uk

LIVERPOOL, Merseyside — HOSTEL

★★★★

Liverpool YHA 25 Tabley Street, Off Wapping, Liverpool L1 8EE
t (0151) 709 8888 **f** (0151) 709 0417
e liverpool@yha.org.uk **w** yha.org.uk

LONGHIRST, Northumberland — HOTEL

★★★

Longhirst Hall Longhirst, Morpeth NE61 3LL **t** (01670) 791348 **f** (01670) 791385
e enquiries@longhirst.co.uk **w** longhirst.co.uk

LONGHORSLEY, Northumberland — HOTEL

★★★

Linden Hall Longhorsley, Morpeth NE65 8XF **t** (01670) 500000 **f** (01670) 500001
e lindenhall@macdonald-hotels.co.uk **w** lindenhall-hotel.co.uk

LONGHORSLEY, Northumberland Map ref 5C1 — SELF-CATERING

★★★★–★★★★★★

Units **15**
Sleeps **2–7**

Low season per wk
£305.00–£650.00
High season per wk
£450.00–£1,375.00

Awaiting
NAS rating

Beacon Hill Farm Holidays, Morpeth

contact Mr Alun Moore, Beacon Hill House, Longhorsley, Morpeth NE65 8QW **t** (01670) 780900 **f** (01670) 780901
e alun@beaconhill.co.uk **w** beaconhill.co.uk

Access   abc

General

Leisure

Unit

Payment Credit/debit cards, cash/cheques

Three newly built cottages (aiming for mobility level 2) with roll-in showers. Four other cottages with ramps, wide doors etc.

We have 15 cottages on our beautiful 350-acre farm; marvellous views to coast and hills; a tranquil place of beauty with 40 acres of Beech woods. Indoor pool, sauna, steam room, jacuzzi, Laconium, gym, resident beautician. Tennis, games room, fly-fishing. Winner: England's Self-Catering Holiday of the Year 2000.

open All year
nearest shop 2 miles
nearest pub 2 miles

From A1(M) turn left 1 mile north of the start of the A697, north of Morpeth. Take the 2nd left signposted to Beacon Hill.

LOWER WHITLEY, Cheshire — GUEST ACCOMMODATION

♦♦♦

Tall Trees Lodge Tarporley Road, Lower Whitley, Warrington WA4 4EZ
t (01928) 790824 **f** (01928) 791330
e booking@talltreeslodge.co.uk **w** talltreeslodge.co.uk

LYTHAM ST ANNES, Lancashire — HOTEL

★★★

The Chadwick Hotel South Promenade, Lytham St Annes FY8 1NP
t (01253) 720061 **f** (01253) 714455

Check it out

Information on accommodation listed in this guide has been supplied by proprietors. As changes may occur you should remember to check all relevant details at the time of booking.

LYTHAM ST ANNES, Lancashire Map ref 4A1 — HOTEL

Rating Applied For

B&B per room per night
s £40.00–£60.00
d £80.00–£120.00
HB per person per night
£60.00–£85.00

The St Annes Hotel

69-71 South Promenade, Lytham St Annes FY8 1LZ **t** (01253) 713108
f (01253) 726674 **e** enquiries@st-annes-hotel.com
w st-annes-hotel.com

Situated in picturesque Lytham St Annes overlooking the beach. Working closely with the Disability Rights Commission, this luxurious and contemporary hotel has been exclusively designed to be accessible for all! Spacious bedrooms, stunning lounges and excellent food all ensure your stay with us will be one to remember.

open All year
bedrooms 4 double, 11 twin, 6 single, 2 family, 3 suites
bathrooms 24 en suite

M55 jct 4, follow signs for airport, then promenade. Left at T-junction, past Pontins and 1st road on right. Follow promenade road.

Access ☺ 🅱 abc •: ☑ 🏇

General ☎ P♿ ✂ 🎱 🗐 ❄

Leisure ☌

Rooms ♨ 📺 🖐 📷 ☕ 🔌 ♨ 🛏 🚽

Payment Credit/debit cards, cash/cheques

Hydrotherapy pool, ramped access, lift, level-access shower rooms, ceiling track hoist, profiling electric beds, Internet cafe, entertainment, conference room.

MANCHESTER, Greater Manchester — GUEST ACCOMMODATION

♦♦♦

Luther King House Brighton Grove, Wilmslow Road, Manchester M14 5JP
t (0161) 224 6404 **f** (0161) 248 9201

MANCHESTER, Greater Manchester — HOSTEL

★★★

Manchester YHA Potato Wharf, Castlefield, Manchester M3 4NB
t 0870 770 5950 **f** 0870 770 5951
e manchester@yha.org.uk **w** yhamanchester.org.uk

MARWOOD, County Durham — SELF-CATERING

★★★★

Hauxwell Grange Cottages (The Stone Byre and Curlew Cottage)
contact Mrs Val Pearson, Hauxwell Grange, Marwood, Barnard Castle DL12 8QU
t (01833) 695022 **f** (01833) 695022
e hauxwellvmp@supaworld.com **w** hauxwellgrangecottages.co.uk

MILLOM, Cumbria — HOSTEL

★★★

Duddon Estuary YHA Borwick Rails, Millom LA18 4JU
t (01229) 773937 **f** (01229) 773937
e duddon@yha.org.uk **w** duddonyha.org.uk

MORECAMBE, Lancashire — SELF-CATERING

★★★

Eden Vale Luxury Holiday Flats contact Mr John Coombs,
Eden Vale Luxury Holiday Flats, 338 Marine Road Central, Morecambe LA4 5AB
t (01524) 415544

NEWTON-ON-RAWCLIFFE, North Yorkshire — SELF-CATERING

★★★★

Let's Holiday contact John Wicks, Let's Holiday, Mel House,
Newton-on-Rawcliffe YO18 8QA **t** (01751) 475396 **f** (01751) 475396
e holiday@letsholiday.com **w** letsholiday.com

NORTHALLERTON, North Yorkshire — GUEST ACCOMMODATION

◆◆◆◆

Lovesome Hill Farm Lovesome Hill, Northallerton DL6 2PB
t (01609) 772311 **f** (01609) 774715
e pearsonlhf@care4free.net

OAKWORTH, West Yorkshire — SELF-CATERING

★★★–★★★★★

Bronte Country Cottages contact Ms Clare Pickles, Bronte Country Cottages,
Westfield Farm, Tim Lane, Haworth, Keighley BD22 7SA
t (01535) 644568 **f** (01535) 646686
e clare@brontecountrycottages.co.uk **w** brontecountrycottages.co.uk

OSWALDKIRK, North Yorkshire — SELF-CATERING

★★★★

Angel Cottage contact Jane Sweeney, Angel Cottage, Wheatfield, Newton Grange,
Oswaldkirk YO62 5YG **t** (01439) 788493
e jane.sweeney@lineone.net

PATELEY BRIDGE, North Yorkshire — GUEST ACCOMMODATION

◆◆◆

Greengarth Greenwood Road, Harrogate HG3 5LR **t** (01423) 711688
w bedandbreakfastexplorer.co.uk

PATRINGTON, East Riding of Yorkshire — CAMPING & CARAVANNING

★★★★★

Patrington Haven Leisure Park Ltd Patrington Haven, Patrington, Hull HU12 0PT
t (01964) 630071 **f** (01964) 631060
e info@patringtonhavenleisurepark.co.uk **w** phlp.co.uk

PICKERING, North Yorkshire — SELF-CATERING

★★★★

Eastgate Cottages contact Mr & Mrs Kevin & Elaine Bedford, Eastgate Cottages,
117 Eastgate, Pickering YO18 7DW **t** (01751) 476653 **f** (01751) 471310
e info@northyorkshirecottages.co.uk **w** eastgatecottages.co.uk

PORTINSCALE, Cumbria — HOTEL

★★★
SILVER AWARD

Derwentwater Hotel Portinscale, Keswick CA12 5RE
t (01768) 772538 **f** (01768) 771002
w derwentwater-hotel.co.uk

PRESTON, East Riding of Yorkshire — GUEST ACCOMMODATION

◆◆◆◆
SILVER AWARD

Little Weghill Farm Weghill Road, Hull HU12 8SX
t (01482) 897650 **f** (01482) 897650
e info@littleweghillfarm.co.uk **w** littleweghillfarm.co.uk

PULFORD, Cheshire — HOTEL

★★★

Grosvenor Pulford Hotel Wrexham Road, Pulford, Chester CH4 9DG
t (01244) 570560 **f** (01244) 570809
e enquiries@grosvenorpulfordhotel.co.uk **w** grosvenorpulfordhotel.co.uk

QUERNMORE, Lancashire — SELF-CATERING

★★★★

Langthwaite Farm Cottages contact Donald and Joan Deering, Langthwaite Farm Cottages, Langthwaite Farm, Lancaster LA2 9EB
t (01524) 62388 **f** (01524) 34143
e info@langthwaitefarmcottages.co.uk **w** langthwaitefarmcottages.co.uk

RAVENSTONEDALE, Cumbria — HOTEL

★★

The Fat Lamb Country Inn Crossbank, Ravenstonedale, Kirkby Stephen CA17 4LL
t (01539) 623242 **f** (01539) 623285
e fatlamb@cumbria.com **w** fatlamb.co.uk

RIMINGTON, Lancashire — SELF-CATERING

★★★★

Higher Gills Farm contact Mrs Freda Pilkington, Higher Gills Farm, Rimington, Clitheroe BB7 4DA **t** (01200) 445370

RUNSWICK BAY, North Yorkshire Map ref 5D3 — GUEST ACCOMMODATION

◆◆◆◆

The Firs

B&B per room per night
d Min £65.00
Evening meal per person
Min £16.50

26 Hinderwell Lane, Runswick, Near Whitby TS13 5HR **t** (01947) 840433
f (01947) 841616 **e** mandy.shackleton@talk21.com **w** the-firs.co.uk

Family-run guesthouse situated at the top of the bank in the picturesque coastal village of Runswick Bay eight miles north of Whitby. Spacious accommodation (all rooms en suite). Private parking. Special breaks available.
bedrooms 3 double, 2 twin,
1 single, 6 family
bathrooms All en suite

General
Rooms
Payment Cash/cheques

SEWERBY, East Riding of Yorkshire — SELF-CATERING

★★★★–★★★★★

Field House Farm Cottages contact Angela & John Foster, Field House Farm Cottages, Jewison Lane, Sewerby YO16 6YG
t (01262) 674932 **f** (01262) 608688
e john.foster@farmline.com **w** fieldhousefarmcottages.co.uk

SHEFFIELD, South Yorkshire — CAMPUS

★★

Tapton Hall of Residence The University of Sheffield, Crookes Road, Sheffield S10 2AZ **t** (0114) 222 8862
e conferences@shef.ac.uk **w** conferencesheffield.com

SHILBOTTLE, Northumberland — SELF-CATERING

★★★–★★★★★

Village Farm contact Mrs Crissy Stoker, Town Foot Farm, Shilbottle, Alnwick NE66 2HG **t** (01665) 575591 **f** (01665) 575591
e crissy@villagefarmcottages.co.uk **w** villagefarmcottages.co.uk

SILVERDALE, Lancashire — SELF-CATERING

★★★★

The Stables contact Mrs Ranford, The Stables, The Stables, Lindeth Road LA5 0TT
t (01524) 702121 **f** (01524) 702226
e conquerors.maryk@virgin.net

SKELWITH FOLD, Cumbria — SELF-CATERING

★★★★★

Crop Howe contact Mrs Susan Jackson, Hart of the Lakes, Old Lake Road, Ambleside LA22 0DH **t** (015394) 33251 **f** (015394) 33110
w heartofthelakes.co.uk

SKIPTON, North Yorkshire — GUEST ACCOMMODATION

♦♦♦

Craven Heifer Inn Grassington Road, Skipton BD23 3LA
t (01756) 792521 **f** (01756) 794442
w cravenheifer.co.uk

SLALEY, Northumberland — SELF-CATERING

★★★★

Rye Hill Farm The Old Byre contact Mrs Elizabeth Courage, Rye Hill Farm, Slaley,
Hexham NE47 0AH **t** (01434) 673259 **f** (01434) 673259
e info@ryehillfarm.co.uk **w** ryehillfarm.co.uk

SLEIGHTS, North Yorkshire — SELF-CATERING

★★★

Groves Dyke Holiday Cottage contact Niall Carson, Groves Dyke,
Woodlands Drive, Sleights YO21 1RY **t** (01947) 811404 **f** (01947) 896474
e relax@grovesdyke.co.uk **w** grovesdyke.co.uk

SOUTH KILVINGTON, North Yorkshire — SELF-CATERING

★★★

Mowbray Stable Cottages contact Mrs Margaret Backhouse,
Mowbray, Stockton Road, South Kilvington, Thirsk YO7 2LY **t** (01845) 522605

STAPE, North Yorkshire — SELF-CATERING

★★★★

Rawcliffe House Farm contact Mr & Mrs Duncan & Jan Allsopp,
Rawcliffe House Farm, Stape, Pickering YO18 8JA
t (01751) 473292 **f** (01751) 473292
e office@yorkshireaccommodation.com **w** yorkshireaccommodation.com

STRETTON, Cheshire — HOTEL

★★★★

The Park Royal Hotel Stretton Road, Stretton, Warrington WA4 4NS
t (01925) 730706 **f** (01925) 730740
e parkroyalreservations@quintessential-hotels.co.uk **w** quintessential-hotels.co.uk

SUMMER BRIDGE, North Yorkshire — SELF-CATERING

★★★★

Helme Pasture, Old Spring Wood contact Mrs Rosemary Helme,
Helme Pasture Old Spring Wood, Hartwith Bank, Summerbridge,
Harrogate HG3 4DR **t** (01423) 780279 **f** (01423) 780994
e info@helmepasture.co.uk **w** helmepasture.co.uk

SWARTHMOOR, Cumbria — SELF-CATERING

★★★–★★★★★

Swarthmoor Hall contact Bill Shaw, Swarthmoor Hall, Swarthmoor Hall Lane,
Swarthmoor, Ulverston LA12 0JQ **t** (01229) 583204 **f** (01229) 583283
e swarthmrhall@gn.apc.org **w** swarthmoorhall.co.uk

THORNTON DALE, North Yorkshire — SELF-CATERING

★★★★

Easthill Farm House and Gardens contact Mrs Diane Stenton,
Easthill Farm House and Gardens, Wilton Road, Thornton Dale, Pickering YO18 7QP
t (01751) 474561
e info@easthill-farm-holidays.co.uk **w** easthill-farm-holidays.co.uk

THORPE BASSETT, North Yorkshire — SELF-CATERING

★★★★

The Old Post Office contact Sandra Simpson, S Simpson Cottages,
The Old Post Office, Thorpe Bassett, Malton YO17 8LU
t (01944) 758047 **f** (01944) 758047
e ssimpsoncottages@aol.com **w** ssimpsoncottages.co.uk

THRELKELD, Cumbria — GUEST ACCOMMODATION

♦♦♦♦

Scales Farm Country Guest House Scales, Threlkeld, Keswick CA12 4SY
t (01768) 779660 **f** (01768) 779510
e scales@scalesfarm.com **w** scalesfarm.com

WAITBY, Cumbria — SELF-CATERING

★★★

Leases contact Mrs Christina Galloway, Leases, Swardale, Kirkby Stephen CA17 4HQ **t** (01768) 371198
e leasesgal@aol.com

WELTON, Cumbria — SELF-CATERING

★★★★–★★★★★

Monkhouse Hill Cottages contact Mr Andy Collard, Monkhouse Hill Cottages, Sebergham, Caldbeck CA15 7HW **t** (01697) 476254 **f** (01697) 476254
e cottages@monkhousehill.co.uk **w** monkhousehill.co.uk

WESTOW, North Yorkshire — GUEST ACCOMMODATION

◆◆◆◆

Blacksmiths Inn Main Street, York YO60 7NE **t** (01653) 618365 **f** (01653) 658483
e info@blacksmithsinn.co.uk **w** blacksmithsinn.co.uk

WETWANG, East Riding of Yorkshire — SELF-CATERING

★★★★

Life Hill Farm Cottage contact Fay Grace, Life Hill Farm, Sledmere, Driffield YO25 3EY **t** (01377) 236224 **f** (01377) 236685
e faygrace@breathemail.net **w** lifehillfarm.co.uk

WHITBY, North Yorkshire — SELF-CATERING

★★★–★★★★★

Captain Cook's Haven contact Anne Barrowman, Captain Cook's Haven, Larpool Lane, Whitby YO22 4NE **t** (01947) 893573 **f** (01947) 893573
w whitbyholidayhomes.co.uk

WILDBOARCLOUGH, Cheshire — SELF-CATERING

★★

Lower House Cottage contact Mrs C Waller, Lower House Cottage, Wildboarclough, Macclesfield SK11 0BL **t** (01260) 227266 **f** (01260) 227266
e sheponthehill@aol.com

WILLERBY, North Yorkshire — HOTEL

★★★

Ramada Hull Grange Park Lane, Hull HU10 6EA
t (01482) 656488 **f** (01482) 655848
e GM.hull@ramadajarvis.co.uk **w** ramadajarvis.co.uk

WINDERMERE, Cumbria — HOTEL

★★★

Burnside Hotel Kendal Road, Windermere LA23 3EP
t 0870 046 8640 **f** 0870 046 8621
e stay@burnsidehotel.com **w** burnsidehotel.com

WINDERMERE, Cumbria — HOTEL

★★★
GOLD AWARD

Holbeck Ghyll Country House Hotel Holbeck Lane, Windermere LA23 1LU
t (01539) 432375 **f** (01539) 434743
e stay@holbeckghyll.com **w** holbeckghyll.com

Key to symbols

Symbols at the end of each entry help you pick out the services and facilities which are most important for your stay. A key to the symbols can be found inside the back-cover flap. Keep this open for easy reference.

WINDERMERE, Cumbria Map ref 5A3 — HOTEL

★★★
GOLD AWARD

B&B per room per night
s £120.00–£149.00
d £140.00–£290.00
HB per person per night
£85.00–£155.00

Linthwaite House Hotel

Crook Road, Bowness-on-Windermere, Windermere LA23 3JA
t (015394) 88600 **f** (015394) 88601 **e** stay@linthwaite.com **w** linthwaite.com

Stylish country-house hotel, hilltop location with spectacular views over Lake Windermere. Beautiful gardens, log fires, comfy sofas, fine wine and 'unstuffy' staff make Linthwaite a great place to unwind.
open All year
bedrooms 19 double, 4 twin, 2 single, 1 family, 1 suite
bathrooms All en suite

Access
General
Rooms

Payment Credit/debit cards, cash/cheques

WINDERMERE, Cumbria — SELF-CATERING

★★★

Beaumont Cottages contact Charles Walmsley, Beaumont, Thornbarrow Road, Windermere LA23 2DG **t** (015394) 45521 **f** 0870 762 3693
e beaumontcottages@aol.com **w** beaumont-cottages.co.uk

WINSFORD, Cheshire — GUEST ACCOMMODATION

◆◆◆

The Winsford Lodge 85-87 Station Road, Winsford CW7 3DE
t (01606) 862008 **f** (01606) 591822
e winsfordlodge@aol.com **w** winsfordlodge.co.uk

WOOLER, Northumberland — SELF-CATERING

★★★★

Fenton Hill Farm Cottages contact Mrs Margaret Logan, Fenton Hill Farm, Wooler NE71 6JJ **t** (01668) 216228 **f** (01668) 216169
e stay@fentonhillfarm.co.uk **w** fentonhillfarm.co.uk

WOOLER, Northumberland — HOSTEL

★★

Wooler YHA 30 Cheviot Street, Wooler NE71 6LW
t 0870 770 6100 **f** 0870 770 6101
e wooler@yha.org.uk **w** yha.org.uk

WRELTON, North Yorkshire — SELF-CATERING

★★★★ – ★★★★★

Beech Farm Cottages contact Mrs Pat Massara, Wrelton, Pickering YO18 8PG
t (01751) 476612 **f** (01751) 475032
e holiday@beechfarm.com

YAPHAM, East Riding of Yorkshire — SELF-CATERING

★★★★ – ★★★★★

Wolds View Holiday Cottages contact Mrs Woodliffe,
Wolds View Holiday Cottages, Mill Farm, Yapham, York YO42 1PH **t** (01759) 302172

YORK, North Yorkshire — HOTEL

Rating Applied For

Groves Hotel St Peters Grove, York YO30 6AQ **t** (01904) 559777 **f** (01904) 627729
e admin@ecsyork.co.uk **w** ecsyork.co.uk

YORK, North Yorkshire — HOTEL

★★★★

Hilton York Tower Street, York YO1 9WD **t** (01904) 648111 **f** (01904) 610317
e carol.edwards@hilton.com **w** york.hilton.com

YORK, North Yorkshire — SELF-CATERING

★★★★ – ★★★★★

York Lakeside Lodges Ltd contact Redeef Manasir, York Lakeside Lodges Ltd, Moor Lane, York YO24 2QU **t** (01904) 702346 **f** (01904) 701631
e neil@yorklakesidelodges.co.uk **w** yorklakesidelodges.co.uk

Stockport Heritage
Where the past comes alive!

Staircase House
Travel through time and touch the past from 1460 to WWII in Staircase House...

      BSL

Hat Works
The UK's only museum dedicated solely to the hatting industry, hats and headwear....

      BSL

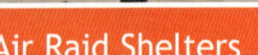

Air Raid Shelters
Step back in time to 1940s war-torn Britain in Stockport's fascinating Air Raid Shelters...

Bramall Hall
Take a trip to Bramall Hall, a magnificent Tudor manor house set in 70 acres of beautiful parkland

 Full disabled access

 Partial disabled access

 Hearing loop

 Disabled toilets

 Disabled lift access

 Guide dogs

BSL British Sign Language tour

 Disabled parking

 Coach parking

For a copy of the Stockport Visitor Guide, please contact our award-winning Tourist Information Centre on

0161 474 4444

or email: tourist.information@stockport.gov.uk

www.stockport.gov.uk/tic

STOCKPORT
METROPOLITAN BOROUGH COUNCIL

Inspirational.
Aspirational. Accessible

The moment you arrive at The Trafford Centre you'll see it's a centre designed with accessibility in mind, with 54 parking spaces reserved for disabled drivers immediately next to the entrance.

Once inside, getting around the 230 stores and 47 restaurants, cafes and bars couldn't be easier with free battery-operated scooters or manual wheelchairs, public areas, lifts and toilet blocks designed for wheelchair use, free lenses for the visually impaired and lots of red-coated assistants ready to help.

With so many accessibility features it's hardly surprising we were awarded the Queen Elizabeth Foundation EASE Award for Ease of Access, Services and Employment for disabled people.

For more information please call Customer Services on 0161 749 1510 or our Shopmobility office on 0161 7478046, or go to our website at www.traffordcentre.co.uk

The
Trafford Centre ®
always ahead

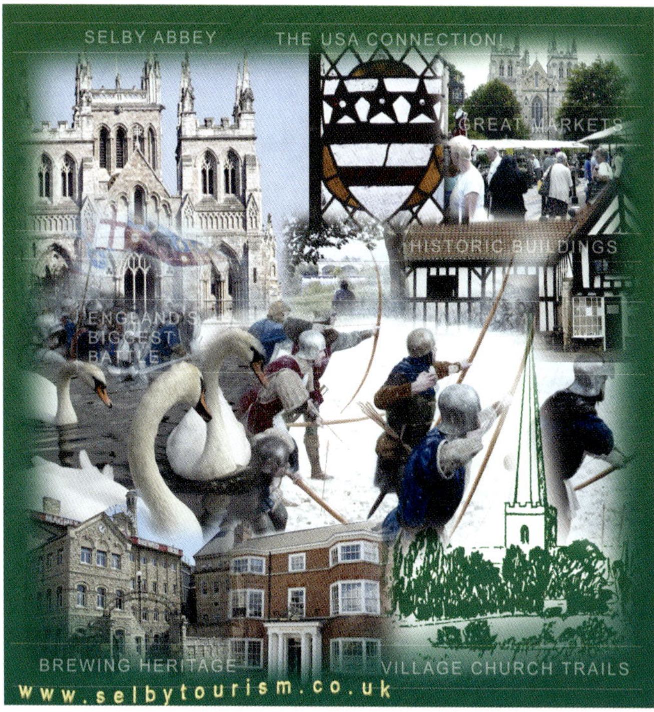

Chester for All

As part of our aim to make Chester a barrier-free city we have opened a **Shopmobility scheme**. Based conveniently close to the main shopping areas and the historic centre, the facility offers easy to use electric scooters and other mobility aids, together with blue badge parking.

Click on **www.cheshireforall.com** for the latest access information on Chester and Cheshire.

The site is regularly updated and will help you plan your visit.

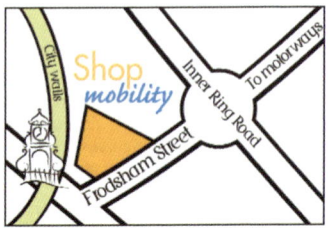

Click on **www.cheshireforall.com** or call **01244 312626**

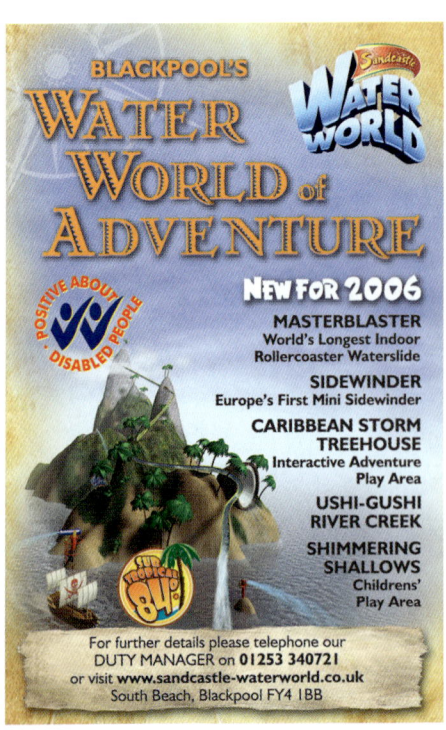

MAKE MY DAY
VISIT BLACKPOOL ZOO

- Fully accessible disabled facilities
- Free wheelchair loan
- Special rates
- Disabled parking

BLACKPOOL ZOO & DINOSAUR Safari

JUNCTION 4 M55 · FREE PARKING

East Park Drive, Blackpool. Tel 01253 830830
www.blackpoolzoo.org.uk

NewcastleGateshead

NewcastleGateshead is a superb short break destination with a fabulous mix of the traditional and the contemporary and is home to one of the most vibrant waterfronts in Europe. The city also is compact, easily accessible, with a great public transport network.

The Tourist Information Centres in NewcastleGateshead can offer information on accessible accommodation and attractions in NewcastleGateshead and North East England.

For further details call or email:
(Newcastle) 0191 277 8000,
tourist.info@newcastle.gov.uk
or (Gateshead) 0191 478 4222,
tourism@gateshead.gov.uk

NewcastleGateshead world-class culture

www.visitNewcastleGateshead.com

It's not eureka! it's my-reka!

Discover the UK's first and foremost museum for children, with 100s of extra-sensory exhibits to explore.

Discovery Road, Halifax
01422 330069 www.eureka.org.uk
EUREKA! the museum for children

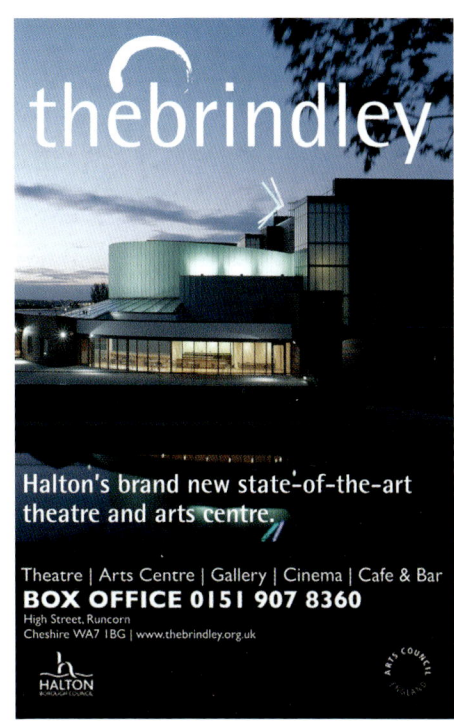

thebrindley

Halton's brand new state-of-the-art theatre and arts centre.

Theatre | Arts Centre | Gallery | Cinema | Cafe & Bar
BOX OFFICE 0151 907 8360
High Street, Runcorn
Cheshire WA7 1BG | www.thebrindley.org.uk

HALTON BOROUGH COUNCIL

ARTS COUNCIL ENGLAND

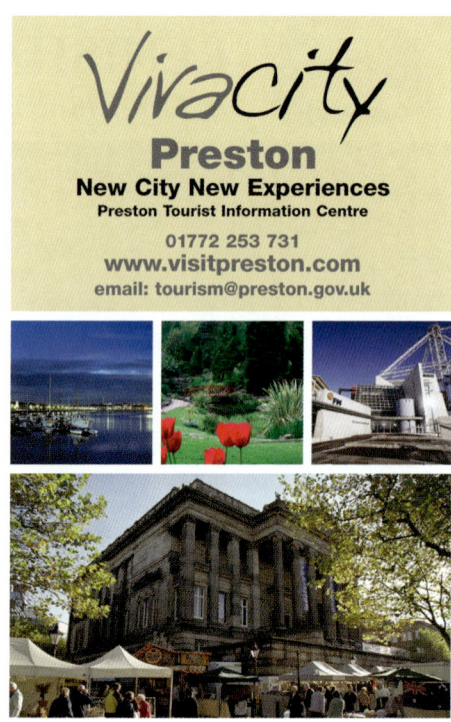
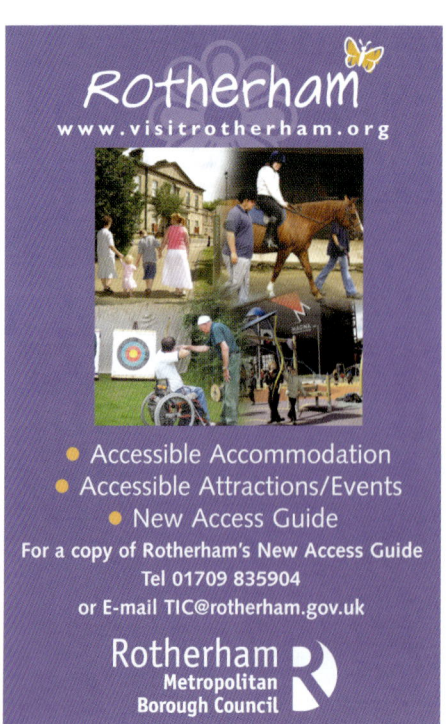
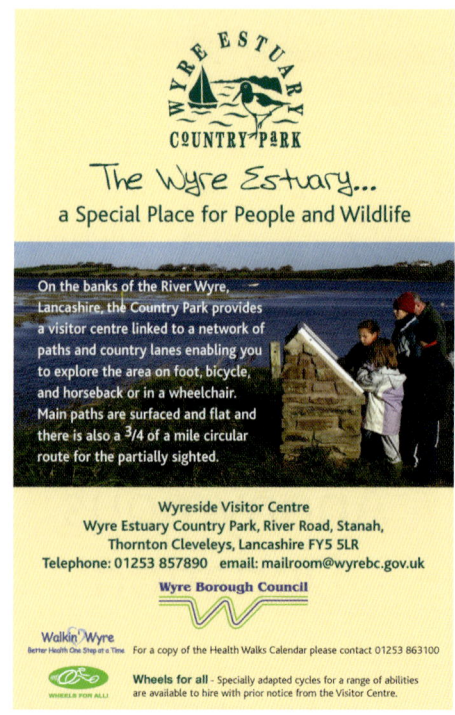

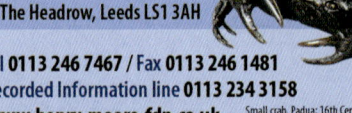

Take a **tour** of England

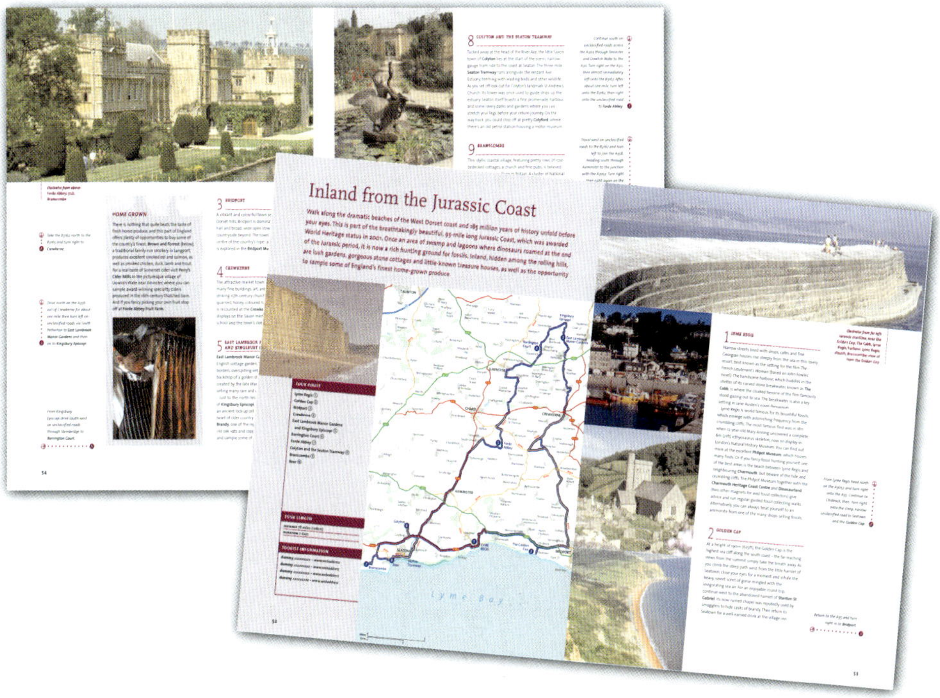

VisitBritain presents a brand new series of **three** inspirational touring guides to the regions of England: South and South West, Northern England and Central England.

Each guide takes you on a fascinating journey through stunning countryside and coastlines, picturesque villages and lively market towns, historic houses and gardens.

- Easy-to-use maps
- Clear directions to follow the route
- Lively descriptions of all the places for you to discover
- Stunning photographs bring each area to life

Touring Central England – £14.99
Touring Northern England – £14.99
Touring South and South West England – £14.99
plus postage and handling

Publication: March 2006

England's Heartland

Bedfordshire Cambridgeshire Derbyshire Essex
Herefordshire Hertfordshire Leicestershire
Lincolnshire Norfolk Northamptonshire
Nottinghamshire Rutland Shropshire Staffordshire
Suffolk Warwickshire West Midlands Worcestershire

Where the **heart** is

Heritage and culture, lazy days and great nights out – it's all on a plate in England's Heartland. Observe a living Victorian community at Blists Hill, Ironbridge Gorge; peer through binoculars at the varied bird life of the Ouse Washes; or paint the town red in Nottingham, with its late night bar and legendary club scene.

Artistic roots

England's Heartland stretches from the Fens of East Anglia to the rugged Welsh border country. With such a rich mix of industry, history, culture and raw natural beauty it's not surprising it inspired so much creative energy. Spot a solitary cottage near Flatford Mill in the Stour Valley, and it immediately hits

you. *The Hay Wain* – a masterpiece by local boy John Constable. On the streets of Stratford-upon-Avon, you just can't avoid references to the town's greatest son. William Shakespeare – England's greatest playwright. Book a seat at the Swan Theatre – home of the Royal Shakespeare Company. His

Share in Sir Benjamin Britten's legacy: be inspired by innovative works and bright new artists at the annual **Aldeburgh Festival**. aldeburgh.co.uk

Previous page picturesque, timeless Cavendish in Suffolk
Above gardeners' delight at Hatfield House, Hertfordshire

words and ideas are just as relevant today. Find out what shaped DH Lawrence's early life in his home town of Eastwood, near Nottingham. See at first hand the decadence of Lord Byron in the gothic Newstead Abbey. On a musical note, Benjamin Britten's Aldeburgh Festival at Snape Maltings, Suffolk, is the place for classical concerts in a rural setting. On Aldeburgh's beach, you can't miss a huge sculpture, The Scallop, dedicated to the composer.

Peer from hides and feel the excitement of quiet anticipation. Marsh harriers, booming bitterns and little terns – over 200 species of birds visit **RSPB Minsmere** annually. **rspb.org.uk**

Nature's playground: gritstone heights, undulating hills, inland waterways, rich earth and wide-open skies

Food-lovers' feast

Has all this culture made you a bit peckish? There's a veritable cornucopia of traditional hearty foods to stop your tummy rumbling. Succulent Melton Mowbray pork pies – so naughty, but so nice. Red Leicester and Stilton – stinky or aromatic – it's up to you! Drop in to Bakewell for a slice of pudding – often imitated, never matched. Is asparagus your favourite veg? Then don't miss the annual asparagus auction at the Fleece Inn in Bretforton in Worcestershire. Head for Britain's food capital, pretty Ludlow on the Welsh borders. Discover what lures so many top chefs to the Ludlow Marches Food and Drink Festival. Lincolnshire plumbread, Malvern spring water, world-famous Worcestershire sauce – the list of epicurean delights continues. Wash it all down with some real ale at Derby's annual CAMRA beer festival. That'll do nicely.

City lights

Remember the Bullring in Birmingham? This is urban regeneration at its most stunning. A space the size of more than 26 football pitches – all dedicated to shopping and entertainment. Fifteen thousand spun aluminium discs later and you have Selfridges' shop front. See it to believe it. The upmarket Mailbox is yet another magnet for shoppers. Hit the town at the canalside Brindleyplace.

Coventry – like a phoenix, it has risen from the destruction of wartime bombing. Basil Spence's remarkable turn of the 1960s modern cathedral vies for the city's skyline with timber-framed buildings and soaring church spires. Back to that phoenix. The Phoenix Initiative is breathing new life into the cathedral area. The impressive Whittle Arch makes its own mark on today's skyline. Soak up the colourful atmosphere of multi-cultural Leicester

Stop off and stare at the impressive, six-storey **Sibsey Trader Windmill** that still works today. Buy some stoneground organic flour or taste the home-made tearoom fare. **english-heritage.org.uk**

or spend time in medieval Nottingham, now the pulsating clubbing capital of the Midlands.

Life on the water

Need to relax? Choose from mile upon mile of sandy and shingle beaches running from Essex to Lincolnshire. Undeniably beautiful is the National Nature Reserve at Holkham, Norfolk. Here, see what is created when creeks, sand dunes, pinewoods, pastures and marshes merge.

Down along the coast at RSPB Minsmere, Suffolk, adjust your binoculars to see just a few of the wading birds and waterfowl that stop over each year. For bustling seaside resorts, try Felixstowe, Southend-on-Sea and Great Yarmouth. For something a bit quieter, seek out the havens of Frinton-on-Sea, Covehithe and Anderby Creek and the coast's numerous quaint fishing villages. Find out what life was like aboard ship with the interactive 'below decks' experience at The Norfolk Nelson Museum in Great Yarmouth.

Moving inland, explore the rivers and dykes in the Fens – spread over Cambridgeshire, Lincolnshire, Norfolk and Rutland. Titchwell and Berney Marshes also make ideal spots for bird-watching. At Fenscape, the interactive Fens discovery centre in Spalding, learn about the unique past of the inhospitable marshland. For lazy days spent with friends and family, what could be more calming than the reed-fringed waterways of the Norfolk Broads? More adventurous? Specially adapted craft at Carsington Sailing Club, Derbyshire, means that 'messing about on the water' is not out of bounds for wheelchair users.

Green fingers

It's easy to brush up on your plant life with such a wonderful choice of gardens to visit. Think small at the Birmingham Botanical Gardens, home to the National Bonsai Collection or get to grips with organic gardening at Ryton Organic Gardens, Warwickshire, where ten glorious acres also provide a haven for wildlife. The renaissance of Trentham, Stoke-on-Trent, has transformed it into one of England's top visitor attractions while Hampton Court

Birmingham's sparkling **Bullring** sets the standards in retail bliss. Shop 'til you drop, then sidle off to Cadbury World to indulge in chocolate heaven. **beinbirmingham.com bullring.co.uk**

Herefordshire, is one of the most ambitious horticultural creations of our time. Original Victorian walls enclose stunning new flower-beds divided by canals and island pavilions. The beautiful gardens at Holdenby House, Northampton, include one of the best-preserved examples of an Elizabethan rose garden. Just smell the fragance.

Great days out

Stately homes. Picture-postcard villages. Historic architecture. Living museums. White-knuckle rides. All the ingredients for a great day out. Spend time in the historic cities of Shrewsbury and Worcester – noted for uneven Tudor half-timbered architecture. Reach for your camera as you pass through Much Wenlock, one of the beautiful black and white villages of Shropshire. Castles and grand homes dot the landscape – Kenilworth Castle and Warwick Castle are favourites. Don't miss the costumed, battle re-enactments in the summer months for a real flavour of life from centuries ago.

For Elizabethan architecture at its most impressive, Hardwick Hall and Chatsworth are hard to beat. Step back into the area's proud industrial past at the Ironbridge Gorge Museums. Have a chat with the working craftsmen at The Black Country Living Museum. Trace the history of fighter planes at the Imperial War Museum Duxford in Cambridgeshire – Europe's premier aviation museum. Hold on tight for hair-raising thrills at Alton Towers in Staffordshire or cheer on your horse at Newmarket, the historical home of British horseracing.

further information

East Midlands Tourism
enjoyeastmidlands.com

East of England Tourist Board
0870 225 4800
visiteastofengland.com

Heart of England Tourism
(01905) 761100
visitheartofengland.com

Above the incredulous bridge spanning Ironbridge Gorge

ABBERLEY, Worcestershire — SELF-CATERING

★★★

Old Yates Cottages contact Mr & Mrs Richard & Sarah Goodman, Stockton Road, Abberley, Worcester WR6 6AT **t** (01299) 896500 **f** (01299) 896065 **e** oldyates@aol.com **w** oldyatescottages.co.uk

ALDEBURGH, Suffolk — HOTEL

★★★
SILVER AWARD

Brudenell Hotel The Parade, Aldeburgh IP15 5BU **t** (01728) 452071 **w** brudenellhotel.co.uk

ALFORD, Lincolnshire — GUEST ACCOMMODATION

◆◆◆◆

Half Moon Hotel and Restaurant 25-28 West Street, Alford LN13 9DG **t** (01507) 463477 **f** (01507) 462916

ALL STRETTON, Shropshire — SELF-CATERING

★★★–★★★★★

Botvyle Farm Holiday Cottages contact Mrs Gill Bebbington, Botvyle Farm, All Stretton, Church Stretton SY6 7JN **t** (01694) 722869 **f** (01694) 722869 **e** enquiries@botvylefarm.co.uk **w** botvylefarm.co.uk

ALTON, Staffordshire — SELF-CATERING

★★★

Jay's Barn contact Mrs Christine Babb, Rest Cottage, Bradley in the Moors, Alton, Stoke-on-Trent ST10 4DF **t** (01889) 507444 **e** jaysbarn@lineone.net **w** jaysbarn.co.uk

ASHOVER, Derbyshire — SELF-CATERING

★★★★★

Holestone Moor Barns contact Mr & Mrs Steve & Vicki Clemerson, Holestone Moor Barns, Holestone Moor Farm, Holestone Moor, Ashover, Chesterfield S45 0JS **t** (01246) 591263 **f** (01246) 591263 **e** hmbarns@aol.com **w** hmbarns.co.uk

ATHERSTONE, Warwickshire Map ref 4B3 — SELF-CATERING

★★★★

Units **6**
Sleeps **1–7**
Low season per wk
£275.00–£495.00
High season per wk
£310.00–£610.00

Hipsley Farm Cottages, Atherstone

contact Mrs Ann Prosser, Waste Farm, Hurley Common, Hurley, Atherstone CV9 2LR **t** (01827) 872437 **f** (01827) 875433
e ann@hipsley.co.uk **w** hipsley.co.uk

Beautifully converted luxury accommodation in the heart of the country. Wainwright – single-storey cottage, one twin bedroom, large living room/kitchen. Brooke – all ground floor, full length windows, two bedrooms, one double, one twin.
open All year
nearest shop 1.75 miles
nearest pub 1 mile

General
Unit
Payment Credit/debit cards, cash/cheques, euros

BARNEY, Norfolk — CAMPING & CARAVANNING

★★★★★

The Old Brick Kilns Little Barney Lane, Barney, Fakenham NR21 0NL
t (01328) 878305

BECK ROW, Suffolk — HOTEL

★★★

Best Western Smoke House Hotel Beck Row, Mildenhall IP28 8DH
t (01638) 713223
w smoke-house.co.uk

BEESTON, Norfolk — SELF-CATERING

★★★

Holmdene Farm contact Mrs Davidson, Holmdene Farm, Syers Lane, Beeston, King's Lynn PE32 2NJ **t** (01328) 701284
e holmdenefarm@farmersweekly.net **w** northnorfolk.co.uk/holmdenefarm

BICTON HEATH, Shropshire — CAMPING & CARAVANNING

★★★★★

Oxon Hall Touring Park Welshpool Road, Bicton Heath, Shrewsbury SY3 5FB
t (01743) 340868 **f** (01743) 340869

BLAXHALL, Suffolk — HOSTEL

★★★

Blaxhall YHA Heath Walk, Blaxhall, Woodbridge IP12 2EA **t** 0870 770 5702
w yha.org.uk

BODHAM, Norfolk — CAMPING & CARAVANNING

★★★★★

Kelling Heath Holiday Park Sandy Hill Lane, Weybourne, Holt NR25 7HW
t (01263) 588181 **f** (01263) 588599

visitBritain.com

Big city buzz or peaceful panoramas? Take a fresh look at Britain and you may be surprised at what's right on your doorstep. Explore the diversity online at visitBritain.com

BOSTON, Lincolnshire Map ref 3A1 — SELF-CATERING

★★★★

Units **8**
Sleeps **1–4**

Low season per wk
£285.00–£325.00

High season per wk
£360.00–£395.00

Elms Farm Cottages, Boston

contact Carol Emerson, Elms Farm Cottages, The Elms, Hubberts Bridge, Boston PE20 3QP **t** (01205) 290840 & 07887 652021
f (01205) 290840 **e** carol@elmsfarmcottages.co.uk
w elmsfarmcottages.co.uk

Access abc 🐾

General

Unit

Payment Cash/cheques

New barn conversion of high-quality cottages, some with wood-burning stoves. En suite facilities, private patio with picnic bench. All cottages are accessible, four with shower rooms especially suitable for wheelchair users. Grass field with wildflower meadow for guests to enjoy. Communal laundry and built-in barbeque.

open All year
nearest shop 2 miles
nearest pub < 0.5 miles

On A1121 (on eastern side or Boston side), 250m from Hubberts Bridge crossroads.

BOTTOMHOUSE, Staffordshire — SELF-CATERING

★★★

Larks Rise contact Mrs Laura Melland, Larks Rise, New House Farm, Bottomhouse, Leek ST13 7PA **t** (01538) 304350
e newhousefarm@btinternet.com **w** staffordshiremoorlandsfarmholidays.co.uk

BRIERLEY HILL, West Midlands — HOTEL

★★★★
♿

Copthorne Hotel Merry Hill Dudley The Waterfront, Level Street, Brierley Hill DY5 1UR **t** (01384) 482882 **f** (01384) 263282
e reservations.merryhill@mill-cop.com **w** millenniumhotels.com

BROSELEY, Shropshire — HOSTEL

★★★
♿

Coalport YHA c/o John Rose Building, High Street, Telford TF8 7HT
t 0870 770 5882
e Ironbridge@yha.org.uk **w** yha.org.uk

BURGH CASTLE, Norfolk — CAMPING & CARAVANNING

★★★★
♿

Burgh Castle Marina and Caravan Park Butt Lane, Great Yarmouth NR31 9PZ
t (01493) 780331 **f** (01493) 780163

BURGH ON BAIN, Lincolnshire — SELF-CATERING

★★★★

Bainfield Lodge contact Mr & Mrs D Walker, Bainfield House, Main Road, Burgh-on-Bain, Market Rasen LN8 6JY **t** (01507) 313540
e dennis.walker1@btinternet.com

CARLTON COLVILLE, Suffolk — HOTEL

★★★
SILVER AWARD
♿

Ivy House Country Hotel Ivy Lane, Oulton Broad, Lowestoft NR33 8HY
t (01502) 501353 **f** (01502) 501539
e admin@ivyhousefarm.co.uk **w** ivyhousefarm.co.uk

CASTLE ACRE, Norfolk — SELF-CATERING

★★★★

Cherry Tree Cottage contact Mr & Mrs Boswell, Wellington House, Back Lane, Castle Acre, King's Lynn PE32 2AR t (01760) 755000 f (01760) 755000
e boswell@paston.co.uk

CHATTISHAM, Suffolk — SELF-CATERING

★★★★

Granary and Stables Cottages contact Margaret Langton, Chattisham Place, Ipswich IP8 3QD t (01473) 652210
w tiscover.co.uk

CHELMARSH, Shropshire — SELF-CATERING

★★★

The Bulls Head Inn Self Catering contact Mr David Baxter, The Bulls Head, Chelmarsh, Bridgnorth WV16 6BA t (01746) 861469 f (01746) 862646
e dave@bullshead.fsnet.co.uk

CHELMSFORD, Essex — GUEST ACCOMMODATION

♦♦♦♦

Boswell House 118 -120 Springfield Road, Chelmsford CM2 6LF t (01245) 287587
w boswellhousehotel.co.uk

CHESHUNT, Hertfordshire — HOSTEL

★★★★★

YHA Lee Valley Village Windmill Lane, Cheshunt, Waltham Cross EN8 9AJ
t (01992) 628392
w yha.org.uk

CHESTERFIELD, Derbyshire — HOTEL

★★
SILVER AWARD

Abbeydale Hotel Cross Street, Chesterfield S40 4TD
t (01246) 277849 f (01246) 558223
w abbeydalehotel.co.uk

CLARE, Suffolk Map ref 3B2 — GUEST ACCOMMODATION

♦♦♦♦
SILVER AWARD

B&B per room per night
s £35.00–£50.00
d Min £70.00
Evening meal per person
£12.00–£20.00

Fiddlesticks

Pentlow, Sudbury CO10 7JW t (01787) 280154 f (01787) 280154
e sarah@fiddlesticks.biz w fiddlesticks.biz

Warm, caring hospitality with Aga cooking. Forty-five minutes or less to Colchester, Bury St Edmunds and Cambridge.
open All year
bedrooms 1 double, 1 single
bathrooms All en suite

General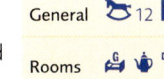

Rooms

Payment Cash/cheques

CLAXBY MOOR, Lincolnshire — SELF-CATERING

★★★★

Pelham Arms Farm contact Mrs Margaret Henderson, Claxby Moor, Market Rasen LN8 3YP t (01673) 828261
e pelhamarmsfarm@btinternet.com w pelhamarmsfarm.co.uk

COTTON, Suffolk — SELF-CATERING

★★★★

Coda Cottages contact Mrs Kate Sida-Nicholls, Poplar Farm, Dandy Corner, Cotton, Stowmarket IP14 4QX t (01449) 780076
w codacottages.co.uk

CRATFIELD, Suffolk — SELF-CATERING

★★★★

Holly Tree Farm Barns contact Ms Rachel Boddy, Holly Tree Farm, Bell Lane, Cratfield, Halesworth IP19 0DN t (01986) 798062
w tiscover.co.uk

CRATFIELD, Suffolk — SELF-CATERING

★★★★

School Farm Cottages **contact** Mrs Claire Sillett, Church Road, Cratfield, Halesworth IP19 0BU **t** (01986) 798844
w schoolfarmcottages.com

CRAVEN ARMS, Shropshire Map ref 4A3 — SELF-CATERING

★★★★

Units **5**
Sleeps **4–12**
Low season per wk
Min £366.00
High season per wk
Max £1,400.00

Upper Onibury Cottages, Craven Arms

contact Mrs Hickman, Upper Onibury Cottages, Upper Onibury, Craven Arms SY7 9AW **t** (01584) 856206 **f** (01584) 856236
e info@shropshirecottages.com **w** shropshirecottages.com

Cottage barn conversions with wheelchair access and disabled facilities on a 2,000-acre estate in beautiful countryside. Attractively furnished with large living areas and farmhouse-style kitchens. Tennis courts, indoor heated pool, gymnasium.
open All year
nearest shop 1.5 miles
nearest pub 0.5 miles

Access	abc
General	
Leisure	
Unit	
Payment	Cash/cheques

CRESSBROOK, Derbyshire — GUEST ACCOMMODATION

♦♦♦♦

Cressbrook Hall Cressbrook, Buxton SK17 8SY **t** (01298) 871289 **f** (01298) 871845
e stay@cressbrookhall.co.uk **w** cressbrookhall.co.uk

CRESSBROOK, Derbyshire — SELF-CATERING

★★★★

Cressbrook Hall Cottages **contact** Mrs Bobby Bailey,
Cressbrook Hall Cottages Ltd, Cressbrook Hall, Cressbrook, Buxton SK17 8SY
t (01298) 871289 **f** (01298) 871845
e stay@cressbrookhall.co.uk

DARLEY MOOR, Derbyshire — SELF-CATERING

★★★–★★★★★

Darwin Forest Country Park **contact** Ms Lyndsey Grayson, Darley Moor, Two Dales, Matlock DE4 5LN **t** (01629) 732428 **f** (01629) 735015
e enquiries@pinelodgeholidays.co.uk
w pinelodgeholidays.co.uk/darwin_forest.ihtml

DARSHAM, Suffolk — SELF-CATERING

★★★★

Granary and The Mallards **contact** Mrs S Bloomfield, Priory Farm, Darsham IP17 3QD **t** (01728) 668459
w holidaysatprioryfarm.co.uk

Accessible index

If you have specific accessible requirements, the Accessible index at the back of the guide lists accommodation under different categories for mobility, hearing and visual impairment.

DEREHAM, Norfolk Map ref 3B1

B&B per room per night
s £70.00–£80.00
d £88.00–£108.00
family max £125.00
Evening meal per person
Min £23.00

Greenbanks Country Hotel and 3 Palms Leisure Pool

Swaffham Road, Wendling, Dereham NR19 2AR **t** (01362) 687742
f (01362) 687760 **e** jenny@greenbankshotel.co.uk
w greenbankshotel.co.uk

Access ☺ 🐾

General 🛏 P♿ ♉ ✕ 🍴 ❄

Leisure 🏊 🛁

Rooms 🖥 📺 🍵 ⛲ 📻 📠

Payment Credit/debit cards, cash/cheques, euros

Special autumn and winter breaks. Superb facilities for disabled and wheelchairs users. Heated hydrotherapy pool for exercise.

Elegant 18thC luxury hotel and excellent restaurant in rural surroundings. Heated indoor swimming pool with full access. Five ground-floor suites for wheelchair users with built in shower rooms. Quality food using local fresh ingredients to create individual dishes adapted for coeliacs and all special diets. Awards for environmental policy and Green Tourism Gold. Queen's Award for Excellence for Sustainable Tourism.
open All year except Christmas
bedrooms 3 double, 2 twin, 1 single, 3 family
bathrooms All en suite

Travelling from Swaffham on the A47 towards Norwich, go 5 miles and turn right at the Wendling sign. Greenbanks is then on your left.

DILHAM, Norfolk

★★★★

Dairy Farm Cottages contact Mr James Paterson, Rumford Ltd, Rumford Limited, Dilham, North Walsham NR28 9PZ **t** (01692) 536883
w dairyfarmcottages.co.uk

Don't forget www.

Web addresses throughout this guide are shown without the prefix www. Please include www. in the address line of your browser. If a web address does not follow this style it is shown in full.

EAST HARLING, Norfolk Map ref 3B2

SELF-CATERING

Units **1**
Sleeps **2–6**

Low season per wk
£310.00–£435.00

High season per wk
£495.00–£655.00

Berwick Cottage, East Harling, Norwich

contact Mrs Miriam Toosey, The Lin Berwick Trust, Eastgate House, Upper East Street, Sudbury CO10 1UB **t** (01787) 372343
f (01787) 372343 **e** info@thelinberwicktrust.org.uk
w thelinberwicktrust.org.uk

Berwick Cottage features state-of-the-art facilities for the disabled in a comfortable, home-from-home setting in a picturesque village well served with shops, pubs, pharmacy and GP. Accommodation comprises one twin-bedded disability bedroom with en suite bathroom; open-plan kitchen/sitting room; two double bedrooms, one with twin beds, and bathroom upstairs.

open All year
nearest shop 0.5 miles
nearest pub < 0.5 miles

From A11 join B1111. Proceed for about 2.5 miles to market place in East Harling. The cottage is in School Lane, to the side of the Nags Head pub.

Access

General

Unit

Payment Cash/cheques

Disability facilities include electrically adjustable Scan 700 beds, overhead hoist, wheelchair-accessible shower, bath with reclining seat, Clos-o-Mat toilet and more.

EDGEFIELD, Norfolk

SELF-CATERING

★★★–★★★★★

Wood Farm Cottages contact Mrs Diana Jacob, Wood Farm Cottages, Edgefield, Holt NR24 2AQ **t** (01263) 587347
w wood-farm.com

ELLASTONE, Staffordshire

SELF-CATERING

★★★★

Dove Farm contact Mrs Jane Stretton, Dove Farm, Dove Street, Ellastone, Ashbourne DE6 2GY **t** (01335) 324357
e jane@dovefarm.co.uk **w** dovefarm.co.uk

FELIXSTOWE, Suffolk

GUEST ACCOMMODATION

◆◆◆

Dorincourt Guesthouse Undercliff Road West, Felixstowe IP11 2AH
t (01394) 270447 **f** (01394) 270447

FOXLEY, Norfolk

SELF-CATERING

★★–★★★★

Moor Farm Stable Cottages contact Mr Paul Davis, Moor Farm, Foxley, Dereham NR20 4QP **t** (01362) 688523
w moorfarmstablecottages.co.uk

84

FRAMLINGHAM, Suffolk — SELF-CATERING

★★★

Boundary Farm contact Mrs Susan Seabrook, Boundary Farm, Saxtead Road, Framlingham, Woodbirdge IP13 9PZ **t** (01728) 621026

FROGHALL, Staffordshire — SELF-CATERING

Rating Applied For

Foxtwood Cottages contact Mr & Mrs Clive & Alison Worrall, Foxtwood Cottages, Foxt Road, Foxt, Stoke-on-Trent ST10 2HJ **t** (01538) 266160
e info@foxtwood.co.uk **w** foxtwood.co.uk

GOULCEBY, Lincolnshire — SELF-CATERING

★★★★

Bay Tree Cottage contact Gordon Reid, Bay Tree Cottage, Goulceby Postford Way, Goulceby LN11 9WD **t** (01507) 343230 **f** (01507) 343920
e goulcebypost@ukonline.co.uk

GRAFTON, Worcestershire — SELF-CATERING

★★★★

Anvil Cottage, Apple Bough and Cider Press contact Mrs Jennie Layton, Grafton Villa Farmhouse, Grafton, Hereford HR2 8ED
t (01432) 268689 **f** (01432) 268689
e jennielayton@ereal.net **w** graftonvilla.co.uk

HADLEIGH, Suffolk — GUEST ACCOMMODATION

♦♦♦♦

Odds and Ends House High Street, Hadleigh, Ipswich IP7 5EJ **t** (01473) 822032

HAGWORTHINGHAM, Lincolnshire — SELF-CATERING

★★★★
Kingfisher Lodge contact Nick Bowser, E.W. Bowser & Son Ltd,
The Estate Office Leverton, Boston PE22 0AA **t** (01205) 870210 **f** (01205) 870602
e office@ewbowser.com

HALLOW, Worcestershire — SELF-CATERING

★★★★

The New Cottage contact Mr & Mrs Michael & Doreen Jeeves, The New Cottage, Bridles End House, Greenhill Lane, Hallow, Worcester WR2 6LG **t** (01905) 640953
e jeeves@thenewcottage.co.uk **w** thenewcottage.co.uk

HANLEY SWAN, Worcestershire — CAMPING & CARAVANNING

★★★★★

Blackmore Camping and Caravanning Club Site Camp Site No 2, Hanley Swan, Worcester WR8 0EE **t** (01684) 310280
w campingandcaravanningclub.co.uk

HARMER HILL, Shropshire — SELF-CATERING

★★★★
Newton Meadows Holiday Cottages contact Mr & Mrs Simcox, Wem Road, Harmer Hill, Shrewsbury SY2 3DZ **t** (01939) 290346 **f** (01939) 290346
e e.simcox@btopenworld.com **w** virtual-shropshire.co.uk/newton

---

visitBritain.com

Get in the know – log on for a wealth of information and inspiration. All the latest news on places to visit, events and quality-assessed accommodation is literally at your fingertips. Explore all that Britain has to offer!

HARTINGTON, Derbyshire Map ref 4B2 — SELF-CATERING

★★★–★★★★★

Units **3**
Sleeps **2–5**

Low season per wk
£175.00–£295.00

High season per wk
£300.00–£450.00

Dairy Cottage, Piggery Place, Shire's Rest,
Buxton

contact Mrs Flower, Dairy Cottage, Piggery Place, Shire's Rest, Newhaven, Hartington, Buxton SK17 0DY **t** (01629) 636268 **f** (01629) 636268 **e** s.flower1@virgin.net **w** oldhousefarm.com

General 🐴 ▥ 🔥 P ✎ Ⓢ

Unit

Payment Cash/cheques

Weekend/mid-week breaks available off-peak.

Piggery Place has character beams and offers level access. Two lovely bedrooms (king-size and twin beds). Wet-floor shower room. Open-plan living area with oak-beamed fireplace and living-flame cast iron stove. Serviced personally to maintain a high standard. We are on site should you need us. A wheelchair-friendly trail leads from the farm. Disabled cycle hire nearby (booking required).
open All year
nearest shop 4.5 miles
nearest pub 2 miles
Located in Newhaven on A5012 near junction to A515.

HERTFORD, Hertfordshire — SELF-CATERING

★★★

Petasfield Cottages contact Miss Helen Clark, Mangrove Lane, Hertford SG13 8AJ **t** (01992) 504201 **w** petasfieldcottages.co.uk

HOLBECK, Nottinghamshire — GUEST ACCOMMODATION

◆◆◆◆◆
GOLD AWARD

Browns The Old Orchard Cottage, Worksop S80 3NF **t** (01909) 720659 **f** (01909) 720659 **e** browns@holbeck.fsnet.co.uk **w** brownsholbeck.co.uk

HORHAM, Suffolk — SELF-CATERING

★★★

Alpha Cottages contact Mr Brian Cooper, Alpha Cottages, Horham IP21 5DX **t** (01379) 384424 **w** tiscover.co.uk

HORNCASTLE, Lincolnshire — HOTEL

★★★

Best Western Admiral Rodney Hotel North Street, Horncastle, Lincoln LN9 5DX **t** (01507) 523131 **f** (01507) 523104 **e** reception@admiralrodney.com **w** admiralrodney.com

HORNING, Norfolk — SELF-CATERING

★★★–★★★★★

King Line Cottages contact Mr Robert King, King Line Cottages, Horning NR12 8LZ **t** (01692) 630297 **w** norfolk-broads.co.uk

HORSINGTON, Lincolnshire — SELF-CATERING

★★★

Wayside Cottage contact Mr & Mrs Ian and Jane Williamson, 72 Mill Lane, Horsington, Woodhall Spa LN10 6QZ **t** (01526) 353101
e will@williamsoni.freeserve.co.uk **w** skegness.net/woodhallspa.htm

HUNSTANTON, Norfolk Map ref 3B1 — HOTEL

★★

B&B per room per night
s £45.00–£59.00
d £70.00–£99.00
HB per person per night
£55.00–£75.00

Caley Hall Hotel

Old Hunstanton Road, Old Hunstanton, Hunstanton PE36 6HH
t (01485) 533486 **f** (01485) 533348 **e** mail@caleyhallhotel.co.uk
w caleyhallhotel.co.uk

General
Rooms

Payment Credit/debit cards, cash/cheques

2 rooms feature specially adapted bathrooms with level-access shower. The hotel has no steps.

Caley Hall Hotel and Restaurant is set around a manor-house dating back to 1648. More recently, the old farm outbuildings have been converted to provide the spacious en suite bedrooms, restaurant and bar. Most of the rooms are on the ground floor, and some feature a four-poster bed or whirlpool bath.
open All year except Christmas and New Year
bedrooms 15 double, 15 twin, 4 single, 5 family, 1 suite
bathrooms All en suite

In Old Hunstanton, on the left-hand side of the A149, just before the turning to the golf course.

ILAM, Staffordshire — SELF-CATERING

★★★★

Beechenhill Cottage and The Cottage by the Pond contact Mrs Sue Prince, Beechenhill Cottage and The Cottage by the Pond, Beechenhill Farm, Ilam, Ashbourne DE6 2BD **t** (01335) 310274 **f** (01335) 310467
w beechenhill.co.uk

ILAM, Staffordshire — HOSTEL

★★★

Ilam Hall YHA Ilam Hall, Ashbourne DE6 2AZ **t** 0870 770 5879 **f** (01335) 350350
e ilam@yha.org.uk **w** yha.org.uk

INGOLDMELLS, Lincolnshire — SELF-CATERING

★★★★

Ingoldale Park contact Mrs Cathryn Whitehead, Ingoldale Park, Roman Bank, Ingoldmells, Skegness PE25 1LL **t** (01754) 872335 **f** (01754) 873887
e ingoldalepark@btopenworld.com **w** ingoldmells.net

IPSWICH, Suffolk — HOTEL

★★★
SILVER AWARD

Courtyard by Marriott Ipswich The Havens, Ransomes Europark, Ipswich IP3 9SJ
t (01473) 272244
w marriotthotels.com

KELLING, Norfolk — HOTEL

★★

The Pheasant Hotel Coast Road, Kelling NR25 7EG **t** (01263) 588382
w pheasanthotelnorfolk.co.uk

KESSINGLAND, Suffolk — SELF-CATERING

Rating Applied For

Four Winds Retreat contact Mr Peter & Jane Garner, Four Winds Retreat,
Kessingland NR33 7RR **t** (01502) 740044
w four-winds-retreat.co.uk

KNIGHTCOTE, Warwickshire Map ref 2C1 — SELF-CATERING

★★★★★

Units **5**
Sleeps **1–10**

Low season per wk
£355.00–£959.00
High season per wk
£470.00–£1,340.00

Knightcote Farm Cottages, Southam

contact Mrs Fiona Walker, The Bake House, Knightcote, Southam CV47 2EF
t (01295) 770637 **f** (01295) 770135 **e** fionawalker@farmcottages.com
w farmcottages.com

Lovingly adapted farm cottages provide luxury with accessibility. Be greeted with chilled wine, freshly arranged flowers and home-made cake. Beautiful beds with soft cotton sheets and lovely en suite bathrooms with fluffy towels.

open All year
nearest shop 2 miles
nearest pub 2 miles

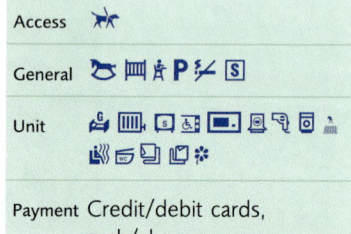

Access

General

Unit

Payment Credit/debit cards, cash/cheques

LEDBURY, Herefordshire — SELF-CATERING

★★★–★★★★★

The Old Kennels Farm contact Mrs J K Wilce, The Old Kennels Farm,
Bromyard Road, Ledbury HR8 1LG **t** (01531) 635024 **f** (01531) 635241
e wilceoldkennelsfarm@btinternet.com **w** oldkennelsfarm.co.uk

LEOMINSTER, Herefordshire — GUEST ACCOMMODATION

♦♦♦

Bramlea Barons Cross Road, Leominster HR6 8RW
t (01568) 613406 **f** (01568) 613406

LINCOLN, Lincolnshire — GUEST ACCOMMODATION

♦♦♦♦

Damon's Motel 997 Doddington Road, Lincoln LN6 3SE
t (01522) 887733 **f** (01522) 887734

LINCOLN, Lincolnshire Map ref 4C2

★★★★

Units **1**

Sleeps **4**

Low season per wk
Min **£290.00**
High season per wk
Max **£350.00**

Cliff Farm Cottage, North Carlton

contact Mrs Rae Marris, Cliff Farm Cottage, Cliff Farm, North Carlton, Lincoln LN1 2RP **t** (01522) 730475 **e** rae.marris@farming.co.uk **w** cliff-farm-cottage.co.uk

General

Unit

Payment Cash/cheques

Short breaks, min 3 nights.

Combine the historic cathedral city of Lincoln with the tranquillity of the countryside. Charming cottage situated three miles north of the city, on a working arable farm with panoramic views over the Trent Valley. Spacious accommodation with level access throughout, wheelchair friendly, fully adapted kitchen and en suite shower room, secluded garden. A warm welcome.

open All year
nearest shop 3 miles
nearest pub 4 miles

From south: A46 left A15 Humber Bridge, 1st left A1500 Gainsborough, 1st left B1398 Lincoln, 2nd left Cliff Farm. From north: A15 south, right A1500.

LITTLE DEWCHURCH, Herefordshire

★★★★

The Granary contact Ms Karen Tibbetts, The Granary, Henclose Farm, Little Dewchurch, Hereford HR2 6PP **t** (01432) 840826 **f** (01432) 840826

LITTLE TARRINGTON, Herefordshire

★★★★

Stock's Cottage contact Mrs Angela Stock, Stock's Cottage, Little Tarrington, Hereford HR1 4JA **t** (01432) 890243 **f** (01432) 890243 **e** stay@stockscottage.co.uk **w** stockscottage.co.uk

LOWESTOFT, Suffolk

★★★

SILVER AWARD

Hotel Victoria Kirkley Cliff, Lowestoft NR33 0BZ **t** (01502) 574433 **w** hotelvictoria.freeserve.co.uk

Check the maps

Colour maps at the front pinpoint all places in which you will find accommodation entries in the regional sections. Pick your location and then refer to the Place index at the back to find the page number.

LUDLOW, Shropshire Map ref 4A3 — SELF-CATERING

★★★

Units **5**
Sleeps **1–6**

Low season per wk
£195.00–£280.00
High season per wk
£275.00–£410.00

Mocktree Barns Holiday Cottages, Ludlow

contact Mr & Mrs Clive & Cynthia Prior, Mocktree Barns Holiday Cottages, Mocktree, Leintwardine, Ludlow SY7 0LY **t** (01547) 540441
e mocktreebarns@care4free.net **w** mocktreeholidays.co.uk

Attractive country cottages (two single storey), easy access, suit couples. Lovely accessible wildlife gardens, gentle walks. Many location attractions. Helpful owners adjacent. Dogs welcome.
open All year
nearest shop 1.5 miles
nearest pub 1 mile

General 🐕 🏛 ♿ P ✂ ⏺ S

Unit 🔧 🏢 ⏺ 📺 🔌 🛏 🔥 📱 📷 ❄

Payment Cash/cheques

MADELEY, Shropshire — CAMPING & CARAVANNING

★★★★★

Severn Gorge Park Bridgnorth Road, Tweedale, Telford TF7 4JB
t (01952) 684789 **f** (01952) 684789
e info@severngorgepark.co.uk **w** severngorgepark.co.uk

MALTBY LE MARSH, Lincolnshire — SELF-CATERING

★★★★

Yew Tree Cottage and The Granary contact Mrs Ann Graves, Grange Farm, Maltby le Marsh, Alford LN13 0JP **t** (01507) 450267
e grangefarm@beeb.net **w** grange-farmhouse.co.uk

Bank holiday
dates for your diary

holiday	2006	2007
January Bank Holiday (Scotland)	2 January	2 January
New Year's Day (England & Wales)	2 January	1 January
New Year's Day (Scotland)	3 January	1 January
Good Friday	14 April	6 April
Easter Monday (England & Wales)	17 April	9 April
Early May Bank Holiday	1 May	7 May
Spring Bank Holiday	29 May	28 May
Summer Bank Holiday (Scotland)	7 August	6 August
Summer Bank Holiday (England & Wales)	28 August	27 August
Christmas Day	25 December	25 December
Boxing Day	26 December	26 December

MALVERN, Worcestershire Map ref 2B1 — SELF-CATERING

★★★★–★★★★★

Units **2**
Sleeps **2–5**
Low season per wk
£308.00–£375.00
High season per wk
£637.00–£693.00

Hidelow House Cottages, Worcester

contact Mrs Pauline Diplock, Hidelow House Cottages,
Hidelow House, Acton Green, Acton Beauchamp,
Worcester WR6 5AH **t** (01886) 884547 **f** (01886) 884658
e stay@hidelow.co.uk **w** hidelow.co.uk

Access abc

General

Unit

Payment Credit/debit cards,
cash/cheques, euros

Range of aids-to-living available,
including profiling bed, hoist,
mattress, shower chairs. Qualified
carers available; profile of local
accessible places.

Worry-free, award-winning luxury holiday accommodation with second-to-none care, service and specialist facilities for disabled guests and their carers. Homely, level-access, spacious single-storey cottages. Roll-in shower rooms, wheelchair-friendly kitchens, accessible landscaped gardens and stunning views across rural Herefordshire. Visitors' information room, payphone, shop, computer/broadband facilities, laundry and drying room all fully accessible.

open All year
nearest shop < 0.5 miles
nearest pub 3 miles

M5, jct 7. A4103 Worcester to Hereford. Turn right at B4220, signposted Bromyard. Hidelow House is 2 miles from this junction on left.

MAYFIELD, Staffordshire — GUEST ACCOMMODATION

◆◆◆◆

Mona Villas Bed and Breakfast 1 Mona Villas, Church Lane, Ashbourne DE6 2JS
t (01335) 343773 **f** (01335) 343773

NAYLAND, Suffolk — SELF-CATERING

★★★★–★★★★★

Gladwins Farm contact Mr Pauline Dossor, Gladwins Farm, Nayland CO6 4NU
t (01206) 262261
w gladwinsfarm.co.uk

NORTH WALSHAM, Norfolk — CAMPING & CARAVANNING

★★★★★

Two Mills Touring Park Yarmouth Road, North Walsham NR28 9NA
t (01692) 405829 **f** (01692) 405829

★★★
Units **1**
Sleeps **1–4**
Low season per wk
£185.00–£225.00
High season per wk
£250.00–£265.00

The Netus Barn, Wickham Skeith, Eye
contact Mrs Joy Homan, Street Farm, Eye IP23 8LP t (01449) 766275
e joygeoff@homansf.freeserve.co.uk

Delightful, sympathetically restored, single-storey period barn, specially adapted with disabled visitor in mind. Patio garden with pleasant rural views. Ideally placed for touring East Anglia. Ample, convenient parking. Dogs welcome.
open All year
nearest shop 2 miles
nearest pub 2 miles

General
Unit
Payment Cash/cheques

◆◆◆◆◆
GOLD AWARD

The Old Lock-Up North End, Wirksworth, Matlock DE4 4FG t (01629) 826272
e wheeler@theoldlockup.co.uk w theoldlockup.co.uk

★★★★
Units **3**
Sleeps **2–4/5**
Low season per wk
£150.00–£200.00
High season per wk
£200.00–£400.00

Common Right Barns, Wisbech
contact Mrs Teresa Fowler, Common Rights Barn,
Plash Drove, Tholomas Drove, Wisbech St Mary, Wisbech PE13 4SP
t (01945) 410424 f (01945) 410424 e teresa@commonrightbarns.co.uk
w commonrightbarns.co.uk

Self-catering properties in renovated, beamed barn buildings. Rural hamlet situation, five miles from the Fenland market town and port of Wisbech. Central for many towns, interests and attractions.
open All year
nearest shop 2 miles
nearest pub < 0.5 miles

Access
General
Unit
Payment Cash/cheques
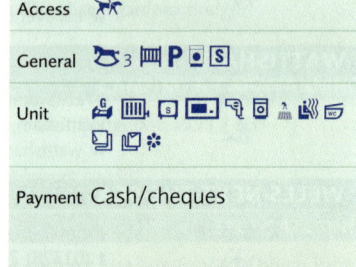

visitBritain.com

Get in the know – log on for a wealth of information and inspiration. All the latest news on places to visit, events and quality-assessed accommodation is literally at your fingertips. Explore all that Britain has to offer!

WOBURN, Bedfordshire Map ref 2C1 — HOTEL

★★★
SILVER AWARD

B&B per room per night
s £110.00–£135.00
d £125.00–£155.00
HB per person per night
£95.00–£125.00

**Awaiting
NAS rating**

The Inn at Woburn

George Street, Woburn, Milton Keynes MK17 9PX **t** (01525) 290441
f (01525) 290432 **e** enquiries@theinnatwoburn.com
w theinnatwoburn.com

Situated in the heart of Woburn village with easy access to the stately home of Woburn Abbey with its many works of great historical interest, as well as the 3,000-acre Deer Park. The award-winning Olivier's Restaurant delivers a superb menu of English continental cuisine.

open All year
bedrooms 37 double, 7 twin, 4 single, 2 family, 7 suites
bathrooms All en suite

Five minutes' drive from jct 13 off the M1. Follow the signs for Woburn and Woburn Abbey.

Access

General

Rooms

Payment Credit/debit cards, cash/cheques, euros

WOODHALL SPA, Lincolnshire Map ref 4D2 — HOTEL

★★★

B&B per room per night
s £92.00–£112.00
d £136.00–£182.00
HB per person per night
£88.00–£134.00

Petwood Hotel

Stixwould Road, Woodhall Spa LN10 6QF **t** (01526) 352411 **f** (01526) 353473
e reception@petwood.co.uk **w** petwood.co.uk

Originally built in the early 1900s, the Petwood Hotel stands in a 30-acre estate and is famous for its magnificent gardens. Individually designed bedrooms. Short holidays available.

open All year
bedrooms 21 double, 13 twin, 6 single, 8 family, 5 suites
bathrooms All en suite

Access

General

Rooms

Payment Credit/debit cards, cash/cheques, euros

Place index

If you know where you want to stay the index at the back of the guide will give you the page number which lists accommodation in your chosen town, city or village. Check out the other useful indexes too.

WOODHALL SPA, Lincolnshire Map ref 4D2 — GUEST ACCOMMODATION

Kirkstead Old Mill Cottage

◆◆◆◆

B&B per room per night
s £36.00–£50.00
d £54.00–£60.00

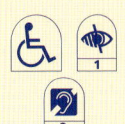

Tattershall Road, Woodhall Spa LN10 6UQ **t** (01526) 353637
f (01526) 352574 **e** barbara@woodhallspa.com **w** woodhallspa.com

A warm welcome awaits you at Barbara and Tony Hodgkinson's sunny, tranquil, riverside home. The superior en suite bedrooms are well-equipped, with the ground-floor one specially designed to accommodate the less mobile with extra wide doors, adjustable beds and a wheel-in shower. The wheelchair-friendly garden has several restful patios.

open All year except Christmas
bedrooms 1 double, 2 twin
bathrooms All en suite

Please see website for travel directions. Full directions supplied at time of booking. Ordnance Survey reference 187602.

Access

General

Rooms

Payment Credit/debit cards, cash/cheques, euros

10% discount on additional weekday nights. Our electric scooter will take you onto the bank of the River Witham.

WOODHALL SPA, Lincolnshire — SELF-CATERING

★★

Mill Lane Cottage contact Mr & Mrs Ian and Jane Williamson, 72 Mill Lane, Woodhall Spa LN10 6QZ **t** (01526) 353101
e will@williamsoni.freeserve.co.uk **w** skegness.net/woodhallspa.htm

WORTWELL, Norfolk — CAMPING & CARAVANNING

★★★★

Little Lakeland Caravan Park Little Lakeland Caravan Park, Wortwell, Harleston IP20 0EL **t** (01986) 788646 **f** (01986) 788646

WYMONDHAM, Norfolk — HOTEL

★★

Best Western Wymondham Consort Hotel Market Street, Wymondham NR18 0BB **t** (01953) 606721
w wymondhamconsorthotel.co.uk

To your credit

If you book by phone you may be asked for your credit card number. If so, it is advisable to check the proprietor's policy in case you have to cancel your reservation at a later date.

Join the Club
great sites, great value, great times.

Folkestone Site

Membership Only £30

Our Club is run by members, for members, that's why our services are so relevant to your needs. Our 92 UK Club Sites are well equipped, with excellent facilities and a legendary reputation for cleanliness. We have over 1,200 certificated Sites in picturesque locations, plus super value Holiday Sites.

The Camping and Caravanning Club welcomes people with disabilities and strives to provide the facilities they need. For many years the Club has had a rolling programme of improvements to its Sites for campers and caravanners with special needs and the vast majority of our Sites now have dedicated disabled facilities. Our annual Sites guide Your Place in the Country - which is free to every member - lists those Sites with disabled facilities.

FREE TO MEMBERS a pack of essential Club publications from Sites Guides and Directories to a monthly magazine and events listing. You'll find them all invaluable.

TO REQUEST A FREE INFORMATION PACK*
OR JOIN WITH YOUR CREDIT CARD DETAILS

Tel: 024 7685 6797

Cost is £30, plus a £5 joining fee which is waived if you pay by continuous credit or debit card transaction or Direct Debit.

PLEASE QUOTE REF 0344

REDUCED SITE CHARGES IF YOU ARE 55 OR OVER
...and Special Deals for Families

GREAT SITES AND GREAT SERVICES FOR OVER 100 YEARS

The Camping and Caravanning Club

The friendly Club

* We will use details you provide for servicing your enquiry and informing you of Member Services. We will disclose your information to our service providers only for these purposes and will not keep it beyond a reasonable period of time.

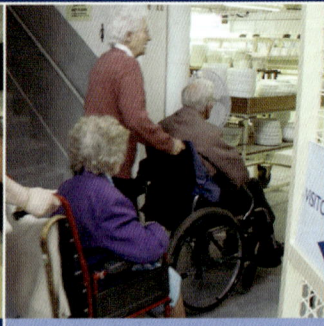

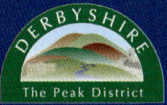
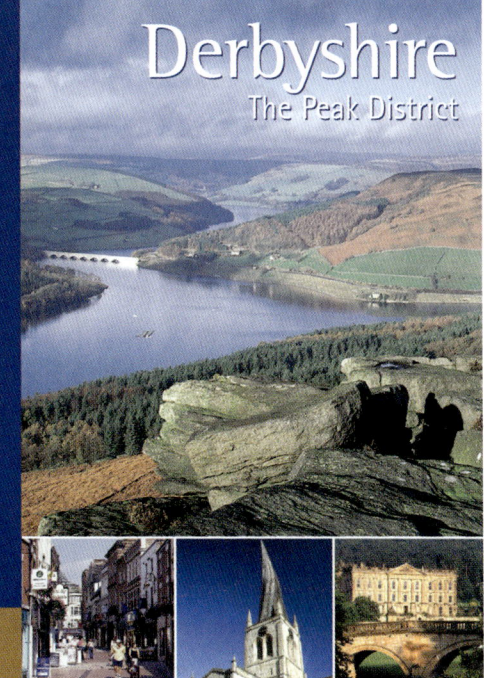

Norfolk

Time to explore

www.visitnorfolk.co.uk

Norfolk Tourism
Room 501A
County Hall
Norwich
Norfolk NR1 2DH

Tel: 01603 222846
Fax: 01603 223104

Always something new to see and do

- Free admission
- Open
  Tues to Sat: 10am - 5pm
  Sun: 12pm - 5pm
  and Bank Holiday Monday
- Fully accessible with lifts to all floors

The New Art Gallery
Gallery Square
Walsall
WS2 8LG

Tel: 01922 654400
www.artatwalsall.org.uk

Walsall Council

Welcome to
Redwings
Horse Sanctuary

Home to rescued horses, ponies and donkeys!

FREE ADMISSION

Meet rescued horses, ponies and donkeys at one of our visitor centres in Norfolk, Suffolk and elsewhere in the UK.

Enquiries including accessibility for our centres

0870 040 0033

Visit www.redwings.co.uk

REDWINGS
HORSE SANCTUARY
A Registered Charity
No.1068911

Registered Charity Number 1068911

Rufford Abbey & Country Park

Visit the Cistercian exhibition in the remains of the Abbey set in beautiful parklands.

Rufford Country Park, Ollerton, Nottinghamshire NG22 9DF
Tel: 01623 822944
Fax: 01623 824840
marilyn.louden@nottscc.gov.uk
www.nottinghamshire.gov.uk/countryparks

Nottinghamshire County Council

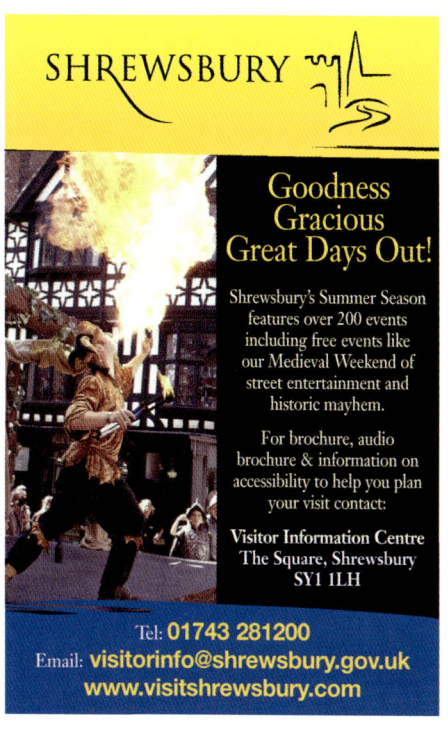

visitBritain.com

Big city buzz or peaceful panoramas? Take a fresh look at Britain and you may be surprised at what's right on your doorstep. Explore the diversity online at visitBritain.com

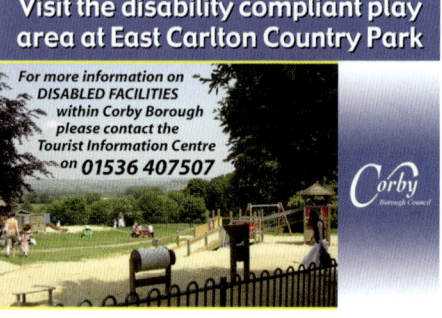

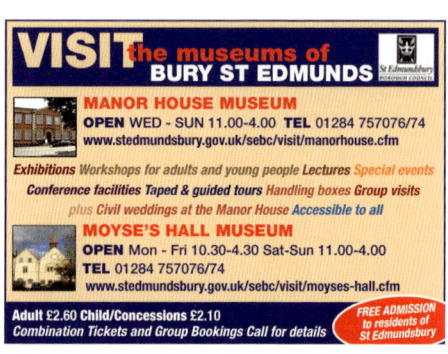

enjoy**England** 🌹
official guides to **quality**

Hotels, Townhouses, Travel Accommodation and Restaurants with Rooms in England 2006

£10.99

Guesthouses, Small Hotels, Bed & Breakfast, Farmhouses, Inns, Campus Accommodation and Hostels in England 2006

£11.99

Self-Catering Holiday Homes and Boat Accommodation in England 2006

£11.99

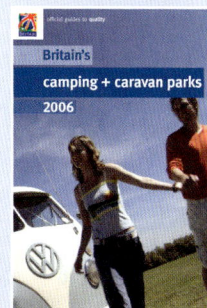

Touring Parks, Camping Parks, Holiday Parks and Holiday Villages in Britain 2006

£8.99

informative, easy to use and great value for money

Somewhere Special in England

£8.99

Families and Pets Welcome in England 2006

£11.99

Places to Stay in the South West 2006

£6.99

Accessible Places to Stay in Britain 2006

£9.99

From good bookshops, online at visitbritaindirect.com or by mail order from:

VisitBritain Fulfilment Centre
t **0870 606 7204** e **fulfilment@visitbritain.org**

visitbritaindirect.com

England's West Country

**Bristol Cornwall Devon Dorset Gloucestershire
Isles of Scilly Somerset Wiltshire**

Wonders of the West

Chill out in hidden bays and sandy coves. Indulge your love of cream teas and clotted cream fudge. Listen to seafaring tales of old in quaint inns. Wonder at the Cerne Abbas Giant and the stunning landscaped gardens at Stourhead, Warminster, where enchanting temples overlook a central lake. There's so much to experience in the wonderful West Country.

Get close to nature

The South West is truly a region of dramatic contrasts: heather-covered Dartmoor and Exmoor National Parks with tumbling rocky rivers, deep wooded gorges and craggy granite tors; brooding Bodmin Moor; 14 Areas of Outstanding Natural Beauty and over 600 miles of dramatic coastline, including the Jurassic Coast, a World Heritage Site. A haven for wildlife, try your hand at moonlight badger watching or otter spotting. Grey seals breed in caves and on undisturbed beaches, while whales, dolphins, porpoises and basking sharks are no

Spot native Exmoor ponies, one of the oldest breeds in the world, as you tour the heather-clad moors and pretty wooded coombes of **Exmoor National Park**.
exmoor-nationalpark.gov.uk

Previous page ponder the mystery of Stonehenge, Wiltshire
Above follow the amazing Forest of Dean Sculpture Trail, Gloucestershire

strangers to the waters off the north coast of Devon and Cornwall. Birdlife in the area is outstanding, from wintering wildfowl at Slimbridge in Gloucestershire to the nesting guillemots and razorbills on Lundy Island. Don't forget the binoculars!

A patchwork of hidden coves, warm sandy beaches, rolling farmland and wild moors all on your doorstep

Down by the sea

How's this for the perfect antidote to modern life? Warm, sandy bays and cosy, sheltered coves. Buckets and spades at the ready – the beach at Woolacombe stretches as far as the eye can see and is the ideal location for the UK National Sandcastle Championships. Newquay is perfect for fun seekers as well as sun seekers, and along the coast bright-white sails scud towards the horizon from the stunning natural harbour at Poole.

Discover Devon's English Riviera, between the rivers Dart and Exe. Here the bustling seaside towns of Torquay, Paignton and Brixham throng with a mix of families, and yachties going ashore for supplies. Get to know some friendly coastal creatures from penguins and puffins to playful fur seals at Living Coasts in Torquay. Away from the beach, lose yourself in one of the West Country's charming fishing villages. Picturesque Clovelly, Port Isaac and Beer all have tales to tell of pirates and shipwrecks.

Awaken your senses... absorb the sights, sounds and scents of the **Eden Project's** sparkling biomes. An unforgettable sanctuary of nature in which to learn and linger.
edenproject.com

Secret gardens

The South West boasts three of the most extraordinary gardens in Britain, if not beyond. Its balmy subtropical climate is a perfect breeding ground for more exotic flora. Delight in the romantic sounding Lost Gardens of Heligan at Pentewan – an 80-acre garden neglected for more than 70 years until 1991. The highlight is the Jungle, a 22-acre steep-sided valley home to some of the lushest vegetation in the country, including bamboos and palms. Be amazed by the remarkable Eden Project, near St Austell, where nature and technology meet head on under enormous glass biomes. It is home to thousands of plants, from Britain's temperate zone and other climatic zones.

More exotic gardens await visitors to the Isles of Scilly – the Abbey Garden at Tresco. Windbreaks shield the garden from the Atlantic gales, leaving plants to grow that you wouldn't expect to see in our northern climes. Home to species from 80 countries, discover cacti, date palms, giant lipstick-red flame trees and rarities like Lobster Claw.

What secrets do the huge 5,000-year-old stones at **Avebury** hide? Perhaps you'll find the answer when you visit this World Heritage Site.
nationaltrust.org.uk

Feast for the senses

Go on – indulge yourself in the South West's delicious specialities. The Cornish pasty tastes especially good washed down with a pint of sweet cider. A bewildering range of fudge and the equally calorific cream teas await those with a sweet tooth. Enjoy mouthwatering scones straight from the oven and topped with indulgent clotted cream.

Cheese is synonymous with the region. Think Cheddar, Double Gloucester and Somerset Brie, while Cornish Yarg, a unique, nettle-wrapped cheese graces the best cheeseboards. Get the best catch of the day at TV chef Rick Stein's Seafood Restaurant, Padstow, or savour exquisite English wines while admiring the view from The Vineyard Restaurant at Three Choirs Vineyards in Newant. End your culinary quest with Julian Temperley's award-winning Somerset cider brandy. Truly scrumptious!

Magic and mystery

Quirky customs and mysterious places abound in the South West. Strange rock formations, mystical festivals, outrageous fertility symbols – even cheese rolling! Overlooked by the majestic Tor, Glastonbury is unlike anywhere else. Today, thousands of people visit, attracted to its mystical charms as well as the world-famous music festival it hosts. Ponder the mysteries of the ancient stone circles of Stonehenge and Avebury – how were such enormous stones transported and arranged? Be amused or outraged by the fantastic chalk drawing of the Cerne Abbas Giant, dominating the hill outside Cerne Abbas.

Chipping Campden in Gloucestershire is the location of the Cotswolds' unique version of the Olympick Games, first held in the 17th century. Gloucestershire is also the home of the annual Cheese Rolling Festival at Cooper's Hill. Competitors from all over the world gather to chase a 7lb Double Gloucester cheese down the hill. What's the reward for their efforts? Yes, you've guessed it – more cheese! Trampling feet pound the earth at the annual International Worm Charming Festival in Blackawton, Devon. The team that persuades the most worms to rise to the surface, wins. It's simple, really.

Resist the temptation to dip your toes at **The Roman Baths**, the best-preserved spa from the ancient world, a monument to the Romans' love of relaxation.
romanbaths.co.uk

Great days out

If you're looking for even more inspiration on great days out, try these for starters. Learn about the history of the railway at Swindon's interactive attraction Steam – Museum of the Great Western Railway and spot the animals at Longleat's famous Safari Park. Meet friendly mute swans and their fluffy cygnets at Abbotsbury Swannery, their home for over 600 years. Relive the seafaring history of the South West at the National Maritime Museum Cornwall in Falmouth, or catch a performance at the stunning cliffside setting of The Minack Theatre at Porthcurno. Finally, take a driving tour around the honey-coloured limestone villages of the Cotswolds. Happy days will be spent exploring the beautiful towns of Cheltenham and Cirencester, and the lovely villages of Bourton-on-the-Water and Castle Combe.

City splendours

The buzzing university cities of Bristol and Bath are filled with attractions. Revel in the Georgian beauty of Bath where townhouses are shaped in elegant crescents – No 1 Royal Crescent is perhaps the finest example of Palladian architecture. Be impressed by the best-preserved Roman religious spa from the ancient world, which lies under the watchful gaze of Bath Abbey.

Enjoy Bristol's infectious vitality. Down by the rejuvenated harbour front discover vibrant bars and restaurants, and the magical At-Bristol – a unique destination bringing science, nature and art to life. Be awestruck by the feat of engineering that is the Clifton Suspension Bridge, the brainchild of Isambard Kingdom Brunel to span the Avon Gorge. Continue your journey to see some of the West's other great cathedral cities. Discover Exeter, Wells and Gloucester and marvel at Salisbury Cathedral with the tallest spire in Britain.

further information

South West Tourism
0870 442 0880
visitsouthwest.co.uk

Above admire Brunel's Clifton Suspension Bridge, Bristol

ABBOTSBURY, Dorset — SELF-CATERING

★★★★–★★★★★  **Gorwell Farm Cottages contact** Mrs Mary Pengelly, M J Pengelly Ltd, Gorwell, Abbotsbury, Weymouth DT3 4JX **t** (01305) 871401
e mary@gorwellfarm.co.uk **w** gorwellfarm.co.uk

ALTON PANCRAS, Dorset — SELF-CATERING

★★★★–★★★★★  **Bookham Court contact** Mr & Mrs Andrew Foot, Whiteways, Bookham, Alton Pancras, Dorchester DT2 7RP **t** (01300) 345511 **f** (01300) 345511
e andy.foot1@btinternet.com **w** bookhamcourt.co.uk

ASHBURTON, Devon Map ref 1C2 — SELF-CATERING

★★★★

Units **2**
Sleeps **2–6**

Low season per wk
Min £245.00
High season per wk
Max £450.00

Wren & Robin Cottages, Newton Abbot

contact Mrs Margaret Phipps, Wren & Robin Cottages, New Cott Farm, Newton Abbot TQ13 7PD **t** (01364) 631421 **f** (01364) 631421
e enquiries@newcott-farm.co.uk **w** newcott-farm.co.uk

Within Dartmoor National Park Robin and Wren cottages sit in a peaceful location with uninterrupted views over farmland and woodland. Beautifully furnished, well equipped, own garden and veranda. Safe parking. Christmas and New Year breaks. Prices all inclusive.

open All year
nearest shop 4 miles
nearest pub 1 mile

General 🐶₃ P ✄ S

Unit (icons)

Payment Credit/debit cards, cash/cheques

ASHBURTON, Devon — CAMPING & CARAVANNING

★★★★ **River Dart Adventures** Holne Park, Ashburton, Newton Abbot TQ13 7NP
t (01364) 652511 **f** (01364) 652020
e enquires@riverdart.co.uk **w** riverdart.co.uk

ASHWATER, Devon Map ref 1C2 — SELF-CATERING

Blagdon Farm Country Holidays, Beaworthy

★★★★–★★★★★★

Units	**8**
Sleeps	**2–6**

Low season per wk
£270.00–£325.00
High season per wk
£695.00–£855.00

contact Mr & Mrs Tucker, Blagdon Farm Country Holidays, Ashwater, Beaworthy EX21 5DF **t** (01409) 211509 **f** (01409) 211510
e enquiry@blagdon-farm.co.uk **w** blagdon-farm.co.uk

Blagdon Farm – award-winning cottages in West Devon. Set in 25 acres of park-like grounds each cottage has its own patio overlooking the two-acre lake. The indoor heated pool and the licensed bistro have their own patios so guests may either sunbathe by the pool or enjoy a meal or drink.

Access abc 🐾

General ☎ ▥ ♿ P ⚒ Ⓢ

Leisure ⌲

Unit ♨ ▦ Ⓢ ☒ ▣ ▤ ⚲ ▣ ♨
🛏 📠 🍽 📺 ✿

Payment Cash/cheques

Mid-week and weekend breaks. Equipment hire, pool hoist, scooters, wheelchairs etc.

open All year
nearest shop 1.5 miles
nearest pub 1.5 miles

A388 Holsworthy to Launceston road. Follow brown information signs to Blagdon Farm.

BATH, Somerset — HOTEL

★★★

Abbey Hotel North Parade, Bath BA1 1LF **t** (01225) 461603 **f** (01225) 447758
w compasshotels.co.uk

BATH, Somerset Map ref 2B2 — GUEST ACCOMMODATION

Carfax Hotel

◆◆◆◆◆

B&B per room per night
s £67.00–£77.00
d £94.00–£142.00
Evening meal per person
£9.00–£17.00

13-15 Great Pulteney Street, Bath BA2 4BS **t** (01225) 462089
f (01225) 443257 **e** reservations@carfaxhotel.co.uk **w** carfaxhotel.co.uk

A trio of Georgian townhouses in the centre of Bath. Lifts to all floors, private car park and garages, wheelchair access to public rooms and affordable prices.
open All year
bedrooms 13 double, 7 twin, 6 single, 4 family, 1 suite
bathrooms All en suite

General ☎ P♿ ⚒ ✕ 🍽 ▣

Rooms ♨ 🕯 ⚲ ♨ 🛏

Payment Credit/debit cards,
cash/cheques

BATH, Somerset Map ref 2B2 — SELF-CATERING

★★★★★

Units **5**
Sleeps **2–4**

Low season per wk
£203.00–£291.00
High season per wk
£328.00–£432.00

Greyfield Farm Cottages, High Littleton

contact Mrs June Merry, Greyfield Farm Cottages, Greyfield Road, High Littleton, Bristol BS39 6YQ **t** (01761) 471132 **f** (01761) 471132 **e** june@greyfieldfarm.com **w** greyfieldfarm.com

Attractive stone cottages in peaceful, private, 3.5-acre setting overlooking the Mendips. The cottages are spacious, fully equipped, warm and very comfortable. Each enjoys its own garden/patio and adjacent safe parking. Free facilities include hot tub, sauna, fitness and barbecue centres plus video/DVD library.

open All year
nearest shop 0.5 miles
nearest pub 0.5 miles

General 🐾 🏢 ⛺ P ⚒ ⊙ S
Unit 🛏 🎛 ⬜ 📺 📷 ⚒ ⊙ 📱 ⬛ 🍴 📖 ✏ ❄

Payment Cash/cheques, euros

Fully flexible bookings and short breaks available all year round. Availability calendar and full details available on our website.

A4 through Bath towards Bristol. Just after leaving Bath, left onto A39 to High Littleton. Greyfield Road for 200yds, bear right. Farm 3rd entrance on left.

BEACON HILL, Dorset — CAMPING & CARAVANNING

★★★

Beacon Hill Touring Park Blandford Road North, Beacon Hill, Nr Lytchett Minster, Poole BH16 6AB **t** (01202) 631631 **f** (01202) 625749 **w** beaconhilltouringpark.co.uk

BEAMINSTER, Dorset — SELF-CATERING

★★★★

Stable Cottage contact Mrs Diana Clarke, Meerhay Manor, Beaminster DT8 3SB **t** (01308) 862305 **f** (01308) 863972 **e** meerhay@aol.com **w** meerhay.co.uk

BEESON, Devon — SELF-CATERING

★★★★

Beeson Farm Holiday Cottages contact Mr & Mrs Robin & Veronica Cross, Beeson Farm Holidays, Beeson Farm, Beeson, Kingsbridge TQ7 2HW **t** (01548) 581270 **f** (01548) 581270 **w** beesonhols.co.uk

BERROW, Somerset — GUEST ACCOMMODATION

◆◆◆◆
SILVER AWARD

Yew Tree House Hurn Lane, Berrow, Burnham-on-Sea TA8 2QT **t** (01278) 751382 **f** (01278) 751382 **w** yewtree-house.co.uk

BETTISCOMBE, Dorset — SELF-CATERING

★★★

Conway Bungalow contact Mrs Margaret Smith, Conway Bungalow, Conway Bungalow, Bettiscombe, Bridport DT6 5NT **t** (01308) 868313 **f** (01308) 868313 **e** info@conway-bungalow.co.uk **w** conway-bungalow.co.uk

BLUE ANCHOR, Somerset Map ref 1D1 — SELF-CATERING

★★★★

Units **4**
Sleeps **1–6**

Low season per wk
£210.00–£320.00

High season per wk
£320.00–£420.00

Primrose Hill Holidays, Blue Anchor, Minehead

contact Mrs Jo Halliday, Primrose Hill Holidays, Wood Lane, Blue Anchor, Minehead TA24 6LA **t** (01643) 821200 **e** info@primrosehillholidays.co.uk **w** primrosehillholidays.co.uk

Terrace of four well-equipped bungalows offering wheelchair-friendly accommodation. Peaceful and secluded environment with amazing panoramic views over Blue Anchor Bay and the Exmoor foothills. Complimentary welcome pack provided. Parking for eight cars.
open All year
nearest shop 0.5 miles
nearest pub 0.5 miles

Access	
General	
Unit	
Payment	Cash/cheques

BOSCASTLE, Cornwall — GUEST ACCOMMODATION

◆◆◆◆

Old Coach House Tintagel Road, Boscastle PL35 0AS **t** (01840) 250398
e parsons@old-coach.demon.co.uk **w** old-coach.co.uk

BOURNEMOUTH, Dorset — GUEST ACCOMMODATION

◆◆◆◆

Wood Lodge Hotel 10 Manor Road, Bournemouth BH1 3EY
t (01202) 290891 **f** (01202) 290892
w woodlodge.com

BOURTON-ON-THE-WATER, Gloucestershire — GUEST ACCOMMODATION

◆◆◆

Kingsbridge and Chester House Hotel Riverside, Bourton-on-the-Water, Cheltenham GL54 2BS **t** (01451) 820286 **f** (01451) 820471
w roomattheinn.info

Quality visitor attractions

VisitBritain operates a Visitor Attraction Quality Assurance Service.

Participating attractions are visited annually by trained, impartial assessors who look at all aspects of the visit, from initial telephone enquiries to departure, customer service to catering, as well as all facilities and activities.

Only those attractions which have been assessed by VisitBritain and meet the standard receive the quality marque, your sign of a 'Quality Assured Visitor Attraction'.

Look out for the quality marque and visit with confidence.

enjoyEngland.com

QUALITY ASSURED VISITOR ATTRACTION

BRATTON, Somerset Map ref 1D1 — SELF-CATERING

★★★★

Units **8**
Sleeps **2–11**
High season per wk
£200.00–£1,250.00

Woodcombe Lodges, Minehead

contact Mrs Nicola Hanson, Woodcombe Lodges, Bratton Lane, Minehead TA24 8SQ **t** (01643) 702789 **f** (01643) 702789
e nicola@woodcombelodge.co.uk **w** woodcombelodge.co.uk

Cherry Lodge and Holly Lodge are both wheelchair accessible with Cherry Lodge being M1 and Holly Lodge M2 which has the additional benefit of a wheel-in shower with seat. Both lodges are very comfortable with wonderful views.

open All year
nearest shop 1 mile
nearest pub 1 mile

M5 jct 24, A39 to Minehead. Follow road out of Minehead towards Porlock then turn west into Woodcombe Lane, then Bratton Lane. Lodges on right just before open country.

General 🐎🏛♿P◉⑤

Unit ♨🏭,💻🛁♨🛏🗄🔌✿

Payment Credit/debit cards, cash/cheques

BRATTON FLEMING, Devon — GUEST ACCOMMODATION

◆◆◆◆◆

Bracken House Country Hotel Bratton Fleming, Barnstaple EX31 4TG
t (01598) 710320
e steve@brackenhousehotel.co.uk **w** brackenhousehotel.co.uk

BRIDGWATER, Somerset — GUEST ACCOMMODATION

◆◆◆◆
SILVER AWARD

Apple View Chedzoy Lane, Bridgwater TA7 8QR
t (01278) 423201 **f** (01278) 423201
w apple-view.co.uk

BRITFORD, Wiltshire — SELF-CATERING

★★★★

The Old Stables contact Mr Giles Gould, The Old Stables, Bridge Farm, Lower Road, Salisbury SP5 4DY **t** (01722) 349002 **f** (01722) 349003
e mail@old-stables.co.uk

BROADCLYST, Devon — SELF-CATERING

★★★★★

Coach House Farm contact Mr & Miss John & Polly Bale, Coach House Farm, Broadclyst, Exeter EX5 3JH **t** (01392) 461254 **f** (01392) 460931
e selfcatering@mpprops.co.uk

BROADCLYST, Devon — SELF-CATERING

★★★★

Hue's Piece contact Mrs Anna Hamlyn, Hue's Piece, Paynes Farm, Broadclyst, Exeter EX5 3BJ **t** (01392) 466720
e annahamlyn@paynes-farm.co.uk **w** paynes-farm.co.uk

BROMHAM, Wiltshire — SELF-CATERING

★★★

Park Farm Cottages contact Mrs Valerie Bourne, Westbrook, Bromham, Chippenham SN15 2EE **t** (01380) 850966
e valandtom2003@aol.com

BUCKLAND-IN-THE-MOOR, Devon | SELF-CATERING

★★★

Pine Lodge Holiday Homes & Cottages South West, 365a Torquay Road, Paignton TQ3 2BT **t** (01803) 663650 **f** (01803) 664037
e holcotts@aol.com **w** swcottages.co.uk

BURTON BRADSTOCK, Dorset | GUEST ACCOMMODATION

♦♦♦

Burton Cliff Hotel Cliff Road, Burton Bradstock, Bridport DT6 4RB
t (01308) 897205 **f** (01308) 898111
e burtoncliffhotel@btopenworld.com **w** burtoncliffhotel.co.uk

CANNINGTON, Somerset | GUEST ACCOMMODATION

♦♦♦♦♦
SILVER AWARD

Blackmore Farm Blackmore Lane, Cannington, Bridgwater TA5 2NE
t (01278) 653442 **f** (01278) 653427
e dyerfarm@aol.com **w** dyerfarm.co.uk

CHARMOUTH, Dorset | SELF-CATERING

★★★

The Poplars contact Mrs Jane Bremner, Wood Farm Caravan and Camping Park, Wood Farm Caravan Park, Axminster Road, Bridport DT6 6BT
t (01297) 560697 **f** (01297) 561243
e holiday@woodfarm.co.uk

CLANVILLE, Somerset | SELF-CATERING

★★★★

Clanville Manor Tallet contact Mrs Snook, Clanville Manor, Clanville Manor, Clanville, Castle Cary BA7 7PJ **t** (01963) 350124 **f** (01963) 350719
e info@clanvillemanor.co.uk **w** clanvillemanor.co.uk

CLEARWELL, Gloucestershire | HOTEL

Rating Applied For

Tudor Farmhouse Hotel and Restaurant High Street, Clearwell, Coleford GL16 8JS **t** (01594) 833046 **f** (01594) 837093
e info@tudorfarmhousehotel.co.uk **w** tudorfarmhousehotel.co.uk

COLEFORD, Gloucestershire Map ref 2A1 | HOTEL

★★★
B&B per room per night
s £60.00–£80.00
d £90.00–£140.00
HB per person per night
£68.00–£113.00

Best Western Speech House Hotel

Forest of Dean, Coleford GL16 7EL **t** (01594) 822607 **f** (01594) 823658
e relax@thespeechhouse.co.uk **w** thespeechhouse.co.uk

Built in 1676 as a hunting lodge for King Charles II, the Speech House Hotel is located in the very heart of the Forest of Dean.
open All year
bedrooms 20 double, 10 twin, 3 single, 3 family, 1 suite
bathrooms All en suite

Access	🏨 abc 🐾
General	🎠 P♿ ❄
Rooms	🛏 📺 🍵 📶 🪜
Payment	Credit/debit cards, cash/cheques

COLYFORD, Devon | SELF-CATERING

★★★★★

Whitwell Farm Cottages contact Mr Mike Williams, Whitwell Farm Cottages, Whitwell Lane, Colyford, Colyton EX24 6HS **t** 0800 092 0419 **f** (01297) 552911
e 100755.66@compuserve.com **w** a5star.co.uk

COLYTON, Devon Map ref 1D2 — SELF-CATERING

★★★★

Units **4**
Sleeps **2–6**

Low season per wk
Min £175.00
High season per wk
Max £695.00

Smallicombe Farm, Colyton

contact Mrs Todd, Smallicombe Farm, Northleigh, Colyton EX24 6BU
t (01404) 831310 **f** (01404) 831431 **e** maggie_todd@yahoo.com
w smallicombe.com

General 🐾 🛏 🚿 **P** ▣ ⑤

Unit 🔧 ▥ ⑤ 🔲 ▦ ⊡ 🔥 ❄

Payment Credit/debit cards, cash/cheques

Short breaks from £99 a couple.

Relax in award-winning converted barns in an Area of Outstanding Natural Beauty. Superb rural views yet close to the World Heritage Coastline between Lyme Regis and Sidmouth. The accommodation is designed to suit the needs of wheelchair users and their carers. It is entirely ground floor and has wheel-in shower rooms.

open All year
nearest shop < 0.5 miles
nearest pub 2 miles

From Honiton High Street take New Street past station, up hill, left at mini-roundabout, then 1st right to top of hill. Left after 2 miles signed 'Slade'.

CORFE CASTLE, Dorset Map ref 2B3

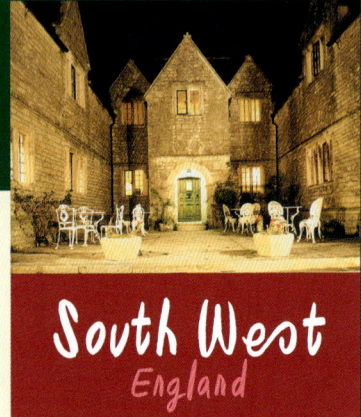

124

COMBE FLOREY, Somerset Map ref 1D1

B&B per room per night
s Min £35.00
d £56.00–£60.00

Redlands

Treble's Holford, Bishops Lydeard, Taunton TA4 3HA
t (01823) 433159 **e** redlandshouse@hotmail.com
w escapetothecountry.co.uk

Access 🐾

General 🛏️12 P🚿 ✂️ 🎛️ ❄️

Rooms 🛁 🛋️ 🍳 ♨️ 📺 📻

Payment Cash/cheques, euros

£365 per week for 2. 10% discount off all rates for DIY breakfast in room.

Barn conversion by a stream at the end of a lane adjacent to the Quantock Hills. Courtyard room has own access with close parking. Twin or six-foot bed. Small cooking/eating area with fridge, microwave and toaster. The owner is a wheelchair user. Three accessible pubs within two miles.

open All year except Christmas and New Year
bedrooms 1 double, 1 twin
bathrooms All en suite

Go under 2 close railway bridges on A358 Minehead Road, 7 miles after Taunton. Left turn to Treble's Holford 1 mile after. Grid ref. 150330.

CORFE CASTLE, Dorset

See previous page.

CROSCOMBE, Somerset
SELF-CATERING

★★★★

St Marys Lodge contact Mrs Jane Hughes, St Mary Mead, Long Street, Croscombe, Wells BA5 3QL **t** (01749) 342157
e janehughes@trtopbox.net **w** st-marys-lodge.co.uk

CURRY MALLET, Somerset
SELF-CATERING

★★★★

Buzzards View Holiday Cottages Group, Spring Mill, Earby, Barnoldswick BB94 0AA **t** 0870 072 3723
w crimsonhillfarm.co.uk

DEERHURST, Gloucestershire
SELF-CATERING

★★★★

Deerhurst Cottages contact Mrs Nicole Samuel, Abbots Court Farm, Deerhurst, Gloucester GL19 4BX **t** (01684) 275845 **f** (01684) 275845
e nic_samuel@hotmail.com **w** deerhurstcottages.co.uk

DULVERTON, Somerset
SELF-CATERING

★★★★

Northmoor House & Lodge contact Mr Robin Nicholson, Northmoor, Northmoor, Dulverton TA22 9QG **t** (01398) 323720 **f** (01398) 324537
e enquiries@bucklandhouse.co.uk **w** northmoorhouse.co.uk

EAST HUNTSPILL, Somerset
GUEST ACCOMMODATION

◆◆◆◆

Merry Farm Merry Lane, Basonbridge, Highbridge TA9 3PS **t** (01278) 783655

ENGLISH BICKNOR, Gloucestershire Map ref 2A1 — GUEST ACCOMMODATION

B&B per room per night
s Min £35.00
d £50.00–£64.00

Dryslade Farm

English Bicknor, Coleford GL16 7PA **t** (01594) 860259 **f** (01594) 860259
e daphne@drysladefarm.co.uk **w** drysladefarm.co.uk

We ensure a relaxed, friendly atmosphere at our 18thC farmhouse on working farm in Royal Forest of Dean, close to Symonds Yat. Level access to all ground-floor rooms. Special diets by arrangement. Dogs welcome.
open All year
bedrooms 1 double, 2 twin
bathrooms All en suite

General	
Rooms	
Payment	Cash/cheques

ERLESTOKE, Wiltshire — GUEST ACCOMMODATION

Longwater Lower Road, Erlestoke, Devizes SN10 5UE
t (01380) 830095 **f** (01380) 830095

EXFORD, Somerset — SELF-CATERING

Westermill Farm contact Mr & Mrs Oliver & Jill Edwards, Westermill Farm, Exford, Minehead TA24 7NJ **t** (01643) 831238 **f** (01643) 831216
e swt@westermill.com **w** westermill.com

FIFEHEAD MAGDALEN, Dorset — SELF-CATERING

Top Stall contact Mrs Kathleen Jeanes, Top Stall, Factory Farm, Fifehead Magdalen, Gillingham SP8 5RS **t** (01258) 820022 **f** (01258) 820022
e factoryfarm@agriplus.net

GOLANT, Cornwall — SELF-CATERING

Penquite Farm Holidays contact Mr & Mrs Varco, Penquite Farm, Golant, Fowey PL23 1LB **t** (01726) 833319 **f** (04017) 2683 3319
e varco@farmersweekly.net **w** penquitefarm.co.uk

HALLEGAN, Cornwall — SELF-CATERING

Country Haven contact Mr & Mrs Peter & Kath Chown, Classic Cottages, Hallegan Manor, Hallegan, Camborne TR14 9LT **t** (01209) 832854 **f** (01209) 831307
e chownpeter@aol.com

HALWILL JUNCTION, Devon — SELF-CATERING

Anglers Paradise contact Mr Zyg Gregorek, Anglers Paradise,
The Gables, Winsford Lane, Halwill Junction, Beaworthy EX21 5XT
t (01409) 221559 **f** (01409) 221559
w anglers-paradise.co.uk

HARRIS MILL, Cornwall — CAMPING & CARAVANNING

Tehidy Holiday Park, Nr Portreath Harris Mill, Illogan, Redruth TR16 4JQ
t (01209) 216489
e holiday@tehidy.co.uk **w** tehidy.co.uk

HARTGROVE, Dorset — SELF-CATERING

Hartgrove Farm contact Mrs Susan Smart, Hartgrove Farm, Hartgrove, Shaftesbury SP7 0JY **t** (01747) 811830 **f** (01747) 811066
e cottages@hartgrovefarm.co.uk **w** hartgrovefarm.co.uk

HIGH BICKINGTON, Devon — SELF-CATERING

★★★★

Country Ways contact Mrs Kate Price, Country Ways, Little Knowle Farm, High Bickington, Umberleigh EX37 9BJ **t** (01769) 560503 **f** (01769) 560503 **e** kate@country-ways.net **w** country-ways.net

HIGHLEADON, Gloucestershire Map ref 2B1 — SELF-CATERING

★★★★
Units **1**
Sleeps **1–2**
Low season per wk
Min £175.00
High season per wk
Min £350.00

Highleadon Holiday Cottages, Newent

contact Mr & Mrs Jonathan & Janet Corbett, Highleadon Holiday Cottages, New House Farm, Newent GL18 1HQ **t** (01452) 790209 **f** (01452) 790209 **e** cjojan@aol.com

Ground-floor cottage on an organic working farm. One double bedroom. Spacious lounge/kitchen/diner. Large shower room. Patio garden. Short breaks. No children.
open All year
nearest shop 4 miles
nearest pub 3 miles

General	P S
Unit	
Payment	Cash/cheques

HOLCOMBE ROGUS, Devon — SELF-CATERING

★★★★

Old Lime Kiln Cottages contact Mrs Sue Gallagher, Whipcott Heights, Holcombe Rogus, Wellington TA21 0NA **t** (01823) 672339 **f** (01823) 672339 **e** bookings@oldlimekiln.freeserve.co.uk

HORSINGTON, Somerset Map ref 2B3 — GUEST ACCOMMODATION

♦♦♦
B&B per room per night
s £35.00–£50.00
d £55.00–£75.00
Evening meal per person
£7.00–£15.00

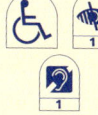

Half Moon Inn

Templecombe BA8 0EF **t** (01963) 370140 **f** (01963) 371450 **e** halfmoon@horsington.co.uk **w** horsington.co.uk

Stone-built 18thC inn in quiet village. Log fires, oak floors, gardens. Evening meals (not Sundays). Four en suite stable rooms. Six new en suites, three disabled-friendly on ground floor with level access, shower seats, grab rails, equipped for visually and hearing impaired visitors. Ample car parking.
open All year except Christmas
bedrooms 4 double, 6 twin
bathrooms All en suite

Three miles south of Wincanton, left off A357. One mile north of Templecombe BR.

Access	abc
General	
Rooms	
Payment	Credit/debit cards, cash/cheques

ILLOGAN, Cornwall — SELF-CATERING

★★★–★★★★★

Trengove Farm Cottages contact Mrs Lindsey Richards, Illogan, Redruth TR16 4PU **t** (01209) 843008 **f** (01209) 843682 **e** richards@farming.co.uk

KILKHAMPTON, Cornwall — SELF-CATERING

★★★★–★★★★★

Forda Lodges & Cottages contact Mr & Mrs Jim & Gillian Chibbett, Forda Lodges, Kilkhampton, Bude EX23 9RZ **t** (01288) 321413 **f** (01288) 321413 **e** forda.lodges@virgin.net **w** fordalodges.co.uk

KILMERSDON, Somerset — SELF-CATERING

★★★★

The Creamery contact Mr & Mrs Susan Knatchbull & Sons, The Creamery, Batch Farm, Kilmersdon, Radstock BA3 5SP **t** (01373) 812337 **f** (01373) 813781 **w** visitsouthwest.co.uk

LANLIVERY, Cornwall — GUEST ACCOMMODATION

♦♦♦

Higher Pennant Farm Guest House Lanlivery, Bodmin PL30 5DD **t** (01208) 873252

LIZARD, Cornwall — HOSTEL

★★★★★

Lizard Point Youth Hostel Yha Lizard, Helston TR12 7NT **t** 0870 770 6120 **f** 0870 770 6121

LONG BREDY, Dorset — SELF-CATERING

★★★★

Whatcombe Stables contact Mrs Jane Peretz, Long Bredy, Dorchester DT2 9HN **t** (01308) 482762 **f** (01308) 482762 **e** janeperetz@compuserve.com

LOOE, Cornwall Map ref 1C3 — SELF-CATERING

★★★★

Units **3**
Sleeps **4–5**

Low season per wk
£170.00–£367.00
High season per wk
£389.00–£530.00

Bocaddon Holiday Cottages, Looe

contact Mrs Alison Maiklem, Bocaddon Holiday Cottages, Lanreath, Looe PL13 2PG **t** (01503) 220192 **f** (01503) 220192 **e** bocaddon@aol.com **w** bocaddon.com

General	🐕 🏛 ♿ P ✂
Leisure	🎣
Unit	📺 📼 📷 ♨ ⚒ 🗄 📖 📁 ✿
Payment	Cash/cheques

All cottages have close parking, level entry, wide doors. Bathrooms have level-entry showers with hoist available over bath and shower.

Unwind, relax and enjoy our tastefully converted barns, nestling peacefully in beautiful countryside. Bocaddon is a 350-acre working farm close to clean beaches, fishing harbours and smugglers' coves! Also close to fabulous gardens and historic houses. All cottages are very wheelchair friendly.

open All year
nearest shop 2 miles
nearest pub 2 miles

From A38, take A390 (East Taphouse). Left onto B3359. After 4 miles, right (Shillamill Lakes). We are 0.25 miles on left-hand side.

LOSTWITHIEL, Cornwall Map ref 1B2 | **SELF-CATERING**

★★★★

Units **1**
Sleeps **2–4**

Low season per wk
£250.00–£300.00
High season per wk
£350.00–£495.00

Chark Country Holidays, Lostwithiel

contact Ms Jenny Littleton, Chark Country Holidays, Chark, Redmoor, Bodmin PL30 5AR **t** (01208) 871118 **e** charkholidays@tiscali.co.uk **w** charkcountryholidays.co.uk

General ⬡🎟♿**P**✂

Unit 🛏🏠🔌🖥📥🔌🔲🔥📢 🍴📻📁❄

Payment Cash/cheques

Excellent value low-season weeks and short breaks available.

Highly praised by our wheelchair guests, Mesyow Chy is comfortable, spacious and well adapted, with level access to patio, garden, duck pond and pets' paddock. An ideal base to explore all of Cornwall's many attractions, with a good choice of restaurants within two miles. Larger groups can be accommodated using adjoining cottages.

open All year
nearest shop 2 miles
nearest pub 1.5 miles

From A30 Bodmin follow signs for Liskeard A38. After roundabout take 2nd right to Lostwithiel. Turn left at roundabout, then after Sweetshouse take 1st right.

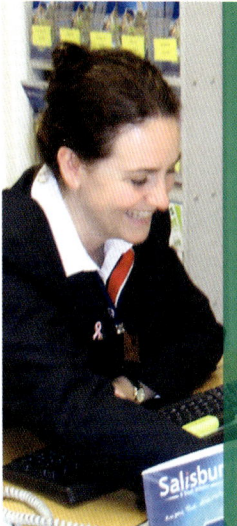

Help before you go

When it comes to your next British break, the first stage of your journey could be closer than you think.

You've probably got a tourist information centre nearby which is there to serve the local community – as well as visitors. Knowledgeable staff will be happy to help you, wherever you're heading.

Many tourist information centres can provide you with maps and guides, and it's often possible to book accommodation and travel tickets too.

You'll find the address of your nearest centre in your local phone book or text the message TIC LOCATE to 64118*.

*Each successful request is charged at 35p (Not available to subscribers of the 3 network)

LOSTWITHIEL, Cornwall Map ref 1B2 — SELF-CATERING

★★★★

Units **2**

Sleeps **1–6**

Low season per wk
£300.00–£450.00

High season per wk
£500.00–£680.00

Hartswheal Barn, Lostwithiel

contact Mrs Wendy Jordan, Hartswheal Barn, Saint Winnow, Downend, Lostwithiel PL22 0RB **t** (01208) 873419 **f** (01208) 873419
e hartswheal@connexions.co.uk
w connexions.co.uk/hartswheal/index.htm

Access abc

General 🐴 6 **P** ✂ 🔲 S

Unit 🔲 ▦ S 🔲 🔲 🔲 🔲 🔲 🔲 🔲 🔲 ❄

Payment Cash/cheques

3-day breaks available in Mar and Apr. Lowered kitchen units in 'Stables'.

The Barn and Stables are part of an old converted granary, within a working farm, with breathtaking views just five miles from the Eden Project. The Stables has a double bedroom, with en suite shower, twin with electric bed, and ceiling hoist tracking to en suite bathroom/wc. The Barn has a double, twin and bunks.

open All year
nearest shop 1 mile
nearest pub 1 mile

Take A38 to Plymouth and Cornwall. Just past Liskeard at Dobwalls, left onto A390 for St Austell. Entrance is off A390 1 mile before Lostwithiel.

LOWER GODNEY, Somerset — GUEST ACCOMMODATION

◆◆◆◆

GOLD AWARD

Double-Gate Farm Godney, Wells BA5 1RX **t** (01458) 832217 **f** (01458) 835612
e doublegatefarm@aol.com **w** doublegatefarm.com

LOWER GODNEY, Somerset — SELF-CATERING

★★★★

Swallow Barn contact Mrs Hilary Millard, Double-Gate Farm Holidays, Double Gate Farm, Godney, Wells BA5 1RX **t** (01458) 832217 **f** (01458) 835612
e doublegatefarm@aol.com **w** doublegatefarm.com

MORETONHAMPSTEAD, Devon — SELF-CATERING

★★–★★★★★

Budleigh Farm contact Mr Arthur Harvey, Moretonhampstead, Newton Abbot TQ13 8SB **t** (01647) 440835 **f** (01647) 440436
e harvey@budleighfarm.co.uk **w** budleighfarm.co.uk

MORTEHOE, Devon — GUEST ACCOMMODATION

◆◆◆◆

SILVER AWARD

The Cleeve House North Morte Road, Mortehoe, Woolacombe EX34 7ED
t (01271) 870719 **f** (01271) 870719
e info@cleevehouse.co.uk **w** cleevehouse.co.uk

MORWENSTOW, Cornwall Map ref 1C2
SELF-CATERING

★★★★

Units **2**

Sleeps **1–8**

Low season per wk
£325.00–£510.00

High season per wk
£675.00–£1,050.00

Cory Farm Cottages, Bude

contact Mrs Edwina Tape, Cory Farm Cottages, Morwenstow,
Bude EX23 9ST **t** (01288) 331735 **f** (01288) 331758
e info@coryfarmcottages.co.uk **w** coryfarmcottages.co.uk

General

Unit

Payment Cash/cheques

Cory Farm is a family-run working
dairy farm situated on the wild
and beautiful north coast of
Cornwall. We offer accessible
accommodation in newly
converted stone farm buildings,
plus a fabulous all-weather
children's play barn. Stunning
views of the surrounding
countryside, sea and Lundy
Island. Towels for hire. Service
dogs welcome.

open All year
nearest shop 1 mile
nearest pub 1 mile

*A39 towards Bude, right turn
signposted Morwenstow. 2nd
right in village. Continue out of
village, right at signpost for
Marsland. Cory Farm is 0.75
miles on the right.*

MOTCOMBE, Dorset Map ref 2B3
GUEST ACCOMMODATION

◆◆◆◆

B&B per room per night
s Min £45.00
d Min £80.00

Awaiting
NAS rating

The Coppleridge Inn

Motcombe, Shaftesbury SP7 9HW **t** (01747) 851980 **f** (01747) 851858
e thecoppleridgeinn@btinternet.com **w** coppleridge.com

Converted farm set in 15 acres of
woodland and meadows. All rooms
ground floor. Bar, restaurant serving
beautifully home-cooked food at
sensible prices. Large car park. Ideal
for exploring Wessex.
open All year
bedrooms 4 double, 4 twin,
2 family
bathrooms All en suite

General

Leisure

Rooms

Payment Credit/debit cards,
cash/cheques

MOUNT HAWKE, Cornwall
SELF-CATERING

★★

Trenerry Lodge contact Mrs Angela Parsons, Trenerry Lodge, Trenerry Farm,
Mingoose, Truro TR4 8BX **t** (01872) 553755 **f** (01872) 553755
e info@babatrenerry.co.uk **w** babatrenerry.co.uk

MUCHELNEY HAM, Somerset — SELF-CATERING

★★★

Hay Loft & Stables contact Mrs Pauline Pickard, Hay Loft & Stables, Dairy House Farm, Muchelney Ham, Langport TA10 0DJ **t** (01458) 253113

NEWTON ABBOT, Devon — SELF-CATERING

★★★★

Rydon Ball contact Mr Ian Butterworth, Holiday Homes & Cottages South West, 365a Torquay Road, Paignton TQ3 2BT **t** (01803) 663650 **f** (01803) 664037
e holcotts@aol.com **w** swcottages.co.uk

NORTH PETHERWIN, Cornwall Map ref 1C2 — SELF-CATERING

★★★★
Units **5**
Sleeps **5–16**

Low season per wk
£250.00–£545.00
High season per wk
£331.00–£960.00

Waterloo Farm, Launceston

Cornish Classic Holidays, Waterloo Farm, North Petherwin, Launceston PL15 8LL **t** (01566) 785386 **e** werreus@agriplus.net
w cornishclassicholidays.co.uk

Luxury disabled access barns for 5-16 people on working farm in beautiful valley. Outdoor swimming pool, games room, river fishing, clay shooting, classic bikes, north Cornwall coast 12 miles.
open All year
nearest shop 5 miles
nearest pub 2 miles

General	
Leisure	
Unit	

Payment Cash/cheques

NORTHLEIGH, Devon — GUEST ACCOMMODATION

♦♦♦♦
SILVER AWARD

Smallicombe Farm Northleigh, Colyton EX24 6BU
t (01404) 831310 **f** (01404) 831431
w smallicombe.com

OKEHAMPTON, Devon — SELF-CATERING

★★★★

Beer Farm contact Mr & Mrs Annear, Beer Farm, Beer Farm, Okehampton EX20 1SG **t** (01837) 840265 **f** (01837) 840245
e info@beerfarm.co.uk **w** beerfarm.co.uk

OLDCROFT, Gloucestershire — SELF-CATERING

★★★★

Cider Press Cottage contact Mr & Mrs Hinton, Cider Press Cottage, 1 Westleigh Villa, St Swithins Road, Oldcroft, Lydney GL15 4NF
t (01594) 510285 **f** (01594) 510285

PAINSWICK, Gloucestershire — HOTEL

★★

The Falcon Hotel New Street, Painswick, Stroud GL6 6UN
t (01452) 814222 **f** (01452) 813377
e bleninns@clara.net **w** falconinn.com

PANCRASWEEK, Devon — SELF-CATERING

★★★

Tamarstone Farm contact Mrs Megan Daglish, Tamarstone Farm, Bude Road, Pancrasweek, Holsworthy EX22 7JT **t** (01288) 381734
e cottage@tamarstone.co.uk **w** tamarstone.co.uk

PARKEND, Gloucestershire — GUEST ACCOMMODATION

♦♦♦

The Fountain Inn & Lodge Fountain Way, Parkend, Lydney GL15 4JD
t (01594) 562189 **f** (01594) 564438
e thefountaininn@aol.com **w** thefountaininnandlodge.com

PLYMOUTH, Devon Map ref 1C2 — HOTEL

★★★

B&B per room per night
s £65.00–£125.00
d £75.00–£145.00
HB per person per night
£90.00–£110.00

Kitley House Hotel and Restaurant

Kitley Estate, Yealmpton, Plymouth PL8 2NW **t** (01752) 881555
f (01752) 881667 **e** sales@kitleyhousehotel.com **w** kitleyhousehotel.com

Historic country-house hotel set in private estate overlooking lake. Popular restaurant and hotel with friendly staff. Ground-floor facilities.
open All year
bedrooms 8 double, 2 twin, 1 single, 1 family, 7 suites
bathrooms All en suite

Access	☺ 🛅 ✈
General	🐎 P♿ ✂ 🍳 ❀
Rooms	🛏 📺 ☕ 🔌
Payment	Credit/debit cards, cash/cheques, euros

PLYMOUTH, Devon — SELF-CATERING

★★★★

Haddington House Apartments contact Mr Fairfax Luxmoore,
42 Haddington Road, Plymouth PL2 1RR **t** (01752) 500383
w abudd.co.uk

PORTREATH, Cornwall Map ref 1B3 — SELF-CATERING

★★★★★

Units   **3**
Sleeps   **1–5**

Low season per wk
£220.00–£300.00
High season per wk
£240.00–£640.00

Higher Laity Farm, Redruth

contact Mrs Lynne Drew, Higher Laity Farm, Portreath Road,
Redruth TR16 4HY **t** (01209) 842317 **f** (01209) 842317
e info@higherlaityfarm.co.uk **w** higherlaityfarm.co.uk

General	🐎 🍳 🛅 P ✂ S
Unit	🛏 🏰 📺 📠 🔌 🗄 ☎ 📻 🔥 🍳 🧺 ❀
Payment	Cash/cheques

Special weekend and mid-week breaks available.

Tastefully converted luxury barns set amidst the Cornish countryside. One cottage, offering master bedroom with en suite and second twin-bedded room, has a fully adapted accessible bathroom with level-access shower. The exceptional accommodation and its proximity to the A30 makes this an ideal base from which to explore. Service dogs welcome.
open All year
nearest shop 1 mile
nearest pub 0.5 miles

From M5 take A30 to Redruth/ Porthtowan slip road towards Redruth. For full travel directions please contact us directly.

POTTERNE, Wiltshire — SELF-CATERING

★★★

Abbotts Ball Farm Cottage contact Mrs V Hazel Hobbs, Pound Hill, Worton Road,
Potterne, Devizes SN10 5PW **t** (01380) 721661
e johnhobbs@abbottsballfarm.freeserve.co.uk

PRESTBURY, Gloucestershire — HOTEL

★★★

The Prestbury House Hotel and Oaks Restaurant The Burgage, Prestbury, Cheltenham GL52 3DN **t** (01242) 529533 **f** (01242) 227076
e enquiries@prestburyhouse.co.uk **w** prestburyhouse.co.uk

ROCHE, Cornwall — SELF-CATERING

Rating Applied For
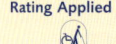

Owls Reach Colbiggan Farm, Roche, St Austell PL26 8LJ **t** (01208) 831597
e info@owlsreach.co.uk **w** owlsreach.co.uk

ST ENDELLION, Cornwall — SELF-CATERING

★★★★

Tolraggott Farm Cottages contact Mrs Harris, Barton Cottage, Tolraggott Farm, St Endellion, Port Isaac PL29 3TP **t** (01208) 880927 **f** (01208) 880927

ST JUST-IN-PENWITH, Cornwall — SELF-CATERING

★★★★

Swallow's End contact Mr & Mrs Beer, Kelynack Moor Farmhouse, Bosworlas, St. Just, Penzance TR19 7RQ **t** (01736) 787011 **f** (01736) 787011
e db.properties@virgin.net **w** westcornwalllets.co.uk

ST MARTIN, Cornwall — SELF-CATERING

★★★★–★★★★★★★

Bucklawren Farm contact Jean Henly, St Martin, Looe PL13 1NZ
t (01503) 240738 **f** (01503) 240481
e bucklawren@btopenworld.com **w** bucklawren.com

SALISBURY, Wiltshire Map ref 2B3 — HOTEL

★★★

B&B per room per night
s £90.50–£115.50
d £125.50–£145.50
HB per person per night
£75.50–£85.50

Grasmere House Hotel

70 Harnham Road, Salisbury SP2 8JN **t** (01722) 338388 **f** (01722) 333710
e grasmerehotel@mistral.co.uk **w** grasmerehotel.com

Set amid 1.5 acres of gardens down to River Nadder with views over watermeadows and Salisbury Cathedral. Salisbury's favourite riverside hotel with accessible public areas.
open All year
bedrooms 14 double, 8 twin, 2 single, 10 family, 1 suite
bathrooms All en suite

Access
General
Rooms
Payment Credit/debit cards, cash/cheques

SALISBURY, Wiltshire — GUEST ACCOMMODATION

♦♦♦♦
GOLD AWARD

Websters 11 Hartington Road, Salisbury SP2 7LG
t (01722) 339779 **f** (01722) 421903
e enquiries@websters-bed-breakfast.com **w** websters-bed-breakfast.com

SOUTHLEIGH, Devon — GUEST ACCOMMODATION

♦♦♦♦

Wiscombe Linhaye Farm Southleigh, Colyton EX24 6JF
t (01404) 871342 **f** (01404) 871342

SPARKFORD, Somerset — CAMPING & CARAVANNING

★★★★

Long Hazel Park High Street, Sparkford, Yeovil BA22 7JH
t (01963) 440002 **f** (01963) 440002
e longhazelpark@hotmail.com **w** sparkford.f9.co.uk/lhi.htm

STATHE, Somerset — SELF-CATERING

★★★★

Walkers Farm Cottages contact Mrs Dianne Tilley, Walkers Farm Cottages, Walkers Farm, Stathe, Bridgwater TA7 0JL **t** (01823) 698229
e info@walkersfarmcottages.co.uk **w** walkersfarmcottages.co.uk

STOKE ABBOTT, Dorset — SELF-CATERING

★★★★

Lewesdon Farm Holidays contact Mr & Mrs Micheal & Linda Smith, Lewesdon Farm Holidays, Lewesdon Farm, Stoke Abbott, Beaminster DT8 3JZ
t (01308) 868270
e lewesdonfarmholiday@tinyonline.co.uk

STOKE ST GREGORY, Somerset Map ref 1D1 — SELF-CATERING

★★★★

Units	5
Sleeps	4–6

Low season per wk
£205.00–£335.00
High season per wk
£335.00–£680.00

Holly Farm, Taunton

contact Rob & Liz Hembrow, Holly Farm, Meare Green, Stoke St Gregory, Taunton TA3 6HS **t** (01823) 490828
f (01823) 490590 **e** robhembrow@btinternet.com **w** holly-farm.com

Relax in the heated, indoor swimming pool (40' x 20'), chill out in the hot tub; the easy-to-use Oxford hoist will lift you in and out. Full underfloor heating to keep you warm. Your spacious, fully equipped cottage has level, adjacent parking with tarmac surfaces.

open All year
nearest shop 1 mile
nearest pub 1 mile

Full directions and map on website.

General 🛏 🏠 ⚓ P Ⓢ

Leisure ☇

Unit 🛋 🏭 📺 📷 ♨ 🎙 📟 📷 ✿

Payment Credit/debit cards, cash/cheques

THELBRIDGE, Devon — SELF-CATERING

★★★–★★★★★

White Witches and Stable Lodge contact Mrs Gillbard, Hele Barton, Hele Barton, Black Dog, Crediton EX17 4QJ **t** (01884) 860278 **f** (01884) 860278
e gillbard@eclipse.co.uk **w** eclipse.co.uk/helebarton

TORQUAY, Devon Map ref 1D2 —

★★

B&B per room per night
s £25.00–£35.00
d £50.00–£70.00

HB per person per night
£35.00–£45.00

Awaiting
NAS rating

Frognel Hall Hotel

Higher Woodfield Road, Torquay TQ1 2LD **t** (01803) 298339
f (01803) 215115 **e** mail@frognel.co.uk **w** frognelhall.co.uk

Beautiful family-run Victorian villa, set in two acres of mature gardens, five minutes away from harbour, cliff walks and beach. Private parking and lift. Sea views. Disabled rooms on ground floor. Licensed bar and restaurant. Entertainment some evenings.

open All year
bedrooms 8 double, 10 twin, 3 single, 6 family
bathrooms 26 en suite, 1 private

Follow signs to Torquay seafront (avoiding town centre). Left to harbour. At clock tower, left towards Babbacombe. Right at lights towards Meadfoot Beach. Hotel 3rd on left.

Access

General

Rooms

Payment Credit/debit cards, cash/cheques

Ground-floor rooms with disabled access. Group discount for parties more than ten.

TORQUAY, Devon —

★★★

South Sands Apartments contact Mr & Mrs Paul & Deborah Moorhouse, South Sands Apartments, Torbay Road, Livermead, Torquay TQ2 6RG
t (01803) 293521 **f** (01803) 293502
e info@southsands.co.uk **w** southsands.co.uk

TRURO, Cornwall Map ref 1B3

GUEST ACCOMMODATION

B&B per room per night
d £50.00–£70.00

Tregoninny Farm

Tresillian, Truro TR2 4AR **t** (01872) 520145
e tregoninny.farm@btopenworld.com **w** tregoninny.com

Access 🏛

General 🛗 P♿ ✂ 🍴 ❄

Rooms 🛏 🛋 🍴 ♨ 🛗 🚾

Payment Cash/cheques

4 specially adapted rooms. Interconnecting doors and lounge areas make Tregoninny perfect for groups. Large accessible conservatory with stunning views.

Set amidst beautiful Cornish countryside with unspoilt panoramic views, the imaginative renovation of traditional barns has created an ideal base to explore all that Cornwall has to offer. Peaceful, comfortable and welcoming with tasteful interior design, four en suite rooms are equipped to very high standards to meet all mobility needs.
open All year except Christmas
bedrooms 4 double, 3 twin, 1 single, 2 suites
bathrooms 8 en suite, 2 private

A30 Carland Cross. Left Truro (A39). Pass Permount Crematorium. 1st exit at next mini roundabout. At traffic signals left St Austell (A390). Lay-by on right, next turning on left.

UGBOROUGH, Devon

SELF-CATERING

★★★★

Venn Farm contact Mrs Stephens, Venn Farm, Ugborough, Ivybridge PL21 0PE
t (01364) 73240 **f** (01364) 73240

VERYAN, Cornwall Map ref 1B3 — SELF-CATERING

★★★★

Units	1
Sleeps	6

Low season per wk
£220.00–£350.00

High season per wk
£350.00–£695.00

Trenona Farm Holidays – Chy Whel, Veryan

contact Mrs Pamela Carbis, Trenona Farm Holidays, Ruan High Lanes, Truro TR2 5JS **t** (01872) 501339 **f** (01872) 501253
e pam@trenonafarmholidays.co.uk **w** trenonafarmholidays.co.uk

Chy Whel is a single-storey cottage with three en suite bedrooms (a double and two twin-bedded rooms). The open-plan lounge/kitchen/diner has all modern comforts and conveniences. The property also has a private garden with patio and lawn area.

open All year
nearest shop 1 mile
nearest pub 2 miles

A30 past Bodmin, A391 to St Austell, A390 towards Truro. Just beyond Probus take A3078 to St Mawes. After 8 miles pass Esso garage, Trenona Farm 2nd on left.

General

Unit

Payment Credit/debit cards, cash/cheques

Short breaks Oct-Mar. 2 bedrooms accessible for wheelchair users.

WEMBDON, Somerset — SELF-CATERING

★★★★

Ash-Wembdon Farm Cottages contact Mr Clarence Rowe, Ash-Wembdon Farm Cottages, Ash-Wembdon Farm, Hollow Lane, Bridgwater TA5 2BD
t (01278) 453097 **f** (01278) 445856
e c.a.rowe@btinternet.com **w** ukcottageholiday.com

WEMBURY, Devon — SELF-CATERING

★★★–★★★★★

Traine Farm contact Mrs Sheila Rowland, Traine Farm, Train Road, Wembury, Plymouth PL9 0EW **t** (01752) 862264 **f** (01752) 862264
e traine.cottages@btopenworld.com **w** traine-holiday-cottages.co.uk

WEST BEXINGTON, Dorset — SELF-CATERING

★★★–★★★★★

Tamarisk Farm Cottages contact Mrs Josephine Pearse, Tamarisk Farm Cottages, Beach Road, West Bexington, Dorchester DT2 9DF
t (01308) 897784 **f** (01308) 897784
e holidays@tamariskfarm.com **w** tamariskfarm.co.uk

Town, country or coast

The entertainment, shopping and innovative attractions of the big cities, the magnificent vistas of the countryside or the relaxing and refreshing coast – this guide will help you find what you're looking for!

WESTON-SUPER-MARE, Somerset Map ref 1D1 — GUEST ACCOMMODATION

♦♦♦

B&B per room per night
s £22.00–£33.00
d £44.00–£56.00

Moorlands Country Guesthouse

Main Road, Hutton, Weston-super-Mare BS24 9QH **t** (01934) 812283
f (01934) 812283 **e** margaret-holt@hotmail.co.uk **w** guestaccom.co.uk/35.htm

Family owned and run 18thC house set in mature landscaped grounds in the pretty village of Hutton. Meals are served at The Old Inn, located almost opposite.
open All year
bedrooms 1 double, 2 twin, 1 single, 2 family
bathrooms 5 en suite

General 🐎 🍽 ❄

Rooms ♿ ☕

Payment Credit/debit cards, cash/cheques

WHITMINSTER, Gloucestershire — SELF-CATERING

★★–★★★★

Whitminster House Cottages **contact** Mrs Teesdale, Whitminster House, Wheatenhurst, Whitminster GL2 7PN **t** (01452) 740204 **f** (01452) 740204
e millard@burwarton-estates.co.uk **w** whitminsterhousecottages.co.uk

WIDECOMBE-IN-THE-MOOR, Devon — SELF-CATERING

★★★–★★★★★

Wooder Manor Holiday Homes **contact** Mrs Angela Bell, Wooder Manor Holiday Homes, Widecombe-in-the-Moor, Dartmoor, Newton Abbot TQ13 7TR **t** (01364) 621391 **f** (01364) 621391
e angela@woodermanor.com **w** woodermanor.com

Bank holiday
dates for your diary

holiday	2006	2007
January Bank Holiday (Scotland)	2 January	2 January
New Year's Day (England & Wales)	2 January	1 January
New Year's Day (Scotland)	3 January	1 January
Good Friday	14 April	6 April
Easter Monday (England & Wales)	17 April	9 April
Early May Bank Holiday	1 May	7 May
Spring Bank Holiday	29 May	28 May
Summer Bank Holiday (Scotland)	7 August	6 August
Summer Bank Holiday (England & Wales)	28 August	27 August
Christmas Day	25 December	25 December
Boxing Day	26 December	26 December

WIMBORNE MINSTER, Dorset Map ref 2B3 — SELF-CATERING

Units **3**
Sleeps **2–4**

Low season per wk
£278.00–£400.00

High season per wk
£375.00–£805.00

Grange Holiday Cottages, Grange, Wimborne

English Country Cottages, Stoney Bank, Barnoldswick BB94 0AA
t 0870 191 7700 **f** (01282) 841539
e ecc.enquiry@holidaycottagesgroup.com
w grangeholidaycottages.co.uk

Access 🐾

General 🛋 ♿ P ✂ S

Unit 🔲 ▦ 📺 📟 🖥 📻 📷 🕯 🔲📺📟📷❄

Payment Credit/debit cards, cash/cheques

Bedrooms can be arranged as doubles or twins to suit your needs.

These cottages are created from a beautiful barn, converted to a high standard with beamed living/dining area and wood-burning stoves. Location is perfect for exploring Dorset and New Forest. They enjoy a courtyard setting in a countryside location. All bedrooms are en suite, with independent wheelchair access and facilities for the disabled.

open All year
nearest shop < 0.5 miles
nearest pub < 0.5 miles

From Wimborne, B3078 towards Cranborne. After 0.75 miles, right towards Furzehill and Holt. After 0.5 miles pass Stocks pub, 250yds, left into Grange. Holiday cottages are 1st right.

WINSFORD, Somerset — CAMPING & CARAVANNING

★★★★

Halse Farm Caravan & Tent Park Winsford, Minehead TA24 7JL
t (01643) 851259 **f** (01643) 851592
w halsefarm.co.uk

WINSLEY, Wiltshire — SELF-CATERING

★★★★

Church Farm Country Cottages contact Mrs Trish Bowles, Church Farm, Winsley, Bradford-on-Avon BA15 2JH **t** (01225) 722246 **f** (01225) 722246
e stay@churchfarmcottages.com **w** churchfarmcottages.com

Check it out

Information on accommodation listed in this guide has been supplied by proprietors. As changes may occur you should remember to check all relevant details at the time of booking.

WOOLACOMBE, Devon Map ref 1C1 |

Sunnymeade Country Hotel

B&B per room per night
s £25.00–£49.00
d £58.00–£72.00
Evening meal per person
Min £16.00

Dean Cross, West Down EX34 8NT **t** (01271) 863668
f (01271) 863668 **e** info@sunnymeade.co.uk **w** sunnymeade.co.uk

Access ☺ 🐾

General 🛏 P♿ ⚡ ♟ ✕ 🍴 ❀

Rooms ♨ 🕯 📺 🛁 ♨ 🛗 📻

Payment Credit/debit cards,
cash/cheques

4 of our 10 en suite rooms are on the ground floor.

The Sunnymeade Country Hotel is a family-run, very friendly and informal hotel close to Exmoor and the beach. Mostly en suite bedrooms, total wheelchair accessibility. The dining room, bar and lounge are on the ground floor (no steps). Wheel-in showers and grab rails etc. BSL signed. Great home-cooked, locally produced food is a speciality.

open All year except Christmas and New Year
bedrooms 4 double, 7 twin, 1 single
bathrooms 10 en suite, 2 private

M5 jct 27, follow A361 north through Barnstaple and on to Braunton. After 3 miles hotel is on right-hand side, just past Foxhunters.

Quality visitor attractions

VisitBritain operates a Visitor Attraction Quality Assurance Service.

Participating attractions are visited annually by trained, impartial assessors who look at all aspects of the visit, from initial telephone enquiries to departure, customer service to catering, as well as all facilities and activities.

Only those attractions which have been assessed by VisitBritain and meet the standard receive the quality marque, your sign of a 'Quality Assured Visitor Attraction'.

Look out for the quality marque and visit with confidence.

YELVERTON, Devon Map ref 1C2

B&B per room per night
s £30.00–£40.00
d £50.00–£60.00

Overcombe Hotel

Old Station Road, Horrabridge, Yelverton PL20 7RA **t** (01822) 853501
f (01822) 853602 **e** enquiries@overcombehotel.co.uk
w overcombehotel.co.uk

Access

General

Rooms

Payment Credit/debit cards,
cash/cheques

*Access to property by ramp. 2
ground-floor bedrooms, double
with standard en suite, twin with
totally flat-floored facilities.*

Offering a warm friendly
welcome in relaxed comfortable
surroundings with a substantial
breakfast using local and home-
made produce. Situated between
Tavistock and Plymouth with
beautiful views over the village
and Dartmoor. Conveniently
located for exploring both Devon
and Cornwall, in particular
Dartmoor National Park and the
adjacent Tamar Valley.
open All year
bedrooms 3 double, 2 twin,
1 single, 2 family
bathrooms All en suite

*From Yelverton follow A386
towards Tavistock. Turn next left
after Horrabridge sign. We are
on right-hand side after short
distance.*

Country ways

**The Countryside Rights of Way Act gives
people new rights to walk on areas of open
countryside and registered common land.**

To find out where you can go and what you can do, as well
as information about taking your dog to the countryside,
go online at countrysideaccess.gov.uk.

And when you're out and about...

Always follow the Country Code

- Be safe – plan ahead and follow any signs
- Leave gates and property as you find them
- Protect plants and animals, and take your litter home
- Keep dogs under close control
- Consider other people

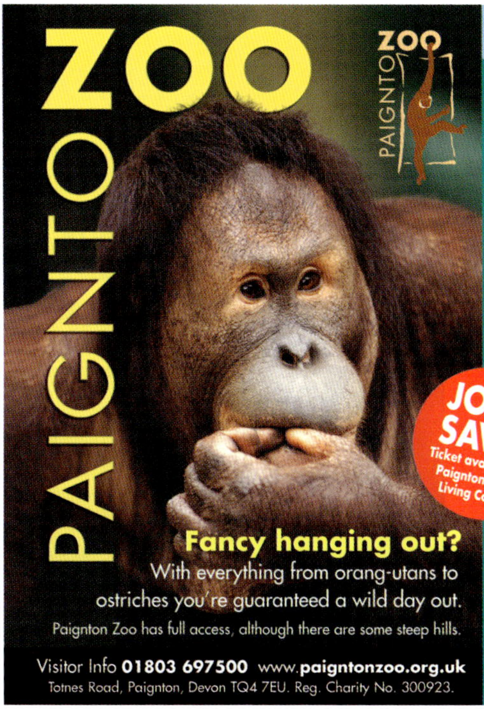
PAIGNTON ZOO
PAIGNTON ZOO
Fancy hanging out?
With everything from orang-utans to ostriches you're guaranteed a wild day out.
Paignton Zoo has full access, although there are some steep hills.
Visitor Info 01803 697500 www.paigntonzoo.org.uk
Totnes Road, Paignton, Devon TQ4 7EU. Reg. Charity No. 300923.
JOINT SAVER
Ticket available for Paignton Zoo & Living Coasts.

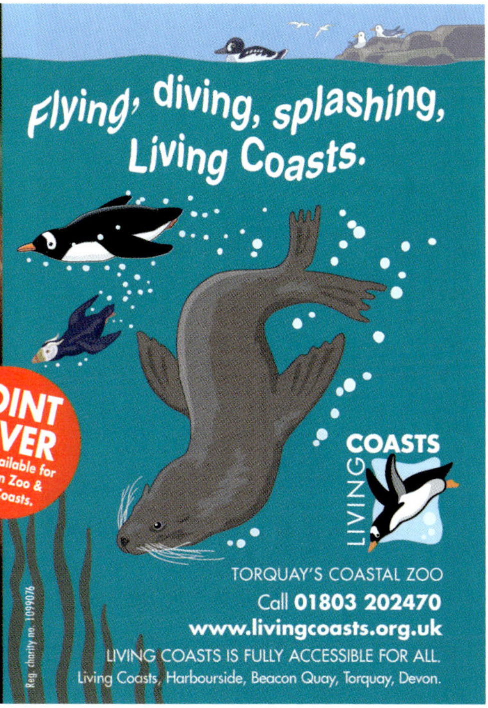
Flying, diving, splashing, Living Coasts.
LIVING COASTS
TORQUAY'S COASTAL ZOO
Call 01803 202470
www.livingcoasts.org.uk
LIVING COASTS IS FULLY ACCESSIBLE FOR ALL.
Living Coasts, Harbourside, Beacon Quay, Torquay, Devon.
Reg. charity no. 1099076

Calvert Trust
Outdoor Activity Centres
for people with disabilities
their families and friends
HOLIDAYS, COURSES, RESPITE CARE AND SELF CATERING IN ENGLANDS BEAUTIFUL COUNTRYSIDE
AALA
Activities include:
Sailing, canoeing, climbing, abseiling, pony riding, trap driving, archery, orienteering and much more.
All with our qualified and experienced staff.
Keswick
Tel: 01768 772255
Fax: 01768 771920
calvert.keswick@dial.pipex.com
Registered Charity Number 270923
Kielder
Tel: 01434 250232
Fax: 01434 250015
enquiries@calvert-kielder.com
Registered Charity Number 511851
Exmoor
Tel: 01598 763221
Fax: 01598 763063
exmoor@calvert-trust.org.uk
Registered Charity Number 1005776
www.calvert-trust.org.uk

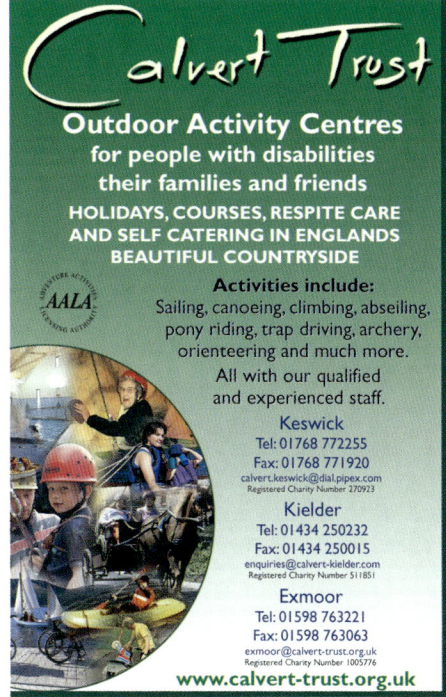

Royal Forest of Dean

The Royal Forest of Dean is an ideal place to visit for people with disabilities. The area's spectacular woodlands offer many All Ability Access Paths and Easy Going Trails, plus many of the area's attractions, inns and accommodation provide a full range of accessible facilities that will make your visit a truly enjoyable one.

For further information call: 01594 812388
or Email: tourism@fdean.gov.uk
Contact the Forestry Commission
on: 01594 833057
to receive a copy of their 'Easy Access' leaflet

The Lost Gardens of **HELIGAN**

www.heligan.com

PAR SANDS HOLIDAY PARK

Cornwall

Par Sands Holiday Park is situated behind the grassysand dunes bordering the beach. For our disabled guests we have a luxury 2 bed caravan built for wheelchair use. For our touring guests we have excellent disabled toilet and shower facilities. The park is flat and we have wheel chair access to the beach.

Par Beach, St. Austell Bay, Cornwall UK, PL24 2AS
Tel: +44 (0)1726 812868 Fax: +44 (0)1726 817899
holidays@parsands.co.uk

Weymouth & Portland, Dorset

For a Weymouth & Portland Holiday Guide or a Guide for Visitors with Special Needs, call: **01305 785747** (Quote TFA) or visit
www.visitweymouth.co.uk

Woodlands Dartmouth

Will Woodlands suit your needs?
INFORMATION 01803 712598

Discover West Dorset

For your **FREE** copy of West Dorset Accessibility Guide contact us 01305 252241 tourism@westdorset-dc.gov.uk

www.westdorset.com

An award winning day out

DairyLand FARM WORLD

New for 2006
The all new supervised ride
"Raging Bulls"

The Bull Pen

Open Daily
10am - 5pm
5 Apr-29 Oct

Pony & Hayrides · Bottle Feeding · Pat-a-pet · Pet Parade
Astra Slides · Drop Slides · Ball Pool & so much more...
INFOLINE 01872 510349
On the A3058 4 miles from Newquay

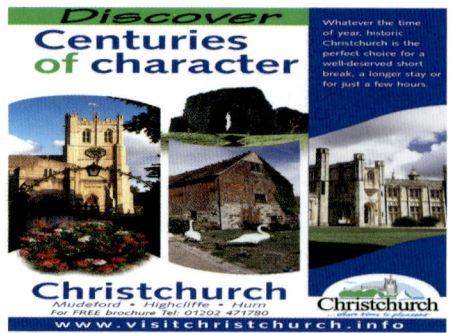

Town, country or coast

The entertainment, shopping and innovative attractions of the big cities, the magnificent vistas of the countryside or the relaxing and refreshing coast – this guide will help you find what you're looking for!

Never has a rose meant so much

Everyone has a trusted friend, someone who tells it straight. Well, that's what the Enjoy England Quality Rose does: reassures you before you check into your holiday accommodation that it will be just what you want, because it's been checked out by independent assessors. Which means you can book with confidence and get on with the real business of having a fantastic break.

enjoy**England**.com

★ ★ ★
SELF CATERING

The **Quality Rose** is the mark of England's *official*, nationwide quality assessment scheme and covers just about every place you might want to stay, using a clear star and diamond rating system: from caravan parks to stylish boutique hotels, farmhouse B&Bs to country house retreats, self-catering cottages by the sea to comfy narrowboats perfect for getting away from it all. Think of the Quality Rose as your personal guarantee that your expectations will be met.

Our ratings made easy

★	Simple, practical, no frills	♦
★★	Well presented and well run	♦♦
★★★	Good level of quality and comfort	♦♦♦
★★★★	Excellent standard throughout	♦♦♦♦
★★★★★	Exceptional with a degree of luxury	♦♦♦♦♦

**Look no further. Just look out for the Quality Rose.
Find out more at** enjoy**England**.com/quality

South East England

Berkshire   Buckinghamshire   East Sussex
Hampshire   Isle of Wight   Kent
London   Oxfordshire   Surrey   West Sussex

Southern **comfort**

Rich in heritage from Roman times to the present day, England's South East is a fascinating melting pot of history, nature and culture. Whether you want to experience the buzz of the big city or the serenity of the countryside, you'll find your desires not just fulfilled, but exceeded.

A place in history

Explore a region that has witnessed some of the most momentous events of British history, from the Battle of Hastings in 1066 to the air raids of the Second World War, the Gunpowder Plot of 1605 and the Great Fire of London in 1666. Delight in seeing some of the country's most familiar landmarks. The gleaming White Cliffs of Dover, the magnificent cathedral at Canterbury, the spires of Oxford and, of course, the tower of Big Ben. Step back in time with the help of East Sussex's Saxon churches and Lullingstone's glorious Roman Villa. It's pure chocolate box territory in the villages of Chiddingstone and Ightham.

Make a beeline for the clean sandy beaches of **Freshwater Bay**. Inland you'll find **Osborne House**, Victoria and Albert's island retreat.
islandbreaks.co.uk
english-heritage.org.uk

Previous page learn to sail at Brighton Marina, East Sussex
Above enjoy a drink in the Three Chimneys pub, Biddenden, Kent

There are modern masterpieces, too. The British Airways London Eye, the Thames Barrier at Greenwich and the Channel Tunnel. All examples of modern engineering at its most innovative and spectacular.

Flamboyant towns and cities, designer shops for retail therapy and more than just a spot of culture

A shore thing

Leave the hurly-burly behind and head instead to the beaches of the south coast. Eastbourne, Bournemouth, Brighton and Margate were all popular playgrounds for the Victorians. Queen Victoria herself frequently stayed at her Isle of Wight home, Osborne House. Today, the south coast is just as hip. Tourists and city dwellers flock here to sample the shopping and cultural scene.

If you're looking for something a bit more peaceful, there are still many gems on this stretch of coastline. Try West Wittering, just down the Sussex coast from Bognor Regis; Pevensey Bay, tucked in between Bexhill and Eastbourne; and Lepe near Southampton in Hampshire.

Many of today's popular resorts have grown out of small fishing villages. Towering net huts in Hastings Old Town are reminiscent of this once thriving trade and are still used by fishermen to this day. Bosham, near Chichester, is arguably the prettiest of harbour villages and it was from here that King Canute

The childhood home of Anne Boleyn, romantic **Hever Castle** stands in magnificent grounds, from the formality of the topiary to the meanderings of the lakeside walk. **hever-castle.co.uk**

reputedly attempted to turn back the tide, sitting on his throne on the site of the present-day quay.

Live like a lord

Discover a life of privilege when you explore the South East's many awe-inspiring castles and palaces. Be enraptured by dreamy Leeds Castle in Kent, named 'the loveliest castle in the world'. In the ultimate romantic gesture, Henry VIII restored it for his first queen, Catherine of Aragon. Other castles waiting to be fallen in love with are those of Hever, Bodiam, Scotney and Windsor. Henry VIII also lived in the magnificent Hampton Court Palace that was opened up to the public by Queen Victoria.

At one with nature

You'll be amazed at how little the region's economic power has affected the beauty of the countryside. It's not for nothing that Kent is called the Garden of England. Commune with nature and take in the more gentle delights of a country garden – it's a nature lover's paradise. Sample the beauty of country gardens such as Sissinghurst Castle Garden near

Don a straw boater and cheer on the crews at the **Henley Royal Regatta** – the height of the social and sporting calendar every summer. **hrr.co.uk**

Cranbrook, the loving creation of Vita Sackville-West. Watch out for wild ponies as they gently graze by the side of paths and bridleways of the New Forest, recently designated a National Park. More ancient tracks run the length of the South Downs Way and the Ridgeway that eventually meets the Thames Path. Feeling full of beans? Catch a ferry over to the Isle of Wight where you can tour round the island in a day, stopping off at Ventnor to explore the renowed Botanic Garden.

Other garden gems include Emmetts in Kent, Polesden Lacey in Surrey and Stowe, near Buckingham. Spend hours in the Royal Botanic Gardens at Kew, the jewel in the crown of English gardens. Explore the garden's incredible 300 acres or wonder at the exotic plants in the world-famous Palm House. All without even leaving London.

Get in the festive spirit

Catch the buzz of a festival or event, whatever the time of year. From rock 'n' pop to hops, from rowing to sailing, from Dickens to dancing round a maypole – the rich tapestry of life. In London, there's the Notting Hill Carnival or The Lord Mayor's Show. The Brighton Festival comes to the hip seaside town every May – a true celebration of the arts. If you're looking for the epitome of elegance, dress up for Glyndebourne's season of opera.

Witness the Sedan Chair Races in the Pantiles of Tunbridge Wells, or see the streets of Broadstairs thronged with Victorian costumes during the Dickens Festival. There's rock, pop and hip hop mixed with a liberal dose of mud at August's Reading Festival. Don't forget the Henley Royal Regatta or Cowes Week – two internationally famous spectacles.

Tempt your tastebuds

Embark on an epicurean journey through the vineyards, breweries, orchards, oyster houses and fine restaurants of the South East. Stock up with juicy strawberries, raspberries and gooseberries at a farm shop, and wash them down with Monks Delight, a Kentish cider infused with honey and spices. Sample ales such as Bishops Finger and Spitfire – oast houses throughout Kent reveal the area's brewing heritage. Oyster connoisseurs flock to Whitstable to sample these

Traverse the Thames across the magnificent **Golden Jubilee Bridges**. Iridescent with light at night, they are London's latest landmarks. **southbanklondon.com**

salty fruits of the sea. Dining out in Bray, near Windsor, is a gastronome's dream. The small town has the distinction of not one, but two Michelin three-starred restaurants, The Fat Duck and The Waterside Inn. You'll find a third at TV mega-chef Gordon Ramsey's eponymous restaurant in Chelsea.

City lights

Exciting, dynamic and cosmopolitan. London has something new and exciting to experience round every corner. Historic Westminster Abbey, the Houses of Parliament and the Tower of London. The new pretenders are Tate Modern, the British Airways London Eye and the stunning reconstruction of Shakespeare's Globe. On rainy days, the Natural History Museum, the V&A and The National Gallery cannot be missed. And the British Museum has outstanding collections that cover world cultures from pre-history to present day.

The West End is abuzz with, bars, restaurants and nightclubs. Catch an all-dancing, all-singing musical or murder mystery at a top theatre. Shopaholics head for Oxford Street, Knightsbridge or the more eclectic markets of Camden, Borough and Spitalfields. Discover the excitement of the London Marathon, cricket at Lord's and Wimbledon fortnight. Relax on a riverboat as it cruises along the Thames east to west from Greenwich to Richmond. Spend a perfect Sunday morning lazing in one of London's green Royal Parks and end with a hearty lunch at one of the city's highly rated gastropubs. It's what Sundays were invented for!

further information

Tourism South East
(023) 8062 5505
visitsoutheastengland.com

Visit London
(020) 7234 5800
visitlondon.com

Above enjoy a relaxing spa break

ASHFORD, Kent Map ref 3B4
HOTEL

★★★★

B&B per room per night
s £75.00–£141.00
d £85.00–£152.00

Awaiting
NAS rating

Ashford International Hotel
Simone Weil Avenue, Ashford TN24 8UX t (01233) 219988 f (01233) 647743
e info@ashfordinthotel.com w ashfordinthotel.com

Ashford International Hotel is the perfect base from which to explore Kent's countryside, coastline, castles, gardens and an ideal venue for every occasion, from conference to private celebration or meeting.
open All year except Christmas
bedrooms 85 double, 82 twin, 8 family, 2 suites
bathrooms All en suite

Access

General

Leisure

Rooms

Payment Credit/debit cards, cash/cheques, euros

ATHERFIELD GREEN, Isle of Wight
SELF-CATERING

★★★★

Atherfield Green Farm Holiday Cottages contact Mr Alistair Jupe, The Laurels, High Street, Newchurch, Sandown PO36 0NJ t (01983) 867613 f (01983) 868214
e alistair.jupe@btinternet.com

BOTLEY, Hampshire
HOTEL

★★★★

Botley Park Hotel, Golf & Country Club Winchester Road, Botley, Southampton SO32 2UA t (01489) 780888 f (01489) 789242
w macdonaldhotels.co.uk

BRACKNELL, Berkshire
HOTEL

★★★★
SILVER AWARD

Coppid Beech Hotel John Nike Way, Bracknell RG12 8TF
t (01344) 303333 f (01344) 301200
e reservations@coppid-beech-hotel.co.uk w coppidbeech.com

CADE STREET, East Sussex
GUEST ACCOMMODATION

◆◆◆◆

Spicers Bed & Breakfast 21 Spicers Cottages, Cade Street, Heathfield TN21 9BS
t (01435) 866363 f (01435) 866363

CANTERBURY, Kent
HOTEL

★★
SILVER AWARD

Ebury Hotel 65-67 New Dover Road, Canterbury CT1 3DX
t (01227) 768433 f (01227) 459187
w ebury-hotel.co.uk

CLIFTONVILLE, Kent
HOTEL

★★

Lonsdale Court Hotel 21-27 Eastern Esplanade, Cliftonville, Margate CT9 2HL
t (01843) 221053 f (01843) 299993
e info@courthotels.com w courthotels.com

DENSOLE, Kent
GUEST ACCOMMODATION

◆◆◆◆

Garden Lodge Canterbury Road, Densole, Folkestone CT18 7BB
t (01303) 893147 f (01303) 894581
e stay@garden-lodge.com w garden-lodge.com

DUCKLINGTON, Oxfordshire
GUEST ACCOMMODATION

◆◆◆

Ducklington Farm Course Hill Lane, Ducklington, Witney OX29 7YL
t (01993) 772175
w country-accom.co.uk

EASTBOURNE, East Sussex HOTEL

★★★
SILVER AWARD

Hydro Hotel Mount Road, Eastbourne BN20 7HZ
t (01323) 720643 **f** (01323) 641167

EASTBOURNE, East Sussex Map ref 3B4 HOTEL

★★★

B&B per room per night
s £30.00–£60.00
d £70.00–£105.00
HB per person per night
£45.00–£65.00

Awaiting
NAS rating

The Langham Hotel

43-49 Royal Promenade, Eastbourne BN22 7AH **t** (01323) 731451
f (01323) 646623 **w** langhamhotel.co.uk

Access 🏛 abc 🐕

General 🛏 🎮 🛗

Rooms 🛋 🛏 🔲 ☕ 🔌 🧺 📺

Payment Credit/debit cards,
cash/cheques

*Some specially adapted rooms.
Special half board rates available
for 7 nights or more.*

The Langham Hotel is a
wheelchair-friendly hotel with
entrance ramp and lift. Many of
the en suite bedrooms have
views over Eastbourne's beautiful
coastline. Facilities include a
comfortable bar, terrace and
restaurant with amazing views
over the sea. The hotel also has
WI-FI Internet throughout public
areas and bedrooms.
open All year
bedrooms 22 double, 38 twin,
21 single, 4 family
bathrooms All en suite
*From M25: M23 south to A23.
A27 east to Lewes and
Eastbourne. Locally: A27 or A259
to Eastbourne seafront. Hotel on
corner of Cambridge Road and
Royal Parade.*

FARNHAM, Surrey Map ref 2C2 SELF-CATERING

★★

Units **2**
Sleeps **1–5**
Low season per wk
£175.00–£350.00
High season per wk
£210.00–£450.00

High Wray, Farnham

contact Mrs Alexine Crawford, High Wray, 73 Lodge Hill Road,
Farnham GU10 3RB **t** (01252) 715589 **e** crawford@highwray73.co.uk
w highwray73.co.uk

Roomy and level ground-floor
apartments specifically designed for
wheelchair users. Wheel-in shower,
parking close by. Sunny patio by
large accessible garden.
open All year
nearest shop 0.5 miles
nearest pub 0.5 miles

General 🛏 🏢 🅿 🚭 🖥

Unit 🛋 🛏 🔲 🖥 🔌 🧺 📺 🍳 📺 ❄

Payment Cash/cheques

GOLDEN GREEN, Kent — SELF-CATERING

★★★★★

Goldhill Mill Cottages contact Mr & Mrs Vernon & Shirley Cole,
Goldhill Mill Cottages, Three Elm Lane, Golden Green, Tonbridge TN11 0BA
t (01732) 851626 **f** (01732) 851881
e vernon.cole@virgin.net **w** goldhillmillcottages.com

HEATHROW AIRPORT, Outer London Map ref 2D2 — HOTEL

★★★★

B&B per room per night
s £69.00–£149.00
d £69.00–£149.00

Awaiting
NAS rating

Park Inn Heathrow

Bath Road, Heathrow UB7 0DU **t** (020) 8759 6611 **f** (020) 8759 3421
e info.heathrow@rezidorparkinn.com **w** parkinn.co.uk

Located at Heathrow Airport with easy access to Royal Windsor, Legoland and Ascot. Health club with gym, indoor swimming pool, sauna, jacuzzi and solarium.
open All year
bedrooms 652 double, 124 twin, 47 single, 47 family, 10 suites
bathrooms All en suite

Access	☺ 🛄 ✈
General	🦢 P& 🍴 🔲
Leisure	🎣 🏊 🏃
Rooms	🛁 S 🍵 🔌 ♨
Payment	Credit/debit cards, cash/cheques, euros

HIGH COGGES, Oxfordshire — GUEST ACCOMMODATION

♦♦♦

Springhill Farm Bed & Breakfast Cogges, Witney OX29 6UL
t (01993) 704919

HIGH HALDEN, Kent — SELF-CATERING

★★★★

The Granary & The Stables contact Mrs Serena Maundrell,
Vintage Years Company ltd, High Halden, Ashford TN26 3JQ
t (01233) 850871 **f** (01233) 850717
e serena@vintageyears.co.uk **w** vintage-years.co.uk

HOLLINGBOURNE, Kent — SELF-CATERING

★★★

1 & 2 Orchard View contact Mr Stuart Winter, Garden of England Cottages,
The Mews Office, 189a High Street, Tonbridge TN9 1BX
t (01732) 369168 **f** (01732) 358817
e holidays@gardenofenglandcottages.co.uk **w** gardenofenglandcottages.co.uk

HOLMBURY ST MARY, Surrey — SELF-CATERING

★★★

Bulmer Farm contact Mrs Gill Hill, Bulmer Farm, Holmbury St Mary,
Dorking RH5 6LG **t** (01306) 730210

Key to symbols

Symbols at the end of each entry help you pick out the services and facilities which are most important for your stay. A key to the symbols can be found inside the back-cover flap. Keep this open for easy reference.

LEWES, East Sussex Map ref 2D3

SELF-CATERING

★★★★

Units **2**
Sleeps **1–10**

Low season per wk
£365.00–£445.00
High season per wk
£440.00–£605.00

Heath Farm, Plumpton Green, Lewes

contact Mr & Mrs Robin & Marilyn Hanbury, Heath Farm, South Road, Plumpton Green, Lewes BN8 4EA **t** (01273) 890712 **f** (01273) 890712
e hanbury@heath-farm.com **w** heath-farm.com

General 🐎🏛️⛺P🔌 ◉S

Unit ♿🏛️🖥️🍴🔌🔘🔥🧹🔒
📋📍❄️

Payment Cash/cheques

Former milking parlour and stables converted into luxury cottages on working family farm. Beautifully and comfortably furnished to highest standard. Level-entry showers. Wonderful countryside, easy access to Brighton, Gatwick, London, National Trust gardens and historic towns and villages. An ideal holiday base.

open All year
nearest shop 1 mile
nearest pub < 0.5 miles

Directions given at time of booking.

LONDON, SE16

HOSTEL

★★

Rotherhithe YHA and Conference Centre 20 Salter Road, London SE16 5PR
t 0870 770 6010 **f** 0870 770 6011
e rotherhithe@yha.org.uk **w** yha.org.uk

LONDON, SW7

HOSTEL

★★★★

YHA South Kensington Baden-Powell House 65-67 Queen's Gate, London SW7 5JS **t** (020) 7590 6900 **f** (020) 7590 6902
w yha.org.uk

LONDON, W2

GUEST ACCOMMODATION

♦♦♦♦

Westland Hotel 154 Bayswater Road, London W2 4HP
t (020) 7229 9191 **f** (020) 7727 1054
e reservations@westlandhotel.co.uk **w** westlandhotel.co.uk

MARDEN, Kent

CAMPING & CARAVANNING

★★★★★

Tanner Farm Touring Caravan & Camping Park Goudhurst Road, Marden, Tonbridge TN12 9ND **t** (01622) 832399 **f** (01622) 832472
e enquiries@tannerfarmpark.co.uk **w** tannerfarmpark.co.uk

MARLOW, Buckinghamshire

GUEST ACCOMMODATION

♦♦♦

Granny Anne's 54 Seymour Park Road, Marlow SL7 3EP **t** (01628) 473086

NEW MILTON, Hampshire

GUEST ACCOMMODATION

♦♦♦♦

St Ursula 30 Hobart Road, New Milton BH25 6EG **t** (01425) 613515

NEWBRIDGE, Isle of Wight — CAMPING & CARAVANNING

★★★★★

The Orchard Holiday Caravan Park Main Road, Newbridge, Yarmouth PO41 0TS
t (01983) 531331 **f** (01983) 531666
e info@orchards-holiday-park.co.uk **w** orchards-holiday-park.co.uk

---

NEWCHURCH, Isle of Wight — CAMPING & CARAVANNING

★★★★★

Southland Camping Park Winford Road, Newchurch, Sandown PO36 0LZ
t (01983) 865385 **f** (01983) 867663

PETHAM, Kent — CAMPING & CARAVANNING

★★★★

Yew Tree Park Stone Street, Canterbury CT4 5PL
t (01227) 700306 **f** (01227) 700306
e info@yewtreepark.com **w** yewtreepark.com

PETWORTH, West Sussex — GUEST ACCOMMODATION

◆◆◆◆◆
SILVER AWARD

Old Railway Station Station Road, Petworth GU28 0JF **t** (01798) 342346
e mlr@old-station.co.uk **w** old-station.co.uk

RUNCTON, West Sussex — SELF-CATERING

★★★★

Cornerstones contact Mrs Higgins, Goodwood Gardens, Runcton,
Chichester PO20 1SP **t** (01243) 839096
e vjrmhiggins@hotmail.com **w** visitsussex.org/cornerstones

RYE, East Sussex Map ref 3B4 — GUEST ACCOMMODATION

◆◆◆◆

B&B per room per night
s £35.00–£45.00
d £50.00–£65.00
Evening meal per person
Min £10.00

Woodlands

Whitebread Lane, Beckley, Rye TN31 6UA **t** (01797) 260524
e robson@woodlandsrye.co.uk **w** woodlandsrye.co.uk

Spacious ground-floor en suite accommodation. Twin adjustomatic beds in bed-sitting room. Shower room designed for wheelchair use. Conservatory opening onto lovely patio suntrap. Parking adjacent. Ideal for touring 1066 Country and Weald of Kent. Relaxed atmosphere – come and go as you wish.

open All year
bedrooms 1 double, 1 family
bathrooms All en suite

On A268 Hawkhurst to Rye Road, 5 miles from Rye. Property is on left 0.5 miles before Beckley (travelling towards Rye) and 0.6 miles after children's farm.

Access 🏛 ⚑

General 🐕 P♿ ✂ ✗ 🎮 ❄

Rooms 📺 ☕ 🍵 ♨ 💷

Payment Cash/cheques

Special rates for week-long stays.
Evening meals by arrangement.

SANDWICH, Kent Map ref 3C3 — SELF-CATERING

★★★★

Units **2**
Sleeps **4–7**

Low season per wk
£300.00–£370.00
High season per wk
£370.00–£650.00

Updown Park Farm, Near Sandwich

contact Mrs Montgomery, Little Brooksend Farm, Birchington CT7 0JW **t** (01843) 841656 **f** (01843) 841656
e info@montgomery-cottages.co.uk **w** montgomery-cottages.co.uk

General 🐎 🏚 ⛺ P Ⓢ

Unit ♨ 🎱 ▬ ▦ 🔄 🧺 ❄

Payment Cash/cheques

Each cottage has an en suite double bedroom with wheelchair access. Short weekend/mid-week breaks available out of season.

Set in 30 acres of Parkland. Two cottages converted from the former dairy. Each having three ground-floor bedrooms, all with own bath/shower rooms, plus twin-bedded room on upper floor. Open-plan living area. Within easy reach of Canterbury, Sandwich, Deal, beaches, Channel ports and Tunnel. Open from March up to and including New Year.

Travel directions given on application.

SHANKLIN, Isle of Wight — SELF-CATERING

★★★

Laramie contact Mrs Sally Ranson, Laramie, Howard Road, Shanklin PO37 6HD
t (01983) 862905
e sally.ranson@tiscali.co.uk

SLINDON, West Sussex — GUEST ACCOMMODATION

♦♦♦♦

Mill Lane House Slindon, Slindon, Arundel BN18 0RP
t (01243) 814440 **f** (01243) 814436

Don't forget www.

Web addresses throughout this guide are shown without the prefix www. Please include www. in the address line of your browser. If a web address does not follow this style it is shown in full.

SWAY, Hampshire Map ref 2C3 — **GUEST ACCOMMODATION**

♦♦♦♦♦
GOLD AWARD

HB per room per night
s £80.00
d £150.00–£160.00
Dinner per person
£19.75–£22.50
(non-residents welcome)

The Nurse's Cottage

Station Road, Sway, Lymington SO41 6BA **t** (01590) 683402
f (01590) 683402 **e** nurses.cottage@lineone.net
w nursescottage.co.uk

Access ☺ 🎒 🐾

General 🛏10 🍴 🍷 ✗ 🍽

Rooms 🛁 📺 📞 📻 🖥 s 🛎 ☕ 🧺 💺

Payment Credit/debit cards, cash

Accommodation: ideal for the less agile, elderly and hearing impaired. Restaurant: suitable for wheelchair users – ramp, disabled wc, etc.

One of the New Forest's most highly acclaimed guest accommodations, The Nurse's Cottage enjoys an enviable reputation for comfort, truly personal service and good food. For over 70 years, this was the cosy cottage home of Sway's successive District Nurses, and all five bedrooms are situated on the ground floor. Numerous awards for accessibility, food, wine, service, etc.

bedrooms 2 double, 2 twin/double, 1 single
bathrooms All en suite

M27 jct 1 follow A337 to Lyndhurst, then Brockenhurst and B3055 to Sway.

TUSMORE, Oxfordshire — **SELF-CATERING**

★★★★

Pimlico Farm Country Cottages contact Mr & Mrs John & Monica Harper, Pimlico Farm Country Cottages, Pimlico Farm, Tusmore, Bicester OX27 7SL
t (01869) 810306 **f** (01869) 810309
e enquiries@pimlicofarm.co.uk

ULCOMBE, Kent — **SELF-CATERING**

★★★★

Apple Pye Cottage contact Mrs Diane Leat, Bramley Knowle Farm, Bramley Knowle Farm, Eastwood Road, Maidstone ME17 1ET
t (01622) 858878 **f** (01622) 851121
e diane@bramleyknowlefarm.co.uk **w** bramleyknowlefarm.co.uk

WINCHESTER, Hampshire — **HOTEL**

★★★

Harestock Lodge Hotel Harestock Road, Winchester SO22 6NX
t (01962) 881870 **f** (01962) 886959
e info@harestocklodgehotel.com **w** harestocklodgehotel.com

WITNEY, Oxfordshire Map ref 2C1

★★★★

| Units | 1 |
| Sleeps | 4 |

Low season per wk
£250.00–£320.00
High season per wk
£420.00–£450.00

Swallows Nest, Witney

contact Mrs Jan Strainge, Springhill Farm Swallows Nest, Cogges, Witney OX29 6UL **t** (01993) 704919 **e** jan@strainge.fsnet.co.uk

Cosy country barn conversion close to Witney, Oxford, Blenheim and nearby Cotswolds. Level access throughout including en suite showers. One zip/link double, one twin (low allergy). Shower chairs etc available.
open All year
nearest shop 1 mile
nearest pub 1 mile

| General | |
| Unit | |

Payment Cash/cheques, euros

TRAVEL BY TRAIN

Trains are changing at South Eastern Trains!
Take a journey through Kent and travel in style
and comfort aboard our improved trains.
With designated wheelchair spaces, accessible toilets,
tactile surfaces and contrasting colours, our trains
are now easier for everyone to use. Automatic on
board announcements and passenger displays
mean you no longer have to guess where you are!

If you need assistance for any part of your train journey,
the Assisted Travel Department are there to help you.
They will happily book assistance for all stages of
your train journey. They can be contacted on:

Freephone 0800 7834524
Textphone 0800 7834548

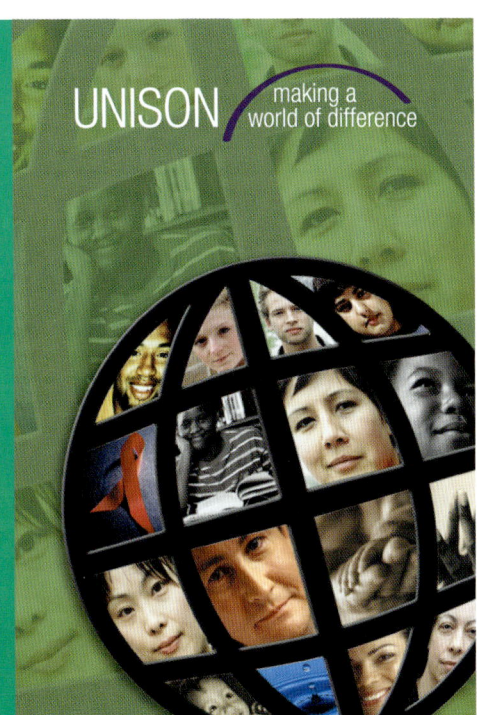

British Transport Police

Every day, millions of people travel by train — very few become victims of crime.

Wherever you travel on a mainline train, the London Underground, or Docklands Light Railway, the officers of the British Transport Police are there to protect and assist you.

Should you need to contact the police in an emergency, please

- ask any member of rail staff to contact us;
- call freephone 0800 40 50 40; or
- dial 999.

If you would like to know more about British Transport Police, or receive a copy of our *Travel Safe* leaflet, write to:

Media & Customer Relations Unit
British Transport Police
25 Camden Road
London NW1 9LN
Telephone: 020 7388 7541

Great value family holidays
Let the fun shine
BUNN Leisure
NEW FOR 2006 BOOK ONLINE
ROSE AWARD CARAVAN 2006
HOLIDAY PARK
Whatever you're seeking from your ideal break in 2006, look no further than Bunn Leisure. We've got all your perfect holiday ingredients by the bucket and spade load... and it's all just 90 minutes from London.
✔ Access for all policy
✔ 4 fantastic Holiday Parks
✔ Choice of disabled access houses and caravans
✔ Sunny Selsey, West Sussex
✔ 1 mile of beach
✔ FREE Kids fun clubs
Book today 01243 606080
www.bunnleisure.co.uk

Visit Guilford and the Surrey Hills
Call 01483 444333
for a free Visitor's Guide
email tourism@guilford.gov.uk
web www.visitguilford.com
www.surreyhills.org
The best of town and country
Guilford and the
Surrey Hills
Area of Outstanding Natural Beauty

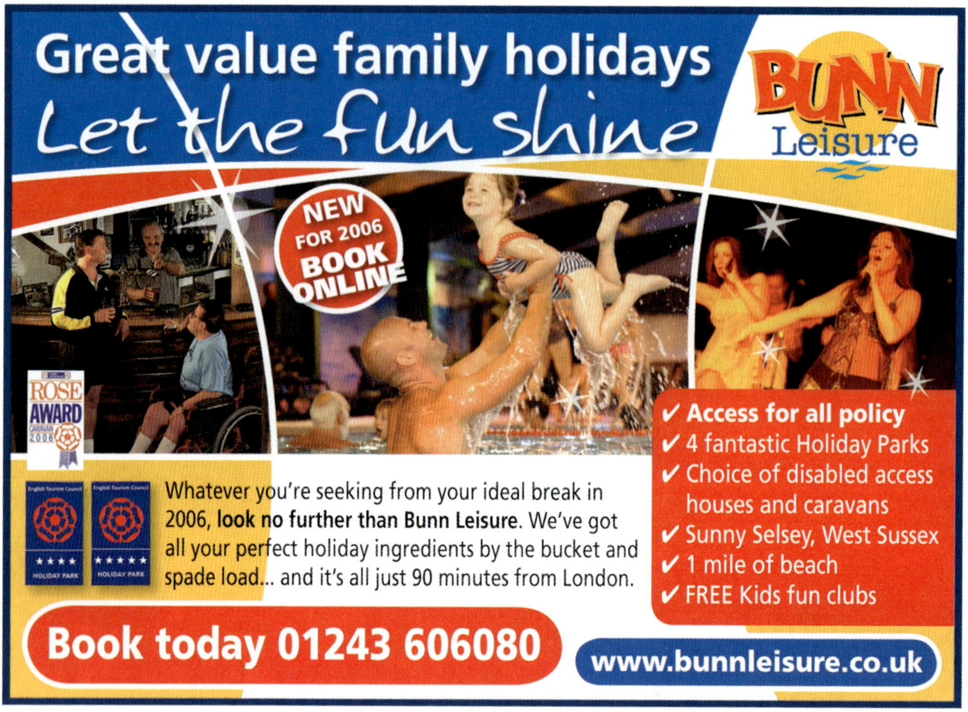

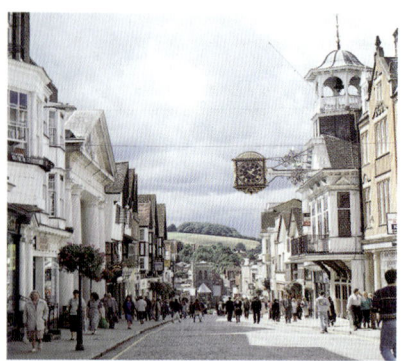

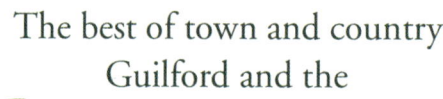

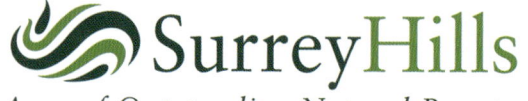

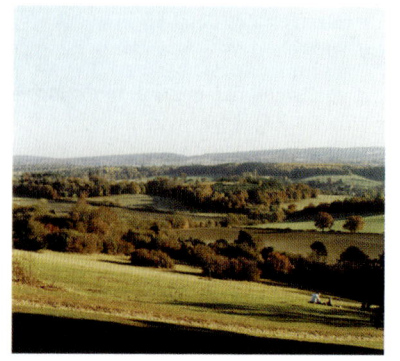

IMPERIAL WAR MUSEUM

The five branches of the Imperial War Museum explore the impact of modern conflict on people's lives through unique historic buildings and fascinating objects, innovative thought-provoking exhibitions and a wide variety of activities for all ages.

IMPERIAL WAR MUSEUM LONDON

The internationally acclaimed museum of twentieth century conflict.

Lambeth Road, London, SE1 6HZ
020 7416 5320/5321

CHURCHILL MUSEUM and CABINET WAR ROOMS

A museum dedicated to Churchill's life housed in his secret wartime headquarters.

Clive Steps, King Charles Street, London, SW1A 2AQ
020 7930 6961

HMS *BELFAST*

Europe's last big gun armoured warship of the Second World War.

Morgan's Lane, Tooley Street, London, SE1 2JH
020 7940 6300

IMPERIAL WAR MUSEUM DUXFORD

World renowned aviation museum and heritage complex.

Cambridgeshire, CB2 4QR
01223 835 000

IMPERIAL WAR MUSEUM NORTH

Iconic new museum illuminating how war shapes lives.

The Quays, Trafford Wharf Rd, Trafford Park, Manchester, M17 1TZ
0161 836 4000

For information about access to our branches please call the numbers above or see our website www.iwm.org.uk

Explore
Lee Valley Regional Park

If you enjoy wildlife, sport, countryside, heritage and fantastic open spaces or are looking for a great place to stay then the Lee Valley Regional Park is the place for you.

The Park is a regional destination for sport and leisure, stretching for 10,000 acres between Ware in Hertfordshire and the River Thames, and provides leisure activities which suit all ages, tastes and abilities.

For more information all about the Park and what you can do call 01992 702 200 or visit
www.leevalleypark.org.uk

Lee Valley Park
Open spaces and sporting places

UP TO
£25 OFF
ENTRY TO LEGOLAND*

*£5 off for up to 5 people (excluding August).

LEGOLAND® Windsor's award-winning facilities allow guests with disabilities and special needs the best possible enjoyment and accessibility. The Park has been designed with the needs of these guests in mind and has been awarded Best Disabled Facility by Group Leisure magazine on numerous occasions.

Terms & Conditions:
- Voucher entitles a maximum of five people to £5.00 off full admission price per person at LEGOLAND Windsor.
- Entrance for children under three years of age is free.
- Voucher must be presented upon entrance into LEGOLAND Windsor and surrendered to the ticket booth operator.
- Not to be used in conjunction with any other offer, reward/loyalty program, 2 Day Pass, Annual Pass, group booking, on-line tickets, rail inclusive offers or an exclusive event or concert.
- Guests are advised that not all attractions and shows may be operational on the day of their visit.
- Height, age and weight restrictions may apply on some rides. Some rides require guests who only just meet the minimum height requirements to be accompanied by a person aged 18 years or over.
- Guests under the age of 14 must be accompanied by a person aged 18 or over.
- This is not for re-sale, is non-refundable and non-transferable.
- The park opens for the 2006 season on 31st March and closes on 29th October 2006.
- Voucher is valid for admissions from 31st March to 29th October 2006 excluding the month of August and selected dates – please check the LEGOLAND website in advance to confirm excluded dates.
- This offer is limited to one per household.
- This offer will apply irrespective of the entrance price at the time of use.
- LEGOLAND Windsor will be closed on selected weekdays in March, April, May, September, October and November.
- PLEASE visit www.LEGOLAND.co.uk in advance to confirm dates and prices.

For great hotel offers go to www.LEGOLAND.co.uk/accommodation

LEGO, the LEGO logo, LEGOLAND and the LEGOLAND logo are trademarks of the LEGO Group. ©2005 The LEGO Group.

300500

BBC TOURS
GET INSIDE THE BBC

Pre-book your tour of BBC Television Centre by calling **0870 6030 304*** or textphone **0870 9030 304**.

bbc.co.uk/tours

*Lines open from 9am to 5pm. Calls are charged at national rate and may be monitored or recorded for training.

barbican   theatre film
             art   education
             dance   music

Great arts for all

Call 020 7638 8891 for a copy of our free access guide to help you plan your visit

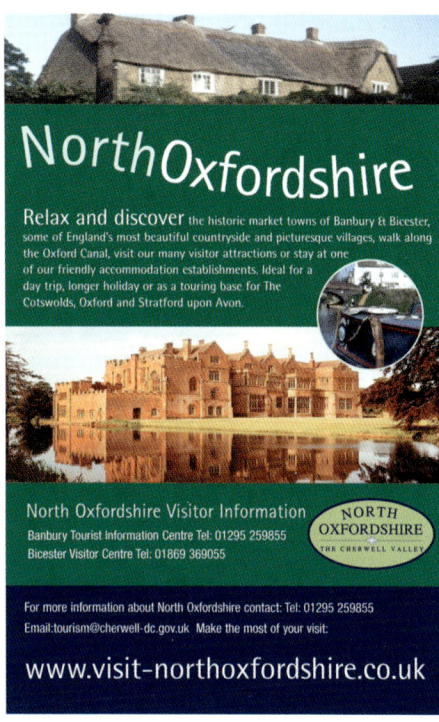

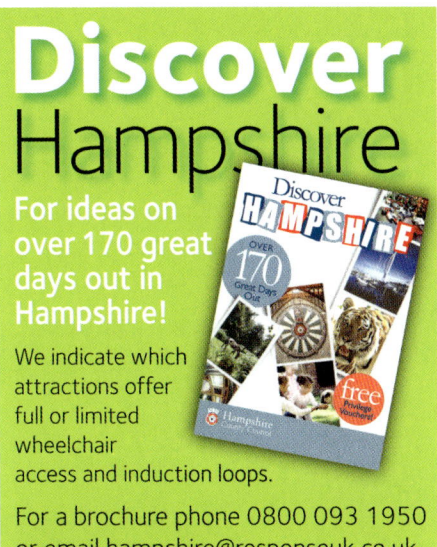

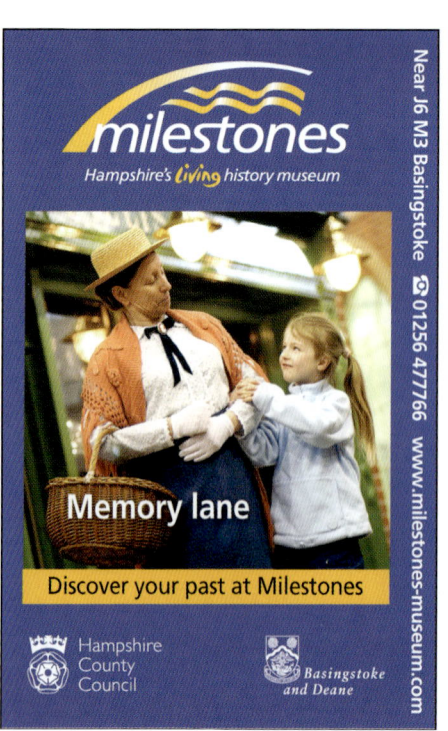

Become a time traveller

Find out what Romans ate for dinner, experience the Great Fire of London, go window shopping in a Victorian street and be amazed by the magnificent Lord Mayor's Coach.

ADMISSION FREE
Close to St Paul's
0870 444 3851
www.museumoflondon.org.uk

MUSEUM OF LONDON

National Portrait Gallery 1856·2006

'There shall be but one mistress here and no master'

Ascribed to Elizabeth I
in response to the Earl of Leicester

www.npg.org.uk
Open daily 10.00 – 18.00
Thursday and Friday until 21.00
St Martin's Place, London
⊖ Leicester Square

History Art Biography Fame
Discover them for Free

150 Years
Collecting for the future

Queen Elizabeth I (detail) by an unknown artist, c.1600
© National Portrait Gallery, London

Herbert Smith

CAPITAL OF THE THAMES VALLEY

Reading

Visitor Centre and Travel Shop

Discover magical days out, fascinating heritage and the best shopping and eating in the South.

Children's Festival
Water Fest
Community Carnival
Real Ale and Jazz Festival
Shakespeare in the Ruins
WOMAD

For information on events, what's on and places to explore
0118 956 6226
e-mail: touristinfo@reading.gov.uk

Open Mon - Fri 9.30am - 5pm (except from 10am Weds)
Sat 9.30am - 4pm.
Church House, Chain Street, Reading, RG1 2HX
Reading

ROYAL Windsor

With 1000 years of history, there's so much to pack in

Call for a free brochure +44 (0)1753 743900
or visit www.windsor.gov.uk

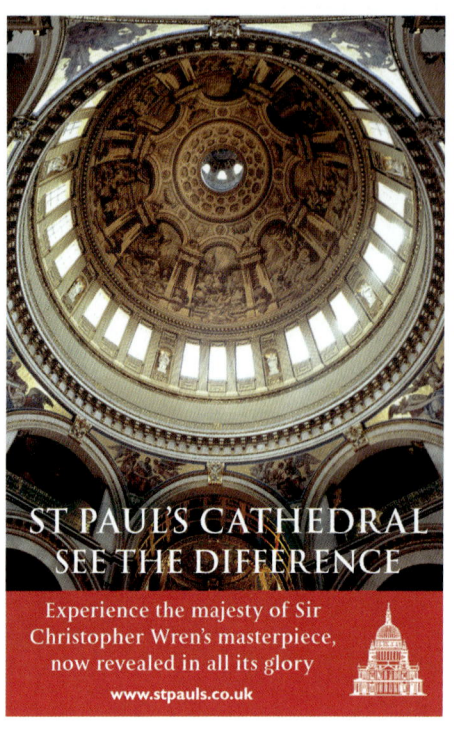

Westminster Cathedral

London SW1

020 7798 9064

gladly supports Tourism for All

Visitors very welcome

Open daily 7am-7pm

www.westminstercathedral.org.uk

Foreign & Commonwealth Office, London

As members of the Employers' Forum on Disability we are dedicated to using the talents of disabled people.

If you are interested in the work of the Foreign & Commonwealth Office you can look us up on our website: www.fco.gov.uk

Worthing Museum and Art Gallery

Open Tuesday to Saturday 10-5. Closed Bank Holidays.

Admission free – Fully accessible

Telephone 01903 239999 ext.1140

Email museum@worthing.gov.uk

Website www.worthing.gov.uk

the Nuffield southampton

Award-Winning Productions Workshops | Sunday Night Specials Poetry Evenings | Community Theatre Community Theatre | Alternative Theatre | Visiting Companies | Studio Bar & Restaurant and so much more...

023 8067 1771 ww.nuffieldtheatre.co.uk

With best wishes from

ALLPORT LIMITED

INTERNATIONAL FREIGHT FORWARDERS

26 Chase Road, London NW10 6QA

Tel: 020 8965 0678   Fax: 020 8965 1340

Anonymous Donation

Escape to the gentle countryside of the Heart of Kent, the Garden of England. Visit our magnificent castles and gardens. For your FREE Holiday Guide with a choice of accessible places to stay, ring:

0800 0288668

Heart of Kent
www.heartofkent.org.uk

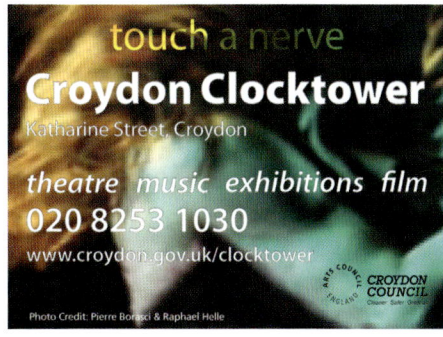

touch a nerve

Croydon Clocktower

Katharine Street, Croydon

theatre music exhibitions film

020 8253 1030

www.croydon.gov.uk/clocktower

CROYDON COUNCIL

Photo Credit: Pierre Borasci & Raphael Helle

Scotland

Scotland the **brave**

Dramatic landscapes and mist on the lochs. Or world-class shopping and an unrivalled arts festival. Can you stay the course on the Malt Whisky Trail? Rediscover yourself in some of Europe's finest landscapes and enjoy a leisurely break or immerse yourself in history and culture.

Take the high road

Wherever your journey in Scotland takes you, you're in for a treat. You might linger in the Borders to explore the dignified ruins of once-powerful abbeys or follow in the footsteps of Rob Roy and Walter Scott through the Trossachs. Perhaps you'll potter around picturesque fishing villages in the Kingdom of Fife, head for Stirling and the battlefield at Brannockburn where Robert the Bruce defeated the English, or drop into Speyside to tickle your taste buds on the Malt Whisky Trail.

If it's drama you're after, venture north for the Highlands, a vast swathe of untamed wilderness where land and sea collide to create stunning perspectives.

Use your nose as well as your mouth to distinguish the malt whiskies produced by the eight renowned distilleries on the **Malt Whisky Trail.** maltwhiskytrail.com

Previous page romantic Eilean Donan Castle, Dornie
Above spectacular panorama of Edinburgh

Discover the most perfect vista at Eilean Donan where the dramatic castle ruins and surrounding mountains are

A unique country of soaring peaks, sparkling lochs and fairytale castles

Pre-historic, volcanic, tropic, antartic... **Our Dynamic Earth** explores the extremes of our planet from the Big Bang, through erupting volcanoes to the chill of polar ice. Try out interactive exhibits in multi-sensory galleries.
dynamicearth.co.uk

reflected in the waters of the loch. Both landscapes and wildlife are at their most spectacular in Scotland's two National Parks – Loch Lomond & The Trossachs, and Cairngorms.

Ancient heritage

Whichever part of Scotland takes your fancy, history is never far away – from the Neolithic ruins of Skara Brae on Orkney to Scotland's dramatic capital city. Here you can browse the specialist shops of the medieval Old Town, visit the castle and uncover 1,000 years of Scotland's tumultuous past or stop for refreshment in Deacon Brodie's Tavern and learn about the devious Edinburgh citizen who inspired Robert Louis Stevenson's tale of Dr Jekyll and Mr Hyde.

Highland fling

And if it's festivals you want – they're here in abundance. Apart from Edinburgh's celebrated arts and fringe festivals, there's traditional music and celebration at the Shetland Folk Festival, caber tossing and games aplenty at the Cowal Highland Gathering and Scotland's national poet Robert Burns is celebrated at venues throughout the Scottish Borders in May each year.

The Scots are fiercely proud of their heritage, which they celebrate in a thousand different ways, from the pomp and splendour of the Edinburgh Military Tattoo to the more intimate appeal of an impromptu ceilidh in a cosy pub. If this leads you to assume that they only look back to the past, a trip to Glasgow will set you straight. Scotland's largest city has reinvented itself to become one of Europe's great cultural capitals. It also has shopping to rival London's best and an abundance of stylish restaurants and cafe bars that will seduce the most adventurous gourmet.

Escape to the outer islands for a unique experience. Dreamy beaches are found in the Outer Hebrides, folk music draws the finest performers to Orkney, and puffins by the million await bird-watchers in Shetland.

further information

VisitScotland
0845 225 5121
visitscotland.com

ABERDEEN, Aberdeenshire Map ref 7D3 — HOTEL

★★★★★

B&B per room per night
s £135.00–£295.00
d £145.00–£325.00

Marcliffe Hotel and Spa

North Deeside Road, Pitfodels, Aberdeen AB15 9YA **t** (01224) 861000
f (01224) 868860 **e** info@marcliffe.com **w** marcliffe.com

Situated in 11 acres of wooded grounds on the A93 to Royal Deeside, yet only five minutes from city centre. Restaurant specialises in local and Scottish produce. Ideal location for visiting Aberdeen city and shire, including castles, distilleries and many other attractions. Wonderful health, beauty and hair spa now open.

open All year
bedrooms 7 twin, 30 double/twin, 5 suites
bathrooms All en suite

From Aberdeen ringroad A90, turn west on A93 direction Braemar. Hotel 1 mile on right after turning onto A93.

Access ☺ 🛄 🐾

General 🐎 P& 🗲 🍴 ⊞ ❄

Leisure 🏊 🏃

Rooms 🔌 ▯ 🍴 🔍 🔦 📺 📠

Payment Credit/debit cards, cash/cheques, euros

Many spa/food packages available. Check website and call hotel for details. Available all year, book 4 days in advance.

COLDSTREAM, Scottish Borders Map ref 6D2 — SELF-CATERING

★★★–★★★★★

Units **2**
Sleeps **4–7**

Low season per wk
£180.00–£200.00
High season per wk
£200.00–£380.00

Little Swinton Cottages, Coldstream

contact Sue Brewis, Leet Villa, Leet Street, Coldstream TD12 4BJ
t (01890) 882173 **e** suebrewis@tiscali.co.uk **w** littleswinton.co.uk

Quiet, single-storey, stone farm cottages with open views. 'Cotoneaster' is fully ramped with large wheelchair adapted bathroom. One double, one king, one single, one twin. Large garden area. Pets and children welcome.

open All year
nearest shop 1.5 miles
nearest pub 1.5 miles

General 🐎 🛏 🚶 P S

Unit 🔌 ▥ S 🔦 📺 📠 🔦 🔦 📠 🍴 ❄

Payment Cash/cheques

EDINBURGH, Edinburgh Map ref 6C2 · GUEST ACCOMMODATION

★★★

B&B per room per night
s £20.00–£70.00
d £40.00–£70.00

Ardgarth Guest House

1 St Mary's Place, Portobello, Edinburgh EH15 2QF t (0131) 669 3021
f (0131) 468 1221 e stay@ardgarth.com w ardgarth.com

Comfortable, warm, family-run guesthouse, fully accessible with roll-in showers. Public transport to city centre is accessible. Parking is directly outside.
open All year except Christmas
bedrooms 4 twin, 3 single, 2 family
bathrooms 4 en suite

Access ☺ abc 🏃

General 🛏 ✕ 🍴

Rooms 🛁 ♨ 📶 🚿 📺 🖂

Payment Credit/debit cards, cash/cheques, euros

GALASHIELS, Scottish Borders Map ref 6C2 · SELF-CATERING

★

Units 12
Sleeps 3–6

High season per wk
Max £325.00

Borders Event Centre, Netherdale, Galashiels

contact Beryl Ewart, Borders Event Centre,
Heriot-Watt University Scottish Borders Campus, Netherdale,
Galashiels TD1 3HF t (01896) 892270 f (01896) 758965
e events_sbc@hw.ac.uk

Flats consist of six single study bedrooms, two toilets, showers, kitchen and lounge. Four on ground floor, two with some disabled facilities. Ideal base for exploring the beautiful Borders. Available during Easter and summer holiday periods.
nearest shop 1.5 miles

General 🛏 P 📺

Unit 🛁 📺 s 📺 📺 📶 📺 ❄

Payment Credit/debit cards, cash/cheques

GATEHOUSE OF FLEET, Dumfries & Galloway Map ref 6B3 — SELF-CATERING

★★–★★★★★

Units **2**
Sleeps **1–6**

Low season per wk
£238.00–£347.00
High season per wk
£392.00–£570.00

Rusko Holidays, Gatehouse of Fleet

contact Beverley Vaux, Rusko Holidays, Gatehouse of Fleet,
Castle Douglas DG7 2BS **t** (01557) 814215
e info@ruskoholidays.co.uk **w** ruskoholidays.co.uk

Access abc 🐾

General 🛏 🏛 🅿 Ⓢ

Unit ♿ ▯ ▭ ▢ 🛏

Payment Credit/debit cards,
cash/cheques

*Wheelchair accessible house has
a bathroom with wet-floor shower
and level access. Special low
season short breaks available.*

Upper Rusko Cottage, a lovely
'haven in the hills' (wheelchair
accessible) and charming, cosy
Garden Cottage (ambulant
disabled) set amid magnificent
scenery in south-west Scotland.
On the edge of Galloway Forest
Park, near accessible beaches
and forest tracks, wonderful
wildlife and historic town. Pets
welcome. The perfect relaxing
break.

open All year

*One and a half hours from
Carlisle, 4 hours from
Manchester and Leeds and 2.5
hours from Edinburgh and
Glasgow. Just off A75 at
Gatehouse of Fleet.*

Scottish **accessible scheme**

All types of accommodation in Scotland are assessed
for wheelchair users and those with limited mobility.
Accommodation entries include one of the following
three mobility symbols.

 Category 1
Accessible to a wheelchair user travelling
independently.

 Category 2
Accessible to a wheelchair user travelling
with assistance.

 Category 3
Accessible to a wheelchair user able to walk
a few paces and up a maximum of three steps.

★★★

B&B per room per night
s Min £47.00
d Min £74.00
Evening meal per person
Min £17.00

Glen Orchy Hotel

20 Knab Road, Lerwick, Shetland ZE1 0AX **t** (01595) 692031
f (01595) 692031 **e** glenorchy.house@virgin.net
w guesthouselerwick.com

General 🐕 P& ✗ 🍴

Rooms 🔆 📺 💆 🍵 ⬆ 🛏 📠

Payment Credit/debit cards,
cash/cheques

*Under-floor heating. Freeview
television. Broadband Internet
access. Authentic Thai cuisine a
speciality. Self-service honesty
bar.*

Town and country on our
doorstep. Adjacent to a 9-hole
practice golf course, free to the
public, yet only 5 minutes' walk
from the harbour and town
centre. An ideal base for
shopping, coastal walks, bird-
watching etc. Pets and well-
behaved children welcome.
open All year
bedrooms 4 double, 8 twin,
7 single, 4 family
bathrooms All en suite

*From airport, A970 to
roundabout then A969 1 mile to
mini-roundabout. Turn right
Knab Road. Glen Orchy House
240yds up hill.*

★★–★★★

Units **2**
Sleeps **2–6**
Low season per wk
£178.00–£338.00
High season per wk
£258.00–£558.00

Bailey Mill Inn, Bailey, Newcastleton

contact Mrs Pamela Copeland, Bailey Mill Inn, Bailey,
Near Newcastleton TD9 0TR **t** (016977) 48617 **e** pam@baileymill.fsnet.co.uk
w holidaycottagescumbria.co.uk

Brookview and Millstream self-
catering apartments on Scottish
Borders (also B&B). Onsite jacuzzi,
sauna, bar and pony-trekking. Ideal
retreat where you can be sure of a
warm welcome.
open All year
nearest shop 7 miles
nearest pub < 0.5 miles

General 🐕 🏛 🚶 P S

Unit 🔆 🍴 📺 📠 ⬆ 📠 🍵 ❄

Payment Credit/debit cards,
cash/cheques

★★★★
Units **10**
Sleeps **2–4**

Low season per wk
£280.00–£420.00
High season per wk
£520.00–£765.00

Balmashie Holiday Cottages, St Andrews, Fife

contact Andrew Pirie, Balmashie Holiday Cottages, St Andrews, Fife KY16 8PN
t (01334) 880666 **f** (01334) 880667 **e** andrew@balmashie.co.uk
w balmashie.co.uk

Well-established, fully equipped and very comfortable cottage facing the sea in quiet, peaceful location. Wheelchair assisted cottage, two twin bedrooms, shower room, open-plan kitchen/living/dining room.
open All year
nearest shop 2.5 miles
nearest pub 2.5 miles

Access
General
Unit
Payment Credit/debit cards, cash/cheques

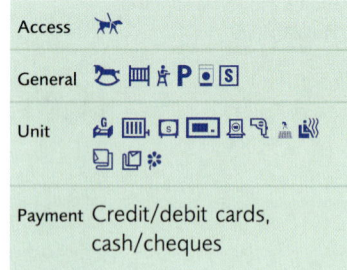

MELFORT PIER & HARBOUR
Argyll, Scotland
COME AND ENJOY EVERY DAY OF YOUR LIFE!

Absorb the tranquillity of glorious Loch Melfort, from your own patio. Seven houses, all with bedrooms on one level, walk in showers, lots of parking and helpful staff ready to assist you. Start any day of the week. Min stay of 2 nights. From £80.00 per night. Pets welcome.
CALL FOR SPECIALS
01852 200 333 www.mellowmelfort.com

Inverclyde is an area of unrivalled beauty, situated along the broad coastal reaches of the River Clyde, with breathtaking views to the Argyll Hills and Scottish Highlands.

Its moorlands, hills and lochs are a haven for the rarest species of Wildlife while its historical attractions celebrate an influential maritime history and industrial past.

A visit to Inverclyde is a visit to remember.

www.inverclyde.gov.uk

Don't forget www.

Web addresses throughout this guide are shown without the prefix www. Please include www. in the address line of your browser. If a web address does not follow this style it is shown in full.

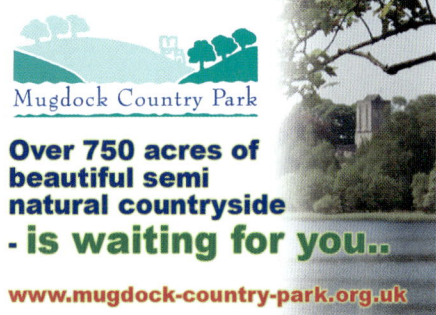

Wales

Land of the ancient Celts

For a small country Wales is big on things to see and do. To start with it has three National Parks, each one featuring very different landscapes, and a turbulent history which comes alive in its many castles. Search out Wales' fascinating industrial heritage and discover its myths and legends.

Nature at its best

In big, bold Snowdonia National Park ascend to the summit of Mount Snowdon on the little mountain railway. Pembrokeshire has Britain's only coastal-based National Park where the sea air fills your lungs and the wildlife captures your attention. The Brecon Beacons National Park is filled with the greenest, grassiest hills imaginable and there are plenty of routes and facilites for the less able.

Cappuccinos and citadels

Europe's youngest capital, Cardiff is just a stone's throw from the Beacons' wide, open spaces. It's cosmopolitan,

The **Centre for Alternative Technology** will fill your head with ideas of how to conserve the earth's natural resources. Wind, water and solar power, energy conservation, organic growing and more.
cat.org.uk

Previous page experience Welsh folklore at the Eisteddfod International Festival, Llangollen
Above melodic strings at Harlech Castle

lively and busy. Join in the cafe culture and don't miss the stunning new waterfront along Cardiff Bay. Make sure you visit the fabulous city-centre castle.

A timeless country of epic mountains, lush green valleys and spectacular coastline

Castles, of course, are what Wales does very well. There are hundreds of them, ranging from Harlech, Beaumaris, Caernarfon and Conwy, part of Edward I's mighty iron ring of castles in the north, to romantic hilltop fortresses such as Carreg Cennen near Llandeilo. Here it's easy to conjure up tales of princes, wizards and dragons from high on the ramparts to the depths of underground passages.

Experience the country's fascinating industrial heritage first-hand in places like the Llechwedd Slate Caverns and the Big Pit at Blaenavon where you can go underground and find out exactly what it was like to work there.

What next?
For all its history, Wales doesn't live in the past. It's an exciting, forward-looking country, full of discovery and adventure. At the Centre for Alternative Technology in mid Wales you'll find the village of the future with lots of child-friendly exhibits and events throughout the year. Test out the interactive, hands-on exhibits at Techniquest, an amazing science centre, and see stars in the planetarium. Visit the National Botanic Garden, created in the new millennium, to unearth a myriad

Travel in style behind a vintage steam locomotive and chug through the beautiful scenery of the Brecon Beacons. Board the **Brecon Mountain Railway** near Merthyr Tydfil.
breconmountainrailway.co.uk

of fascinating plants. For an adrenalin rush, hang on tight and hold your breath at Oakwood Theme Park or ride more sedately on Wales' charming Great Little Trains – scenic narrow-guage railways that puff their way to the loveliest corners of the country.

And there's plenty going on all over Wales. Give your taste buds a treat in September at the Abergavenny Food Festival or at Caerphilly's Big Cheese extravaganza in July. Or for something completely different cheer on the competitors in the extraordinary World Bog Snorkelling Championships near Llanwrtyd Wells on August Bank Holiday Monday. As you would expect, there is music everywhere. Get with the beat at the renowned Brecon International Festival of Jazz or immerse yourself in all things Welsh at the National Eisteddfod near Swansea, both in August.

further information
Wales Tourist Board
0870 121 1251
0870 121 1255 (minicom)
visitwales.com

★★★★

ACCESS STATEMENT

B&B per room per night
s Min £30.00
d £50.00–£55.00
Evening meal per person
£7.50–£15.50

Old Radnor Barn

Station Yard, Talgarth, Brecon LD3 0PE
t (01874) 712102 & 07796 953904   **e** groves@oldradnorbarn.com
w oldradnorbarn.com

Access ☺ 🏛 abc 🐾

General ☎ P♿ ✂ ✕ 🍺 ❄

Leisure 🏃

Rooms 🛏 Ⓢ 🍴 🔌 📻 📺

Payment Credit/debit cards, cash/cheques

Ideally situated for outdoor activities – bookings and arrangements made on your behalf. Special rates for groups and longer stays.

Quality accommodation and service in a 400-year-old Listed barn conversion, situated in the foothills of the Black Mountains within the Brecon Beacons National Park. Ground and first-floor accommodation, level access – suitable for the elderly and disabled. All rooms with en suite/private facilities. Flexible accommodation – extra beds available. Pick-up/drop-off service available.

open All year
bedrooms 2 double,
1 double/twin, 1 family
bathrooms 2 en suite, 2 private

In Talgarth follow signs for public car park. We are on the right, 50m off the junction with High Street.

★★★–★★★★★★

ACCESS STATEMENT

Units   **2**
Sleeps   **2–6**

Low season per wk
£110.00–£320.00
High season per wk
£280.00–£420.00

Madog's Wells, Llanfair Caereinion

contact Ann Reed, Madog's Wells, Llanfair Caereinion, Welshpool SY21 0DE
t (01938) 810446   **f** (01938) 810446   **e** madogswell@btopenworld.com

Compact cosy two-bedroom bungalow (one double, one bunk and single) and spacious three-bedroom bungalow (one double, two twins) in beautiful secluded valley; bird-watching, walking, steam trains, lakes and mountains nearby. Access statement available.
open All year
nearest shop 3 miles
nearest pub 3 miles

General ☎ 🍺 ⛽ P♿ ✂ Ⓢ

Unit 🛏 🏬 Ⓢ 📺 📻📺 ♨ 🔥

🍴 💷 ❄

Payment Cash/cheques

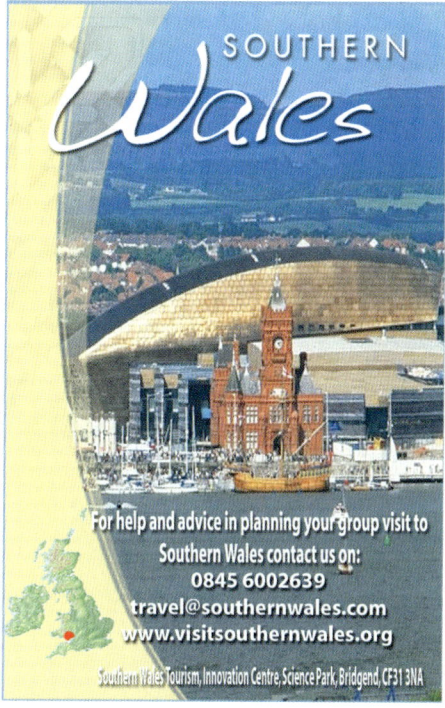

SOUTHERN *Wales*

For help and advice in planning your group visit to
Southern Wales contact us on:
0845 6002639
travel@southernwales.com
www.visitsouthernwales.org

Southern Wales Tourism, Innovation Centre, Science Park, Bridgend, CF31 3NA

Wonderful Woodland Visits

There are some fantastic opportunities to experience
wonderful woodlands in Wales. The five centres
below all offer an opportunity to find out more.

Coed y Brenin Visitor Centre some of the best mountain biking
in the world, walking trails, shop and café. Tel **01341 440666**

Bwlch Nant yr Arian Visitor Centre daily Red Kite feeding
at 3pm BST (2pm winter), walks, mountain biking, café.
Tel **01970 890694**

Garwnant Visitor Centre within the Brecon Beacons
National Park, offers walking trails, a new adventurous
ropes course, café and shop. Tel **01685 723060**

Cwmcarn Forest Drive and Centre forest drive offers 7 miles
of dramatic forests with stunning views, play furniture, BBQ's,
sculpture and mountain bike trails. Tel **01495 272001**

Afan Forest Park exciting walking and mountain biking
available in the Forest Park, café and shop. Tel **01639 850564**

Comisiwn Coedwigaeth Cymru
Forestry Commission Wales

For more information about all Forestry Commission woodlands visit:
www.forestry.gov.uk

BRECON BEACONS NATIONAL PARK

**520 square miles of
impressive landscapes,
atmosphere and
experiences.**

**For a copy of the Disabled and
Easier Access Guide please visit:
www.breconbeacons.org
or phone 01874 624437**

PARC CENEDLAETHOL BANNAU BRYCHEINIOG

Amgueddfa **Lloyd George** Museum

Life & times of the cottage bred boy
who became Prime Minister during
World War I

Easter – October

Tel **01766 522071**
Llanystumdwy, Criccieth, LL52 0SH

Greenacres
nr Porthmadog, North Wales

* Heated Indoor & Outdoor
  Pools with SplashZone
  Activities Programme
* Rory & Bradley Clubs
* Sports Facilities
* Indoor & Outdoor Play Areas
* 9 hole Pitch & Putt
* Nature Reserve
* Bars & Restaurants
* Family Entertainment Day & Night
* Tourers Welcome

GREAT SAVINGS ALL YEAR

Call the Park direct: **0870 40 50 146**
Or visit: www.greenacres-park.co.uk
Or see your local Travel Agent Quote ACCESSGR

Haven

MINFFORDD LUXURY SELF CATERING
ISLE OF ANGLESEY

A range of four superb units of 5 WTB rated
accommodation, sleeping 4/5 and 9
in rural surroundings on Anglesey's east coast,
some with disabled facilities.*

**Hughes-Roberts, Minffordd DULAS,
Isle of Anglesey LL70 9HJ**

Tel **01248 410678** Fax **01248 410378**
e-mail enq@minffordd-holidays.com

www.minffordd-holidays.com

Welsh Access Statement
Owners of all types of accommodation in Wales are required to have a full Access
Statement available for guests.

Northern Ireland

Travel a land of legends and folklore and let the ancient tale of Ireland unfold. A tale older than the pyramids of Egypt, full of turmoil and romance, set against a spectacular backdrop of breathtaking scenery.

Discover the natural wonder of the Giant's Causeway in County Antrim, touch the history embedded in the ancient 'Walls of Derry' and visit the magical region of the Kingdoms of Down, famous for the stunning Mountains of Mourne, its dramatic coastline and acres of forest and parks. Experience warm hospitality, delicious traditional dishes and the universal language of music performed anywhere and everywhere!

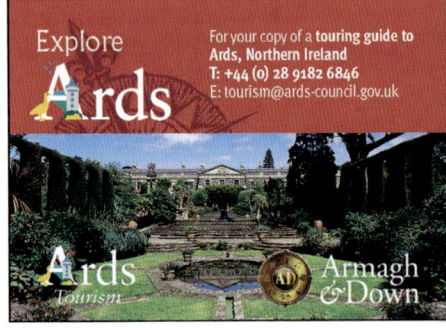

Above Mountains of Mourne, County Down

Further **information**

Quality assurance schemes

When you're looking for a place to stay, you need a rating system you can trust. Quality ratings are your clear guide to what to expect, in an easy to understand form. The system puts great emphasis on quality and is based on research which shows exactly what consumers are looking for when choosing accommodation. Properties are visited annually by trained, impartial assessors, so you can be confident that your accommodation has been thoroughly checked and rated for quality before you make a booking.

VisitBritain uses one to five stars to rate hotels and self-catering holiday homes and one to five diamonds (stars from January 2006) to rate guest accommodation.

Look out, too, for VisitBritain's Gold and Silver Awards for hotels and guest accommodation. These are awarded to properties achieving the highest overall levels of quality within their star or diamond rating. Gold and Silver Awards are based solely on the quality provided.

Camping and caravan parks are rated according to The British Graded Holiday Parks Scheme, operated jointly by the national tourist boards for England, Scotland, Wales and Northern Ireland, and are awarded one to five stars.

Quality ratings and awards are your sign of quality assurance, giving you the confidence to book the accommodation that will meet your expectations.

Hotels

In a one star hotel you will find an acceptable level of quality, services and a range of facilities. Moving up the one to five star rating scale, you will find progressively higher quality standards providing ever better guest care as well as a wider range of facilities and a higher level of services.

★ **At a ONE STAR hotel you will find:** Practical accommodation with a limited range of facilities and services, but a high standard of cleanliness throughout. Friendly and courteous staff to give you the help and information you need to enjoy your stay. Dining room/eating area offering breakfast to guests. Alcoholic drinks will be served in a bar or lounge. 75% of bedrooms will have en suite or private facilities.

★★ **At a TWO STAR hotel you will find (in addition to what is provided at one star):** Good overnight accommodation with more comfortable and better equipped bedrooms – all with en suite or private facilities and colour TV. A relatively straightforward range of services and a personal style of service. Food and drink are of a higher standard. A restaurant/dining room for breakfast every day and dinner at least five days a week.

★★★ At a THREE STAR hotel you will find (in addition to what is provided at one and two star): Very good accommodation offering significantly greater quality and a higher standard of facilities and services, and usually more spacious public areas and bedrooms. A more formal style of service with a receptionist on duty. Room service of continental breakfast. Laundry service available. Greater attention to quality of food.

★★★★ At a FOUR STAR hotel you will find (in addition to what is provided at one, two and three star): Accommodation offering excellent comfort and quality; all bedrooms with en suite bath, fitted overhead shower and wc. Strong emphasis on food and drink. Staff will have very good technical and social skills, anticipating and responding to your needs and requests. Room service for all meals; light refreshments and snacks available 24 hours.

★★★★★ At a FIVE STAR hotel you will find (in addition to what is provided at one, two, three and four star): Spacious, luxurious accommodation of the highest international quality, facilities, services and cuisine. Striking accommodation throughout, with a range of extra facilities. You will feel very well cared for by professional, attentive staff

providing flawless guest services. A hotel setting the highest standards for the industry, with an air of luxury, exceptional comfort and a very sophisticated ambience.

Guest Accommodation

The rating reflects the unique character of guest accommodation, and covers areas such as cleanliness, service and hospitality, bedrooms, bathrooms, food quality and visitor expectations of this sector. The quality of what is provided is more important to visitors than a wide range of facilities and services. Therefore, the same minimum requirement for facilities and services applies to all guest accommodation from one to five diamonds (stars from January 2006), while progressively higher levels of quality and customer care must be provided for each of the one to five diamonds.

♦ At ONE DIAMOND guest accommodation you will find: An acceptable overall level of quality and helpful service. Accommodation offering, as a minimum, a full cooked or continental breakfast. Other meals, where provided, will be freshly prepared. You will have a comfortable bed, with clean bed linen and towels and fresh soap. Adequate heating and hot water available at reasonable times for baths or showers at no extra charge.

♦♦ At TWO DIAMOND guest accommodation you will find (in addition to what is provided at one diamond): A good overall level of quality and comfort, with a greater emphasis on guest care in all areas.

♦♦♦ At THREE DIAMOND guest accommodation you will find (in addition to what is provided at one and two diamond): A very good overall level of quality. For example, good-quality, comfortable bedrooms; well-maintained, practical decor; a good choice of quality items available for breakfast; other meals, where provided, will be freshly cooked from good-quality ingredients. A greater degree of comfort provided for you, with good levels of customer care.

♦♦♦♦ At FOUR DIAMOND guest accommodation you will find (in addition to what is provided at one, two and three diamond): An excellent overall level of quality in all areas and customer care showing very good levels of attention to your needs.

♦♦♦♦♦ At FIVE DIAMOND guest accommodation you will find (in addition to what is provided at one, two, three and four diamond): An exceptional overall level of quality. For example, breakfast offering a wide choice of high-quality fresh ingredients; other meals, where provided, featuring fresh, seasonal and often local ingredients. Excellent levels of customer care, anticipating your needs.

NB. En suite and private bathrooms contribute to the quality score at all diamond levels. Please check when booking or see entry details.

Self-Catering Holiday Homes

Based on a one to five star rating, all self-catering properties have to meet an extensive list of minimum requirements to take part in the scheme. The more stars, the higher the overall level of quality you can expect to find.

Establishments at higher rating levels also have to meet some additional requirements for facilities.

Minimum entry requirements include the following:

- High standards of cleanliness throughout
- Clear pricing and booking conditions
- Local information to help you make the most of your stay
- Comfortable accommodation with a range of furniture to meet your needs
- Colour television (where signal available) at no extra charge
- Kitchen equipped to meet all essential requirements.

★ At a ONE STAR property you will find: An acceptable overall level of quality, with furniture, furnishings and fittings all in sound condition, and offering good standards of cleanliness.

★★ At a TWO STAR property you will find (in addition to what is provided at one star): A good overall level of quality. A good standard of cleanliness and maintenance.

★★★ At a THREE STAR property you will find (in addition to what is provided at one and two star): A good to very good overall level of quality, with very good standards of cleanliness. Ample space and good quality furniture and fittings.

★★★★ At a FOUR STAR property you will find (in addition to what is provided at one, two and three star): An excellent overall level of quality with greater attention to detail. High standards of cleanliness. Layout of property more likely to be designed with guest comfort in mind.

★★★★★ **At a FIVE STAR property you will find (in addition to what is provided at one, two, three and four star):** An exceptional overall level of quality, with the highest standards throughout including cleanliness, maintenance, range of equipment and guest care. Outstanding attention to detail with many personal touches.

Many self-catering establishments have a range of accommodation units in the building or on the site, and in some cases the individual units may have different star ratings. In such cases, the entry shows the range available.

Camping and Caravan Parks

Parks are required to meet progressively higher standards of quality as they move up the scale from one to five stars:

★ **Acceptable** To achieve this grade, the park must be clean with good standards of maintenance and customer care.

★★ **Good** All the above points plus an improved level of landscaping, lighting, refuse disposal and maintenance. May be less expensive than more highly rated parks.

★★★ **Very good** Most parks fall within this category; three stars represent the industry standard. The range of facilities provided may vary from park to park, but they will be of a very good standard and will be well maintained.

★★★★ **Excellent** You can expect careful attention to detail in the provision of all services and facilities. Four star parks rank among the industry's best.

★★★★★ **Exceptional** Highest levels of customer care will be provided. All facilities will be maintained in pristine condition in attractive surroundings.

As well as the star rating, all parks have a designator to help you choose the one that's right for you.

If you want to hire a caravan holiday home for a short break or longer holiday, or are looking to buy your own holiday home, then a **Holiday Park** is for you.

If you're planning to take your own touring caravan, motor home or tent, look for a **Touring Park**.

Where you see **Camping Park** this means that there are pitches available for tents only.

Many parks offer combinations of these designators. For example, Holiday and Touring Park or Touring and Camping Park.

Campus and Hostel Accommodation

For details of the rating system for campus and hostel accommodation see page 13.

While the majority of accommodation included in this guide has been quality rated by VisitBritain, some establishments have been assessed to similar criteria by either the AA, VisitScotland or Wales Tourist Board.

Advice and information

Making a booking

When enquiring about accommodation, make sure you check prices and other important details. You will also need to state your requirements clearly and precisely, for example:

- Arrival and departure dates, with acceptable alternatives if appropriate.
- Accessible requirements.
- The type of accommodation you need; for example, room with twin beds.
- The terms you want; for example, room only, bed and breakfast, half board, full board.
- Number of people in your party and the ages of any children.
- Special requirements, such as a garden, cot or special diet.

Booking by letter or email

Misunderstandings can easily happen over the telephone, so we strongly advise you to confirm your booking in writing if there is time.

Deposits

When you book your self-catering holiday, the proprietor will normally ask you to pay a deposit immediately, and then to pay the full balance before your holiday date. This safeguards the proprietor in case you decide to cancel at a late stage or simply do not turn up. He or she may have turned down other bookings on the strength of yours and may find it hard to re-let if you cancel.

If you make your hotel or guest accommodation reservation weeks or months in advance, you may also be asked for a deposit. The amount will vary according to the time of year, the number of people in your party and how long you plan to stay. The deposit will then be deducted from the final bill.

In the case of camping and caravan parks the full charge often has to be paid in advance. This may be in two instalments – a deposit at the time of booking and the balance by, say, two weeks before the start of the booked period.

Payment on arrival

Some establishments, especially large hotels in big towns, ask you to pay for your room on arrival if you have not booked it in advance. This is especially likely to happen if you arrive late and have little or no luggage. If you are asked to pay on arrival, it is a good idea to see your room first, to make sure it meets your requirements.

Cancellations
Legal contract
When you accept accommodation that is offered to you, by telephone or in writing, you enter a legally binding contract with the proprietor. This means that if you cancel your booking, fail to take up the accommodation or leave early, the proprietor may be entitled to compensation if he cannot re-let for all or a good part of the booked period. You will probably forfeit any deposit you have paid, and may well be asked for an additional payment.

At the time of booking you should be advised of what charges would be made in the event of cancelling the accommodation or leaving early. If this does not happen you should ask, to avoid any future disputes. The proprietor cannot make a claim until after the booked period, and during that time every effort should be made by the proprietor to re-let the accommodation. If there is a dispute it is sensible for both sides to seek legal advice on the matter. If you do have to change your travel plans, it is in your own interests to let the proprietor know in writing as soon as possible, to give them a chance to re-let your accommodation.

And remember, if you book by telephone and are asked for your credit card number, you should check whether the proprietor intends charging your credit card account should you later cancel your reservation. A proprietor should not be able to charge your credit card account with a cancellation fee unless he or she has made this clear at the time of your booking and you have agreed. However, to avoid later disputes, we suggest you check whether this is the intention.

Insurance
A travel or holiday insurance policy will safeguard you if you have to cancel or change your holiday plans. You can arrange a policy quite cheaply through your insurance company or travel agent. Some hotels offer their own insurance schemes and many self-catering agencies insist their customers take out a policy when they book their holiday.

Arriving late
If you know you will be arriving late in the evening, it is a good idea to say so when you book. If you are delayed on your way, a telephone call to say that you will be late will help prevent any problems when you arrive.

Service charges and tipping
These days many places levy service charges automatically (normally only applicable for hotel accommodation). If they do, they must clearly say so in their offer of accommodation at the time of booking. Then the service charge becomes part of the legal contract when you accept the offer of accommodation.

If a service charge is levied automatically, there is no need to tip the staff, unless they provide some exceptional service. The usual tip for meals is 10% of the total bill.

Telephone charges
Hotels can set their own charges for telephone calls made through their switchboard or from direct-dial telephones in bedrooms. These charges are often much higher than telephone companies' standard charges (to defray the cost of providing the service).

Comparing costs

It is a condition of VisitBritain's quality assurance schemes that a hotel's unit charges are on display by the telephones or with the room information. But in practice it is not always easy to compare these charges with standard telephone rates. Before using a hotel telephone for long-distance calls, you may decide to ask how the charges compare.

Security of valuables

Many establishments allow you to deposit your valuables with the proprietor or manager during your stay, and we recommend you do this as a sensible precaution. Make sure you obtain a receipt for them. Some places do not accept articles for safe custody, and in that case it is wisest to keep your valuables with you.

Disclaimer

Some proprietors put up a notice that disclaims liability for property brought on to their premises by a guest. In fact, they can only restrict their liability to a minimum laid down by law (The Hotel Proprietors Act 1956). Under that Act, a proprietor is liable for the value of the loss or damage to any property (except a motor car or its contents) of a guest who has engaged overnight accommodation, but if the proprietor has the notice on display as prescribed under that Act, liability is limited to £50 for one article and a total of £100 for any one guest. The notice must be prominently displayed in the reception area or main entrance. These limits do not apply to valuables you have deposited with the proprietor for safekeeping, or to property lost through the default, neglect or wilful act of the proprietor or his staff.

Comments and complaints

The law

Places that offer accommodation have legal and statutory responsibilities to their customers, such as providing information about prices, providing adequate fire precautions and safeguarding valuables. They must also abide by the Trades Description Acts 1968 and 1972 when they describe their accommodation and facilities. All the places featured in this guide have declared that they do fulfil all applicable statutory obligations.

Information

The proprietors themselves supply the descriptions of their establishments and other information for the entries, (except VisitBritain Ratings and Awards). VisitBritain cannot guarantee the accuracy of information in this guide, and accepts no responsibility for any error or misrepresentation. All liability for loss, disappointment, negligence or other damage caused by reliance on the information contained in this guide, or in the event of bankruptcy or liquidation or cessation of trade of any company, individual or firm mentioned, is hereby excluded. We strongly recommend you check all details when you book.

Problems

Of course, we hope you will not have cause for complaint, but problems do occur from time to time. If you are dissatisfied with anything, make your complaint to the management immediately. Then the management can take action at once to investigate the matter and put things right. The longer you leave a complaint, the harder it is to deal with it effectively. In certain circumstances, VisitBritain may look into complaints. However, VisitBritain has no statutory control over establishments or their methods of operating. VisitBritain cannot become involved in legal or contractual matters, nor can they get involved in seeking financial recompense.

If you do have problems that have not been resolved by the proprietor and which you would like to bring to our attention, please write to: Quality in Tourism, Farncombe House, Broadway, Worcestershire WR12 7LJ.

Code of conduct and conditions of participation for hotels, guest accommodation and self-catering holiday homes

The proprietor/management is required to undertake and observe the following Code of Conduct:

- To maintain standards of guest care, cleanliness and service appropriate to the type of establishment;

- To describe accurately in any advertisement, brochure or other printed or electronic media, the facilities and services provided;

- To make clear to visitors exactly what is included in all prices quoted for accommodation, including taxes, and any other surcharges. Details of charges for additional services/facilities should also be made clear;

- To give a clear statement of the policy on cancellations to guests at the time of booking ie by telephone, fax, email, as well as information given in a printed format;

- To adhere to, and not to exceed prices quoted at the time of booking for accommodation and other services;

- To advise visitors at the time of booking, and subsequently if any change, if the accommodation offered is in an unconnected annexe or similar and to indicate the location of such accommodation and any difference in comfort and/or amenities from accommodation in the establishment;

- To give each visitor on request details of payments due and a receipt, if required;

- To deal promptly and courteously with all enquiries, requests, bookings and correspondence from visitors;

- To ensure complaint handling procedures are in place and that complaints received are investigated promptly and courteously and that the outcome is communicated to the visitor;

- To give due consideration to the requirements of visitors with disabilities and visitors with special needs, and to make suitable provision where applicable;

- To provide public liability insurance or comparable arrangements and to comply with all applicable planning, safety and other statutory requirements;

- To allow a VisitBritain representative reasonable access to the establishment on request, to confirm the Code of Conduct is being observed.

Conditions for participation

All establishments participating in VisitBritain's quality assurance schemes are required to:

- Meet or exceed the minimum entry requirements for a rating in the relevant accommodation sector;

- Observe the Code of Conduct;

- Be assessed annually, or following a complaint, by authorised representatives of VisitBritain;

- Pay an annual participation fee;

- Complete an annual information collection questionnaire either online or by post as required.

Change of ownership

When an establishment is sold, the existing rating cannot be transferred to the new owner, unless otherwise agreed by VisitBritain in writing. The new owner is required to make an application for participation in VisitBritain's quality assessment schemes.

Signage

Where an establishment, for whatever reason, ceases to participate in the schemes, all relevant display signs and print material must be removed. Use of ratings should always be accompanied by the VisitBritain quality marque. Any listing in a VisitBritain publication/ website and within the tourist information centre network is conditional on continued participation in the quality assessment schemes. Failure to observe these conditions may result in the establishment becoming ineligible to display or use the VisitBritain endorsement in any form whatsoever.

Code of conduct & conditions for participation for caravan & camping parks

In addition to fulfilling its statutory obligations, including having applied for a certificate under the Fire Precautions Act 1971 (if applicable) and holding public liability insurance, and ensuring that all caravan holiday homes/chalets for hire and the park and all buildings and facilities thereon, the fixtures, furnishings, fittings and decor are maintained in sound and clean condition and are fit for the purposes intended, the management undertakes to observe the following code of conduct:

- To ensure high standards of courtesy and cleanliness; catering and service appropriate to the type of park.

- To describe to all visitors and prospective visitors the amenities, facilities and services provided by the park and/or caravan holiday homes/chalets whether by advertisement, brochure, word of mouth or other means.

- To allow visitors to see the park or caravan holiday homes/chalets for hire, if requested, before booking.

- To present grading awards and/or any other national tourist board awards unambiguously.

- To make clear to visitors exactly what is included in prices quoted for the park or caravan holiday homes/ chalets, meals and refreshments, including service charge, taxes and other surcharges. Details of charges, if any, for heating or for additional services or facilities available should also be made clear.

- To adhere to, and not to exceed, prices current at time of occupation for caravan holiday homes/chalets or other services.

- To advise visitors at the time of booking, and subsequently if any change, if the caravan holiday home/chalet or pitch offered is in a different location or on another park, and to indicate the location of this and any difference in comfort and amenities.

- To give each visitor, on request, details of payments due and a receipt if required.

- To advise visitors at the time of booking of the charges that might be incurred if the booking is subsequently cancelled.

- To deal promptly and courteously with all visitors and prospective visitors, including enquiries, reservations, correspondence and complaints.

- To allow a national tourist board representative reasonable access to the park and/or caravan holiday homes/chalet whether by prior appointment or on an unannounced assessment, to confirm that the Code of Conduct is being observed and that the appropriate quality standard is being maintained.

- The operator must comply with the provision of the caravan industry Codes of Practice.

Bank holiday
dates for your diary

holiday	2006	2007
January Bank Holiday (Scotland)	2 January	2 January
New Year's Day (England & Wales)	2 January	1 January
New Year's Day (Scotland)	3 January	1 January
Good Friday	14 April	6 April
Easter Monday (England & Wales)	17 April	9 April
Early May Bank Holiday	1 May	7 May
Spring Bank Holiday	29 May	28 May
Summer Bank Holiday (Scotland)	7 August	6 August
Summer Bank Holiday (England & Wales)	28 August	27 August
Christmas Day	25 December	25 December
Boxing Day	26 December	26 December

About the
guide entries

Entries

All the accommodation featured in this guide has been quality assessed or has applied for assessment. Proprietors have paid to have their establishment featured in either a standard entry (includes description, facilities and prices) or enhanced entry (photograph and extended details).

Locations

Places to stay are generally listed under the town, city or village where they are located. If a place is in a small village or the countryside, you may find it listed under a nearby town (providing it is within a seven-mile radius).

Place names are listed alphabetically within each regional section of the guide, along with the name of the ceremonial county they are in and their map reference. Complete addresses for rental properties are not given and the town(s) listed may be a distance from the actual establishment. Please check the precise location at the time of booking.

Map references

These refer to the colour location maps at the front of the guide. The first figure shown is the map number, the following letter and figure indicate the grid reference on the map. Some entries were included just before the guide went to press, so they do not appear on the maps.

Addresses

County names, which appear in the town headings, are not repeated in the entries. When you are writing, you should of course make sure you use the full address and postcode.

Telephone numbers

Booking telephone numbers are listed below the accommodation address for each entry. Area codes are shown in brackets.

Prices

The prices shown are only a general guide; they were supplied to us by proprietors in autumn 2005. Remember, changes may occur after the guide goes to press, so we strongly advise you to check prices when you book your accommodation.

There are many different ways of quoting prices for accommodation. Prices are shown in pounds sterling and include VAT where applicable. Some places also include a service charge in their standard tariff.

Bed and breakfast, the prices shown are per room for overnight accommodation with breakfast. The double room price is for two people. (If a double room is occupied by one person there is sometimes a reduction in price.)

Half board, the prices shown are per person per night for room, evening meal and breakfast. These prices are usually based on two people sharing a room.

Evening meal, the prices shown are per person per night.

Some places only provide a continental breakfast in the set price, and you may have to pay extra if you want a full English breakfast.

According to the law, hotels with at least four bedrooms or eight beds must display their overnight accommodation charges in the reception area or entrance. In your own interests, do make sure you check prices and what they include.

Self-catering, prices are shown per unit per week and include VAT.

Camping and caravan parks, touring pitch prices are based on the minimum and maximum charges for one night for two persons, car and either caravan or tent. (Some parks may charge separately for car, caravan or tent, and for each person and there may be an extra charge for caravan awnings.) Minimum and maximum prices for caravan holiday homes are given per week.

Children's rates

Many places charge a reduced rate for children, especially if they share a room with their parents. Some places charge the full rate, however, when a child occupies a room which might otherwise

have been let to an adult. The upper age limit for reductions for children varies between establishments, so check this when you book.

Seasonal packages and special promotions

Prices often vary through the year and may be significantly lower outside peak holiday weeks. Many places offer special package rates – fully inclusive weekend breaks, for example – in the autumn, winter and spring.

Bathrooms

(hotels and guest accommodation)
Each accommodation entry shows you the number of en suite and private bathrooms available. En suite bathroom means the bath or shower and wc are contained behind the main door of the bedroom. Private bathroom means a bath or shower and wc solely for the occupants of one bedroom, on the same floor, reasonably close and with a key provided. Some establishments may also provide public bathrooms, normally with a bath, sometimes with a shower attachment. If the availability of a bath is important to you, remember to check when you book.

Meals

(hotels and guest accommodation)
It is advisable to check availability of meals and times when making your booking. Some smaller places may ask you at breakfast or midday whether you want an evening meal. The prices shown in each entry are for bed and breakfast or half board, but many places also offer lunch.

Symbols

The at-a-glance symbols included at the end of each entry show many of the services and facilities available at each establishment. You will find the key to these symbols on the back-cover flap – open it out and check the meanings as you go.

Smoking

Some places prefer not to accommodate smokers, and in such cases the descriptions or symbols in each entry make this clear.

Alcoholic drinks

All hotels in this guide will be licensed and most will have a bar, some B&B guest accommodaton may also be licensed to serve alcohol. The licence may be restricted – to diners only, for example – so you may want to check this when you book. If a bar is available this is shown by the ♀ symbol in guest accommodation entries.

A note about hotels

There is no restriction on any property that provides serviced accommodation using the word hotel in the title. Hotels with a star rating meet all the requirements for the one star hotel standard. They will have an alcohol licence and usually offer meals in addition to breakfast.

Hotel establishments with a guest accommodation rating meet the minimum entry requirements for the guest accommodation standard but do not automatically meet the hotel one star requirements.

Payment accepted

The types of payment accepted by an establishment are listed in the payment accepted section. If you plan to pay by card, check that the establishment will take your particular card before you book. Some proprietors will charge you a higher rate if you pay by credit card rather than cash or cheque. The difference is to cover the percentage paid by the proprietor to the credit card company.

When you book by telephone, you may be asked for your credit card number as confirmation. But remember, the proprietor may then charge your credit card account if you cancel your booking. See under Cancellations on page 199.

Over the next few years Switch debit cards will be phased out and replaced by the globally recognised Maestro.

Awaiting confirmation or rating

At the time of going to press some establishments featured in this guide were awaiting assessment for either their new quality or National Accessible Scheme rating. Rating Applied For indicates this.

Getting around Britain

Britain is a country of perfect proportions – big enough to find a new place to discover, yet small enough to guarantee it's within easy reach. Getting from A to B can be easier than you think...

Planning your journey

Make **transportdirect.info** your first portal of call! It's the ultimate journey-planning tool to help you find the best way from your home to your destination by car or public transport. Decide on the quickest way to travel by comparing end-to-end journey times and routes. You can even buy train and coach tickets and find out about flights from a selection of airports.

In the air

With so many low-cost domestic flights, air travel really is an option. It is particularly important that you give an airline advance notice of any special requirements at the time of booking. It's also advisable to confirm that these requirements have been noted a day or so before your flight, and to check in early.

Train it

Let the train take the strain – the National Rail network is illustrated on page 209. If you need assistance on your journey you should give as much advance notice as possible to the train company with which you are travelling.

Turn to pages 210 and 211 for a useful list of contacts.

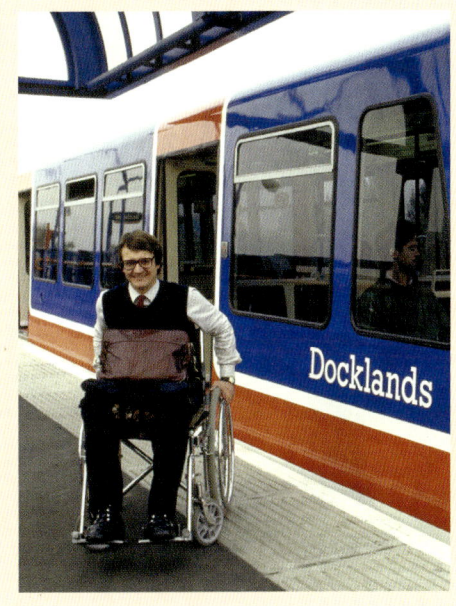

In which region is the English county I wish to visit?

If you know what English county you wish to visit you'll find it in the regional section shown below.

county	region	county	region
Bedfordshire	England's Heartland	London	South East England
Berkshire	South East England	Lincolnshire	England's Heartland
Bristol	England's West Country	Merseyside	England's North Country
Buckinghamshire	South East England	Norfolk	England's Heartland
Cambridgeshire	England's Heartland	North Yorkshire	England's North Country
Cheshire	England's North Country	Northamptonshire	England's Heartland
Cornwall	England's West Country	northern Lincolnshire	England's North Country
County Durham	England's North Country	Northumberland	England's North Country
Cumbria	England's North Country	Nottinghamshire	England's Heartland
Derbyshire	England's Heartland	Oxfordshire	South East England
Devon	England's West Country	Rutland	England's Heartland
Dorset	England's West Country	Shropshire	England's Heartland
East Riding of Yorkshire	England's North Country	Somerset	England's West Country
East Sussex	South East England	South Yorkshire	England's North Country
Essex	England's Heartland	Staffordshire	England's Heartland
Gloucestershire	England's West Country	Suffolk	England's Heartland
Greater Manchester	England's North Country	Surrey	South East England
Hampshire	South East England	Tees Valley	England's North Country
Herefordshire	England's Heartland	Tyne and Wear	England's North Country
Hertfordshire	England's Heartland	Warwickshire	England's Heartland
Isle of Wight	South East England	West Midlands	England's Heartland
Isles of Scilly	England's West Country	West Sussex	South East England
Kent	South East England	West Yorkshire	England's North Country
Lancashire	England's North Country	Wiltshire	England's West Country
Leicestershire	England's Heartland	Worcestershire	England's Heartland

To help readers we do not refer to unitary authorities in this guide.

By train

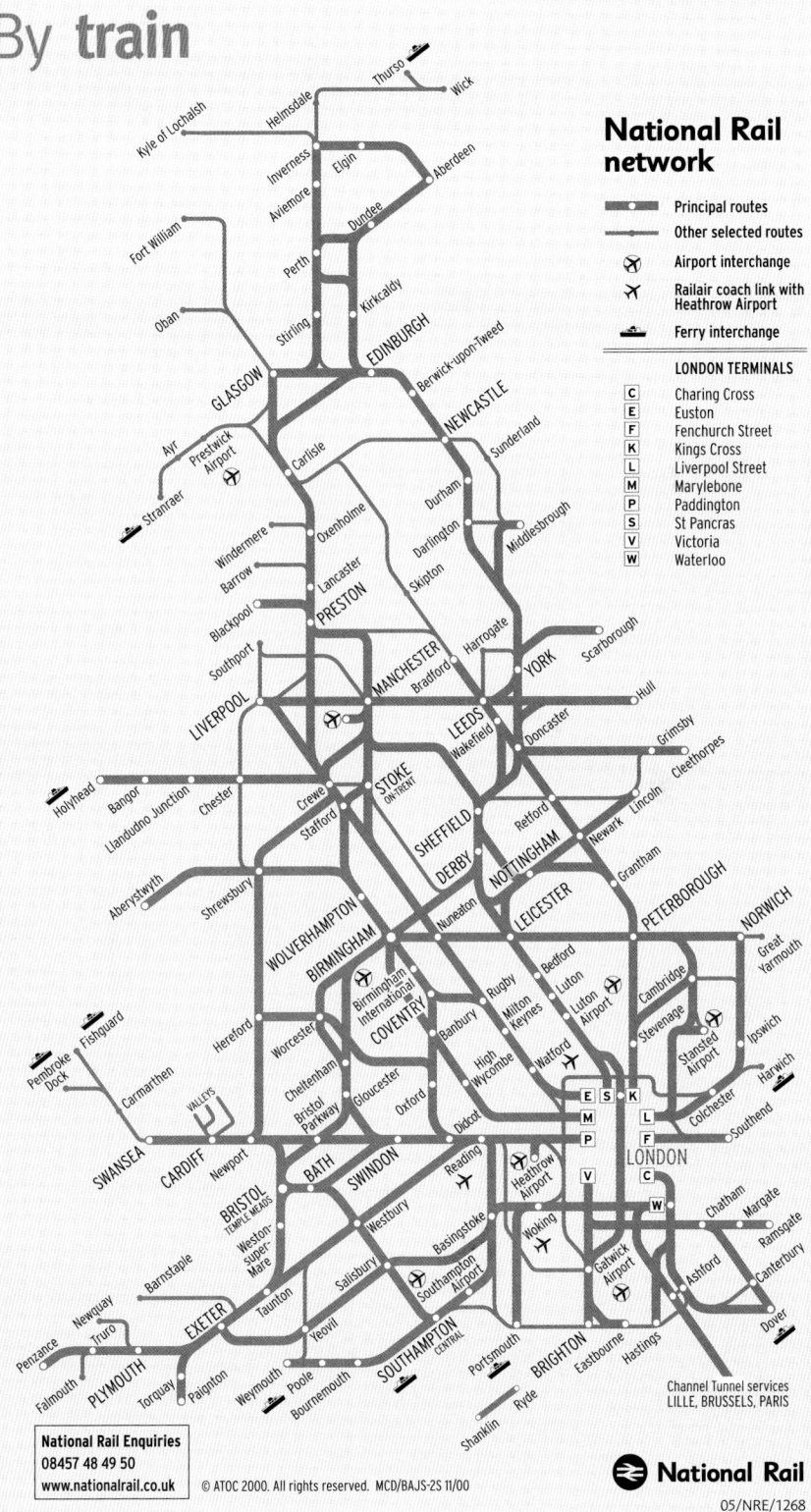

National Rail network

- Principal routes
- Other selected routes
- ✈ Airport interchange
- ✈ Railair coach link with Heathrow Airport
- ⛴ Ferry interchange

LONDON TERMINALS

C	Charing Cross
E	Euston
F	Fenchurch Street
K	Kings Cross
L	Liverpool Street
M	Marylebone
P	Paddington
S	St Pancras
V	Victoria
W	Waterloo

Channel Tunnel services
LILLE, BRUSSELS, PARIS

National Rail Enquiries
08457 48 49 50
www.nationalrail.co.uk

National Rail

© ATOC 2000. All rights reserved. MCD/BAJS-2S 11/00

05/NRE/1268

Travel information

general travel information

Streetmap	streetmap.co.uk	
Transport Direct	transportdirect.info	
Transport for London	tfl.gov.uk	(020) 7222 1234
Travel Services	departures-arrivals.com	
Traveline	traveline.org.uk	0870 608 2608

car & car hire

AA	theaa.com	0870 600 0371
Green Flag	greenflag.co.uk	0845 246 1557
RAC	rac.co.uk	0870 572 2722
Alamo	alamo.co.uk	0870 599 4000*
Avis	avis.co.uk	0870 010 0287
Budget	budget.co.uk	0870 156 5656
Easycar	easycar.com	0906 333 3333
Enterprise	enterprise.com	0870 350 3000*
Hertz	hertz.co.uk	0870 844 8844*
Holiday Autos	holidayautos.co.uk	
National	nationalcar.co.uk	0870 400 4560
Thrifty	thrifty.co.uk	(01494) 751600*

air

Airport information	a2btravel.com/airports
A2B Airways (Belfast City/Isle of Man to Blackpool)	a2bairways.com
Air Southwest	airsouthwest.com
Air Wales	airwales.com
BMI	flybmi.com
BMI Baby	bmibaby.com
BNWA (Isle of Man to Blackpool)	flybnwa.co.uk
British Airways	ba.com
British International (Isles of Scilly to Penzance)	islesofscillyhelicopter.com
Eastern Airways	easternairways.com
Easyjet	easyjet.com
Flybe	flybe.com
Jet2.com	jet2.com
Rockhopper (Channel Islands)	rockhopper.aero
Ryanair	ryanair.com
Skybus (Isles of Scilly)	skybus.co.uk
VLM	flyvlm.com

Phone numbers listed are for general enquiries unless otherwise stated.
*Booking line only

bus & coach

Megabus	megabus.com	
National Express	nationalexpress.com	0870 580 8080
Shearings Holidays	shearingsholidays.com	(01942) 824824
Wallace Arnold Holidays	wallacearnold.com	(0113) 263 4234

train

National Rail Enquiries	nationalrail.co.uk	0845 748 4950
The Trainline	thetrainline.com	
UK train operating companies	rail.co.uk	
Arriva Trains	arriva.co.uk	0845 748 4950
c2c	c2c-online.co.uk	0845 744 4422*
Central Trains	centraltrains.co.uk	0870 609 6060
Chiltern Railways	chilternrailways.co.uk	0845 600 5165
First Great Western	firstgreatwestern.co.uk	0845 700 0125*
Gatwick Express	gatwickexpress.co.uk	0845 850 1530
GNER	gner.co.uk	0845 722 5225*
Heathrow Express	heathrowexpress.com	0845 600 1515
Hull Trains	hulltrains.co.uk	(01482) 606388
Island Line	island-line.co.uk	0845 748 4950
Merseyrail	merseyrail.org	0845 748 4950
Midland Mainline	midlandmainline.com	0845 712 5678
Northern Rail	northrail.org	0845 748 4950
One Railway	onerailway.com	0845 600 7245
Silverlink	silverlink-trains.com	0870 512 5240
South Eastern Trains	setrains.co.uk	0870 603 0405
South West Trains	southwesttrains.co.uk	0845 600 0650
Southern	southernrailway.com	0870 830 6000
Stansted Express	stanstedexpress.com	0845 850 0150
Thameslink	thameslink.co.uk	0845 748 4950
Transpennine Express	tpexpress.co.uk	0845 600 1671
Virgin Trains	virgintrains.co.uk	0845 722 2333*
Wagn	wagn.co.uk	0870 850 8822
Wessex Trains	wessextrains.co.uk	0870 900 2320

ferry

Ferry information	sailanddrive.com	
Condor Ferries (Channel Islands)	condorferries.co.uk	0845 345 2000
The Isle of Man Steam Packet Company and Sea Cat	steam-packet.com	0870 552 3523
Isles of Scilly Travel	islesofscilly-travel.co.uk	0845 710 5555
Red Funnel (Isle of Wight)	redfunnel.co.uk	0870 444 8898
Wight Link (Isle of Wight)	wightlink.co.uk	0870 582 7744

Accessible Schemes
index

Establishments listed have a detailed entry in this guide – use the property index to find the page number. At the front of the guide you can find information about the different schemes.

England

Mobility level 1

Century Hotel Blackpool	Applied	England's North Country
Mellwaters Barn Bowes	★★★★	England's North Country
East Greystone Farm Cottages Gainford	★★★★	England's North Country
The Cornmill Kirkbymoorside	◆◆◆◆ SILVER	England's North Country
Linthwaite House Hotel Windermere	★★★ GOLD	England's North Country
Hipsley Farm Cottages Atherstone	★★★★	England's Heartland
Upper Onibury Cottages Craven Arms	★★★★	England's Heartland
Greenbanks Country Hotel and 3 Palms Leisure Pool Dereham	◆◆◆◆	England's Heartland
Caley Hall Hotel Hunstanton	★★	England's Heartland
Mocktree Barns Holiday Cottages Ludlow	★★★	England's Heartland
Lyth Hill House Shrewsbury	◆◆◆◆ GOLD	England's Heartland
Bluebell, Bonny, Buttercup & Bertie Sibton	★★★★	England's Heartland
Common Right Barns Wisbech	★★★★	England's Heartland
Petwood Hotel Woodhall Spa	★★★	England's Heartland
Wren & Robin Cottages Ashburton	★★★★	England's West Country
Blagdon Farm Country Holidays Ashwater	★★★★–★★★★★	England's West Country
Carfax Hotel Bath	◆◆◆◆◆	England's West Country
Greyfield Farm Cottages Bath	★★★★★	England's West Country
Primrose Hill Holidays Blue Anchor	★★★★	England's West Country
Best Western Speech House Hotel Coleford	★★★	England's West Country
Dryslade Farm English Bicknor	◆◆◆◆	England's West Country
Bocaddon Holiday Cottages Looe	★★★★	England's West Country
Hartswheal Barn Lostwithiel	★★★★	England's West Country
Cory Farm Cottages Morwenstow	★★★★	England's West Country
Waterloo Farm North Petherwin	★★★★	England's West Country
Trenona Farm Holidays – Chy Whel Veryan	★★★★	England's West Country

🚶 Mobility level 1 continued

Moorlands Country Guesthouse *Weston-super-Mare*	♦♦♦	England's West Country
Overcombe Hotel *Yelverton*	♦♦♦♦	England's West Country
High Wray *Farnham*	★★	South East England
Updown Park Farm *Sandwich*	★★★★	South East England
The Nurse's Cottage *Sway*	♦♦♦♦♦ GOLD	South East England

♿ Mobility level 2

Rothay Manor *Ambleside*	★★★ SILVER	England's North Country
Mellwaters Barn *Bowes*	★★★★	England's North Country
Brentwood Farm Cottages *Burton in Lonsdale*	★★★★	England's North Country
East Greystone Farm Cottages *Gainford*	★★★★	England's North Country
Westwood Lodge Ilkley Moor *Ilkley*	★★★★–★★★★★	England's North Country
Barkinbeck Cottage *Kendal*	★★★	England's North Country
The Firs *Runswick Bay*	♦♦♦♦	England's North Country
Elms Farm Cottages *Boston*	★★★★	England's Heartland
Fiddlesticks *Clare*	♦♦♦♦ SILVER	England's Heartland
Dairy Cottage, Piggery Place, Shire's Rest *Hartington*	★★★–★★★★	England's Heartland
Knightcote Farm Cottages *Knightcote*	★★★★★	England's Heartland
Hidelow House Cottages *Malvern*	★★★★–★★★★★	England's Heartland
Norfolk Cottages *Norfolk/Suffolk border*	★★★★	England's Heartland
Acorn Cottage *Sandy*	★★★★	England's Heartland
The Netus Barn *Wickham Skeith*	★★★	England's Heartland
Common Right Barns *Wisbech*	★★★★	England's Heartland
Wren & Robin Cottages *Ashburton*	★★★★	England's West Country
Blagdon Farm Country Holidays *Ashwater*	★★★★–★★★★★	England's West Country
Woodcombe Lodges *Bratton*	★★★★	England's West Country
Redlands *Combe Florey*	♦♦♦♦	England's West Country
Highleadon Holiday Cottages *Highleadon*	★★★★	England's West Country
Bocaddon Holiday Cottages *Looe*	★★★★	England's West Country
Hartswheal Barn *Lostwithiel*	★★★★	England's West Country
Cory Farm Cottages *Morwenstow*	★★★★	England's West Country
Kitley House Hotel and Restaurant *Plymouth*	★★★	England's West Country
Higher Laity Farm *Portreath*	★★★★★	England's West Country
Holly Farm *Stoke St Gregory*	★★★★	England's West Country
Trenona Farm Holidays – Chy Whel *Veryan*	★★★★	England's West Country
High Wray *Farnham*	★★	South East England
Heath Farm *Lewes*	★★★★	South East England
Updown Park Farm *Sandwich*	★★★★	South East England
Swallows Nest *Witney*	★★★★	South East England

♿ Mobility level 3 Independent

Mellwaters Barn *Bowes*	★★★★	England's North Country
Stonecroft and Swallows Nest *Cockfield*	★★★★	England's North Country
The St Annes Hotel *Lytham St Annes*	Applied	England's North Country
Knightcote Farm Cottages *Knightcote*	★★★★★	England's Heartland

♿ Mobility level 3 Independent continued

Cliff Farm Cottage *Lincoln*	★★★★	England's Heartland
Hidelow House Cottages *Malvern*	★★★★–★★★★★★	England's Heartland
Newlands Country House *Southwold*	♦♦♦♦	England's Heartland
Kirkstead Old Mill Cottage *Woodhall Spa*	♦♦♦♦	England's Heartland
Blagdon Farm Country Holidays *Ashwater*	★★★★–★★★★★★	England's West Country
Primrose Hill Holidays *Blue Anchor*	★★★★	England's West Country
Smallicombe Farm *Colyton*	★★★★	England's West Country
Mortons House Hotel *Corfe Castle*	★★★ GOLD	England's West Country
Half Moon Inn *Horsington*	♦♦♦	England's West Country
Chark Country Holidays *Lostwithiel*	★★★★	England's West Country
Hartswheal Barn *Lostwithiel*	★★★★	England's West Country
Tregoninny Farm *Truro*	♦♦♦♦	England's West Country
Sunnymeade Country Hotel *Woolacombe*	♦♦♦	England's West Country
Woodlands *Rye*	♦♦♦♦	South East England

♿ Mobility level 3 Assisted

Mellwaters Barn *Bowes*	★★★★	England's North Country
The St Annes Hotel *Lytham St Annes*	Applied	England's North Country
Berwick Cottage *East Harling*	★★★	England's Heartland
Spixworth Hall Cottages *Norwich*	★★★–★★★★★	England's Heartland
Park House Hotel *Sandringham*	★★ SILVER	England's Heartland
Blagdon Farm Country Holidays *Ashwater*	★★★★–★★★★★★	England's West Country
Hartswheal Barn *Lostwithiel*	★★★★	England's West Country
Grasmere House Hotel *Salisbury*	★★★	England's West Country
Tregoninny Farm *Truro*	♦♦♦♦	England's West Country
Grange Holiday Cottages *Wimborne Minster*	★★★★	England's West Country

🔊 Hearing impairment level 1

Mellwaters Barn *Bowes*	★★★★	England's North Country
Elms Farm Cottages *Boston*	★★★★	England's Heartland
Highleadon Holiday Cottages *Highleadon*	★★★★	England's West Country
Half Moon Inn *Horsington*	♦♦♦	England's West Country
Sunnymeade Country Hotel *Woolacombe*	♦♦♦	England's West Country
The Nurse's Cottage *Sway*	♦♦♦♦♦ GOLD	South East England

🔊 Hearing impairment level 2

The St Annes Hotel *Lytham St Annes*	Applied	England's North Country
Berwick Cottage *East Harling*	★★★	England's Heartland
Kirkstead Old Mill Cottage *Woodhall Spa*	♦♦♦♦	England's Heartland

👁 Visual impairment level 1

Century Hotel *Blackpool*	Applied	England's North Country
Elms Farm Cottages *Boston*	★★★★	England's Heartland
Kirkstead Old Mill Cottage *Woodhall Spa*	♦♦♦♦	England's Heartland
Half Moon Inn *Horsington*	♦♦♦	England's West Country

👁 Visual impairment level 2

Berwick Cottage *East Harling*	★★★	England's Heartland

Awaiting National Accessible Scheme rating

Beacon Hill Farm Holidays *Longhorsely*	★★★★–★★★★★★	England's North Country
The Inn at Woburn *Woburn*	★★★ SILVER	England's Heartland
The Coppleridge Inn *Motcombe*	♦♦♦♦	England's West Country
Frognel Hall Hotel *Torquay*	★★	England's West Country
Ashford International Hotel *Ashford*	★★★★	South East England
The Langham Hotel *Eastbourne*	★★★	South East England
Park Inn Heathrow *Heathrow Airport*	★★★★	South East England

Scotland

Mobility level 1

Marcliffe Hotel and Spa *Aberdeen*	★★★★★	Scotland
Little Swinton Cottages *Coldstream*	★★★–★★★★★	Scotland
Ardgarth Guest House *Edinburgh*	★★★	Scotland
Rusko Holidays *Gatehouse of Fleet*	★★–★★★★★	Scotland

Mobility level 2

Bailey Mill Inn *Newcastleton*	★★–★★★★	Scotland
Balmashie Holiday Cottages *St Andrews*	★★★★	Scotland

Mobility level 3

Borders Event Centre *Galashiels*	★	Scotland
Rusko Holidays *Gatehouse of Fleet*	★★–★★★★★	Scotland
Glen Orchy Hotel *Lerwick*	★★★	Scotland

Wales

Access Statement

Old Radnor Barn *Brecon*	★★★★	Wales
Madog's Wells *Llanfair Caereinion*	★★★–★★★★★★	Wales

Quick
reference index

If you're looking for a specific facility use this index to see-at-a-glance detailed accommodation entries that match your requirements. Use the property index to find the page number.

⊠ Induction loop system at reception

Century Hotel *Blackpool*	Applied	England's North Country
The St Annes Hotel *Lytham St Annes*	Applied	England's North Country
Half Moon Inn *Horsington*	♦♦♦	England's West Country
Grasmere House Hotel *Salisbury*	★★★	England's West Country
Ashford International Hotel *Ashford*	★★★★	South East England

⊺ Typetalk available

The St Annes Hotel *Lytham St Annes*	Applied	England's North Country
Sunnymeade Country Hotel *Woolacombe*	♦♦♦	England's West Country
The Nurse's Cottage *Sway*	♦♦♦♦♦ GOLD	South East England

⊠ Adapted kitchen

Mellwaters Barn *Bowes*	★★★★	England's North Country
Stonecroft and Swallows Nest *Cockfield*	★★★★	England's North Country
Berwick Cottage *East Harling*	★★★	England's Heartland
Knightcote Farm Cottages *Knightcote*	★★★★★	England's Heartland
Cliff Farm Cottage *Lincoln*	★★★★	England's Heartland
Hidelow House Cottages *Malvern*	★★★★–★★★★★★	England's Heartland
Spixworth Hall Cottages *Norwich*	★★★–★★★★★	England's Heartland
Acorn Cottage *Sandy*	★★★★	England's Heartland
Blagdon Farm Country Holidays *Ashwater*	★★★★–★★★★★★	England's West Country
Primrose Hill Holidays *Blue Anchor*	★★★★	England's West Country
Smallicombe Farm *Colyton*	★★★★	England's West Country
Chark Country Holidays *Lostwithiel*	★★★★	England's West Country
Hartswheal Barn *Lostwithiel*	★★★★	England's West Country
Cory Farm Cottages *Morwenstow*	★★★★	England's West Country
Grange Holiday Cottages *Wimborne Minster*	★★★★	England's West Country
High Wray *Farnham*	★★	South East England
Rusko Holidays *Gatehouse of Fleet*	★★–★★★★	Scotland

Refer to the property index for page numbers.

✶ Facilities for service dogs

Century Hotel Blackpool	Applied	England's North Country
Mellwaters Barn Bowes	★★★★	England's North Country
Stonecroft and Swallows Nest Cockfield	★★★★	England's North Country
East Greystone Farm Cottages Gainford	★★★★	England's North Country
Westwood Lodge Ilkley Moor Ilkley	★★★★–★★★★★★	England's North Country
The St Annes Hotel Lytham St Annes	Applied	England's North Country
Linthwaite House Hotel Windermere	★★★ GOLD	England's North Country
Elms Farm Cottages Boston	★★★★	England's Heartland
Upper Onibury Cottages Craven Arms	★★★★	England's Heartland
Greenbanks Country Hotel and 3 Palms Leisure Pool Dereham	♦♦♦♦	England's Heartland
Berwick Cottage East Harling	★★★	England's Heartland
Knightcote Farm Cottages Knightcote	★★★★★	England's Heartland
Hidelow House Cottages Malvern	★★★★–★★★★★★	England's Heartland
Park House Hotel Sandringham	★★ SILVER	England's Heartland
Acorn Cottage Sandy	★★★★	England's Heartland
Common Right Barns Wisbech	★★★★	England's Heartland
Kirkstead Old Mill Cottage Woodhall Spa	♦♦♦♦	England's Heartland
Blagdon Farm Country Holidays Ashwater	★★★★–★★★★★★	England's West Country
Primrose Hill Holidays Blue Anchor	★★★★	England's West Country
Best Western Speech House Hotel Coleford	★★★	England's West Country
Redlands Combe Florey	♦♦♦♦	England's West Country
Half Moon Inn Horsington	♦♦♦	England's West Country
Kitley House Hotel and Restaurant Plymouth	★★★	England's West Country
Grange Holiday Cottages Wimborne Minster	★★★★	England's West Country
Sunnymeade Country Hotel Woolacombe	♦♦♦	England's West Country
The Langham Hotel Eastbourne	★★★	South East England
Park Inn Heathrow Heathrow Airport	★★★★	South East England
Woodlands Rye	♦♦♦♦	South East England
The Nurse's Cottage Sway	♦♦♦♦♦ GOLD	South East England
Marcliffe Hotel and Spa Aberdeen	★★★★★	Scotland
Ardgarth Guest House Edinburgh	★★★	Scotland
Rusko Holidays Gatehouse of Fleet	★★–★★★★★	Scotland
Balmashie Holiday Cottages St Andrews	★★★★	Scotland
Old Radnor Barn Brecon	★★★★	Wales

Index to
display advertisers

All display advertisers are listed below.

Index by property name

All accommodation with a detailed entry in this guide is listed below.

Establishments listed here have a detailed entry in this guide.

Index by
place name

The following places all have detailed accommodation entries in this guide. If the place where you wish to stay is not shown, the location maps (starting on page 22) will help you find somewhere to stay in the area.

Index by place name

Published by: VisitBritain, Thames Tower, Blacks Road, London W6 9EL in partnership with England's tourism industry enjoyEngland.com
Publishing Manager: Tess Lugos
Production Manager: Iris Buckley
Compilation, design, copywriting, production and advertisement sales: Jackson Lowe Marketing, 173 High Street, Lewes, East Sussex BN7 1YE
t (01273) 487487 jacksonlowe.com
Typesetting: Marlinzo Services, Somerset and Jackson Lowe Marketing
Maps: © VisitBritain 2006. Digital data base designed and produced by ESR Cartography.
Printing and binding: Emirates Printing Press, Dubai, United Arab Emirates
Cover design: Eugenie Dodd Typographics

Photography credits: britainonview.com/Daniel Bosworth/Martin Brent/CWTB NWDA Grant Pritchard/Rod Edwards/Adrian Houston/Pawel Libera/McCormick-McAdam/Andrew Perris/Grant Pritchard/Ingrid Rasmussen/Wales Tourist Board Photo Library; Exmoor National Park Authority; Fens Tourism Group; Zac Macaulay; manchesterimages.com; One NorthEast Tourism;

Our Dynamic Earth; RSPB/Andy Hay; Brian Slater; VisitScotland/Scottish Viewpoint; Vitalise; Richard Waites

Front cover: Mortons House Hotel, Corfe Castle, Dorset (britainonview.com/Rod Edwards)

Important note: The information contained in this guide has been published in good faith on the basis of information submitted to VisitBritain by the proprietors of the premises listed, who have paid for their entries to appear. VisitBritain cannot guarantee the accuracy of the information in this guide and accepts no responsibility for any error or misrepresentation. All liability for loss, disappointment, negligence or other damage caused by reliance on the information contained in this guide, or in the event of bankruptcy, or liquidation, or cessation of trade of any company, individual or firm mentioned, is hereby excluded to the fullest extent permitted by law. Please check carefully all prices, ratings and other details before confirming a reservation.

© British Tourist Authority (trading as VisitBritain) 2006
ISBN 0 7095 8146 7

A VisitBritain Publishing guide